# Global E

# Dictionary of
# BUSINESS

**David Hicks**
**Andrew Betsis & Sean Haughton**

Edited by
**D.S. PAUL**

# Contents

| | Page: |
|---|---|
| **Preface** | 3 |
| **Dictionary** | 7 |
| **Business Letters Writing Guide** | 335 |
| **Useful phrases for Business Letters** | 344 |
| **British versus American words and phrases** | 349 |

GLOBAL ELT LTD, 2013
www.globalelt.co.uk
email: orders@globalelt.co.uk

*Dictionary of Business by David Hicks*
*Copyright © 2013*
**Published by arrangement with Goodwill Publishing House, India**
*All rights reserved. First published in 2012 by* **Goodwill Publishing House, India**

All rights reserved. No part of this publication may be reproduced, stored in a retrieval system, or transmitted in any form or by any means, electronic, mechanical, photocopying, recording or otherwise, without the prior permission in writing of the Publisher. Any person who does any unauthorised act in relation to this publication may be liable to criminal prosecution and civil claims for damages.

- *Global ELT Dictionary of Business* - ISBN: 978-1-78164-115-6
*Copyright for pages 335 - 351 :* © *Global ELT, 2013*

# PREFACE

Business comprises all management activities carried out in the course of running a company, firm or enterprise such as controlling, leading, monitoring, organising and planning. A business is also stated as a legally recognised organisation designed to provide goods, services, or both to consumers or do tertiary business in exchange for money. Businesses are predominant in capitalist economies, in which most businesses are privately owned and are typically formed to earn profit that will increase the wealth of its owners. Taking financial risks to earn profit is an important feature of privately-owned business. However, the state-owned business is not for-profit.

The essence of business is the state of being busy, either as an individual or society as a whole, doing commercially viable and profitable work. The term 'business' has at least three usages, depending on the scope: (i) the singular usage, viz. that conducted by a particular company or corporation; (ii) the generalised usage, which refers to a particular market sector such as trading in consumer durables; and (iii) the compound forms such as agribusiness. The third category may also be the broadest meaning to include all activities by the community of suppliers of goods and services. Although the forms of business ownership vary by jurisdiction, there are several common forms:

**Sole proprietorship:** It is a for-profit business owned by one person. The owner may operate on his/her own or may employ others. The owner of the business has unlimited liability for the debts incurred by the business.

**Partnership:** It is a form of for-profit business owned by two or more persons. In most forms of partnerships, each partner has unlimited liability for the debts incurred by the business. There are three typical classifications of partnerships, viz. general partnerships, limited partnerships, and limited liability partnerships.

**Corporation:** It can be either public or private in nature. A public company is often listed on the stock exchange and typically has unlimited liability. Privately-owned companies have limited liability and are often signified by the term 'Pvt Ltd'. The relevant jurisdiction normally specifies the rules of incorporation, i.e. whether rules are replaceable, who is responsible for making decisions and how the directors of the company may be elected.

**Cooperative:** It is a limited liability entity that can be organised for-profit or not for-profit. A for-profit cooperative differs from a for-profit corporation in that it has members, as opposed to shareholders, who share decision-making authority. Cooperatives may be classified as either consumer cooperatives or worker cooperatives. Cooperatives are fundamental to the ideology of economic democracy.

There are many types of businesses, and because of this, businesses are classified in many ways. Agriculture and mining businesses are concerned with the production of raw material such as plants or minerals. Financial businesses include banks and other companies that generate profit through investment and management of capital. Information businesses generate profits primarily from the resale of intellectual property and include movie studios, publishers and packaged software companies.

Manufacturers make products from raw materials or component parts, which they then sell at a profit. Companies that make physical goods such as cars or pipes, are considered manufacturers.

Real estate businesses deal with constructing commercial buildings at prime locations or blocks of residential apartments in large cities. They generate profit from the selling, renting, and development of properties, homes, and buildings. Retailers and distributors act as middlemen in getting goods produced by manufacturers to the intended consumer, generating a profit as a result of providing sales or distribution services.

Service businesses offer intangible goods or services and typically generate a profit by charging for labour or other services provided to government, other businesses, or consumers. Organisations ranging from house decorators to consulting firms, restaurants, and even entertainers are types of service businesses. Transportation businesses deliver goods and take individuals from location to location, generating a profit on the transportation costs. Utilities produce public services such as heat, electricity, or sewage treatment, and are usually government controlled.

Management in all business and organisational activities are the acts of getting people together to accomplish desired goals and objectives efficiently and effectively. Management comprises planning, organising, staffing, leading or directing, and controlling an organisation or a group of one or more persons or entities, or efforts for the purpose of accomplishing a goal. Resourcing encompasses the deployment and manipulation of human resources, financial resources, technological resources, and natural resources.

Because organisations can be viewed as systems, business management can also be defined as human actions, including design, carried out to facilitate the production of useful outcomes from a system.

Businesses are so varied that any dictionary that attempts to provide terms relating to this area has to draw from a number of sources. *Dictionary of Business* is the result of an exhaustive information search of various authentic sources including textbooks, journals, sites, as well as interaction with experts in the field. It contains simple terms, which provide basic information on the subject, as well as complex terms, which relate to latest business practices, not just in India but all over the world. Since business is one of the fields expanding rapidly with the development of most regions within the country and many nations across continents, many new terms have come about with the application of latest technologies as well as framing of new rules and regulations. Moreover, with the increasing acceptance of theories of business management due to the expansion of education, the field of business is becoming vaster still. This dictionary contains all such new terms.

Each term has been explained in simple language and lucid manner for easy understanding by the readers. Other distinguishing features of this dictionary are precise, standard definitions of many technical terms and easy illustrations to provide better comprehension of complex terms relating to business principles.

It will prove useful to the students and teachers of business management and researchers in this field. It will also prove useful to businessmen, entrepreneurs, exporters, importers, and all those concerned with any form of business, including manufacturing and trade. To those who wish to know about various aspects of business, it will provide for a richly rewarding and stimulating reading.

**D.S. Paul**

It is estimated that each of us in business today spends about 50% of our time writing correspondence. Often, the ubiquitous letter or email is, therefore, the best opportunity to make a positive first impression on prospective clients. As such, our Business Letters and E-mails Writing Guide, outlining as it does simple, effective conventions for writing professional-looking correspondence, is a must-read for all business people.

And all professionals, native-speaker or otherwise, use so-called stock phrases in their correspondence, which is what makes our Useful Phrases section so utterly relevant, too.

In the Global marketplace, English is the lingua franca, it's true, but there remain subtle differences in usage between the various so-called 'Englishes'. Our dictionary's British versus American Words and Phrases section takes some of the key business-related terminology from both sides of the Atlantic and highlights the cultural nuances of lexicology that those operating in today's business world simply must be aware of.

**Andrew Betsis & Sean Haughton**

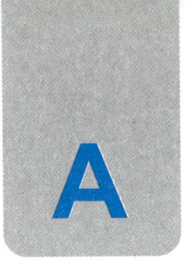

## abandonment
It can be defined as giving up the ownership of something covered by an insurance policy, assuming that it has been lost. In case the insurer agrees to abandonment, it will pay less claim. If the lost things/goods are recovered subsequently, they become the property of insurer. In other words, such goods are abandoned to the insurance company.

## ABC (activity-based costing)
The term refers to a costing method that breaks down overhead costs into specific activities in order to distribute more accurately the costs in product costing. Such costing is also applied to customer and vendor management.

## ABC classification
It refers to a method for prioritising items on the basis of product of the annual demand and the unit cost. The high annual money volume items are classified as 'A' items while the low annual money volume items are classified as 'C' items. Based on Pareto's law, the ABC classification system advises us to manage 'A' items more carefully which means that these items should be ordered and counted more often. They should be located closer to the door and be forecasted more carefully, whereas 'C' items are not very important from the investment point of view and therefore should be ordered rarely, and there is no need to count them often.

## ABC method/analysis
It is an analysis of a range of items, stock levels, customers, sales territories, etc. categorised into three groups: (i) A, very important; (ii) B, important; and (iii) C, having marginal significance. The object is to sort the total into categories which should be handled and controlled in different ways. In the case of customers, for example, the A customers are the responsibility of the sales manager

and warrant regular visits, while the C customers, whose turnover and potential are insignificant, might not necessitate frequent visits.

## ABC stratification

It denotes a method used to categorise inventory into groups based upon certain activity characteristics. Examples of ABC stratifications include ABC by velocity; ABC by sales money; ABC by quantity sold or consumed; ABC by average inventory investment; ABC by margin, etc. Such stratification is used to develop inventory planning policies.

## abilene paradox

It is a phenomenon first observed by Jerry Harvey, Professor of Management Science at George Washington University (US). It states that people individually or in groups often support a group activity which they may not really agree with, or justify it for spurious reasons.

## ability to follow instructions test

The term refers to personnel selection and vocational guidance test devised as part of the engineering apprentice test battery of the former National Institute of Industry Psychology in the UK.

## ability to pay

It refers to a pay theory which implies that wage and salary levels should be based on a company's profitability, e.g. increased profits mean higher pay levels, but lower profits seldom mean pay reductions.

## absence culture

The term refers to an organisation culture which accepts absenteeism up to certain level as norm. In companies where such culture prevails, officers and workers take occasional days off without any justification for this.

## absolute cost advantage

The term denotes cost advantage that a country enjoys in producing certain goods as compared to costs in other countries. The cost of producing a good varies among different countries due to cheap availability of certain resources, i.e. labour, raw materials, and energy. In some countries, multi-national companies (MNCs)

Dictionary of Business

take advantage of these cost differences by buying products from countries which have these advantages.

## absorption costing

It refers to the cost accounting system in which the overheads of a company are charged to the production through the process of absorption. Costs are initially apportioned to cost centres where they are absorbed, using absorption rates.
In absorption costing, various methods are used for assigning overheads, e.g. the rate of cost per unit system, the standard cost rate used in conjunction with standard costing, direct materials cost percentage rate, direct wages cost percentage rate, labour hour rate, and machine hour rate.

## absorption rate

The term denotes the rate calculated in an absorption costing system in advance of an accounting period to charge the overheads to the production of that period. Such rate is used during the accounting period to obtain the absorbed overhead by the following formula:

Actual production achieved × Absorption rate

## acceptable quality level (AQL)

It can be defined as maximum percentage or number of defective items allowable under acceptance sampling, etc.

## acceptability criteria

It refers to a limit placed upon the degree of non-conformance permitted in material or products, expressed in definitive operational terms. It is also called acceptance criteria.

## acceptance

It refers to the following:
1. An action by an authorised representative of the acquirer by which the acquired assumes ownership of products as a partial or complete performance of contract.
2. The signatures of a person on a bill of exchange indicating that the person on whom the bill is drawn, has accepted its conditions.
3. A bill of exchange that has been accepted.
4. Agreement to accept the terms of an offer.

**Dictionary of Business**

## acceptance credit

The term refers to a credit facility with a bank to an agreed percentage of the value of shipments within specified periods for a company which has a large volume of export business. The bank undertakes to accept bills of exchange drawn on it up to the agreed maximum amount. These bills are then readily discountable with a discount house. Similar credit facilities may be granted against the collection of bills where the exporters normally draw bills of exchange on their overseas buyers which they duly assign to the bank by way of security.

## acceptance criteria

It refers to the criteria that a product must meet to successfully complete a test phase, or meet delivery requirements.

## acceptance house

It refers to a financial house, generally a merchant bank, specialised in lending money on the security of bills of exchange or adding its name as endorser to a bill drawn on another party. A particular service provided to exporters by an acceptance house is the granting of acceptance credit facilities.

## acceptance number

The term is used for maximum number of defective units in the sample that will still permit the acceptance of the inspection lot or batch.

## acceptance sampling

It is a form of statistical quality control in which a sample of items is inspected and tested, the results of which enable one to make a decision as to accept or reject the total quantity of items.

With attribute sampling plans, acceptance decisions are based on a count of the number of defects and sampling. With variable sampling plans, these decisions are based on measurements. Plans requiring only a single sample set are known as single sampling plans. For example, a single attribute sampling plan with a sample a=1 requires that a sample of 100 units be inspected. If the number of defective pieces in that sample is one or zero, the lot is accepted, otherwise it is rejected.

## acceptance supra protest

It means payment of a bill of exchange after it has been dishonoured, by a person willing to save the honour of the drawer. It is also known as acceptance for honour.

## acceptance test

It denotes the following:
1. A formal testing conducted to determine whether a system satisfies its acceptance criteria and to enable the acquirer to determine whether or not to accept the system.
2. A test made in the progress of a project with the aim of checking that the finished work will be fit for its purpose.

## acceptance use policy

The term is used for rules of permitted behaviour on a particular portion of the Internet.

## acceptor

It refers to the drawee of a bill of exchange after its acceptance, e.g. the acceptor has accepted liability by signing on the face of bill.

## acceptability criteria

It refers to a limit placed upon the degree of non-conformance permitted in material or products, expressed in definitive operational terms. It is also called acceptance criteria.

## accessibility

It can be defined as the degree to which a market segment can be reached and served.

## access provider

The term is used for a company providing services to an organisation or individual to access the Internet.

## accident analysis

In business, it implies the use of analytical techniques to identify the cause of accidents, to identify potential hazards at a place of work, and to draw action plans for reducing the risks of injury to workers, as well as damage to system.

## accident book

It denotes a record (kept in a register) of personal injuries suffered by employees at a place of work.

### accident insurance
It refers to the following:
1. An insurance policy that pays a specified amount of money to the policyholder in case of permanent disability of any type caused by an accident.
2. Also, an insurance policy that pays a sum of money to the dependants of policyholder in the event of his/her death.

### accommodation endorser
The term is used for an individual or bank that endorses a loan to another party, e.g. a company may endorse a bank loan to its subsidiary. The endorser, in such case, becomes guarantor and is liable to the bank in case of default.

### accommodation note
It denotes a document in which one party acts as guarantor for another party in terms of creditworthiness.

### accord and satisfaction
It refers to the making and completion of an agreed variation of a contract. 'Accord' means agreement for variation of contract and 'satisfaction' means satisfactory completion of contract after variation.

### account
It refers to the following:
1. An account maintained by a bank in which a deposited money is kept.
2. A debit statement from one person to another. A provider of goods and services may render an account to a client for this purpose.
3. Also, in advertising or marketing, a commission or fee is received from a client, in return for the service.
4. A named segment of a ledger recording transactions relevant to the person.

### accountancy conventions
The term implies basic practices and assumptions concerned with the proportion of account. These conventions are: consistency, conservation, accounting entity, etc. Nowadays, accountancy conventions are giving way to agreed accountancy standards.

### accountant
It refers to a person who has passed the accountancy examination of a recognised accountancy body like college or institute, and has completed the required work

Dictionary of Business

experience. An accountant's responsibility centres on collating, recording and communicating financial information, preparing accounts and periodic financial statements like Profit and Loss A/c, Balance Sheet, etc.

## accounting
It can be described as principles and techniques used in establishing, recording, maintaining, and analysing financial transactions. Usually, it involves the design of systems and procedures, keeping records to ensure that the recording and handling of each transaction is undertaken in a proper manner.

## accounting cycle
It is a collective process of recording and processing the accounting events of a company. It is a methodical set of rules to ensure the accuracy and conformity of financial statements. It is also known as bookkeeping cycle.

## accounting event
It refers to a transaction recognised by the accounting recording system. Events are recorded as debit and credit entries.

## accounting method
The term can be referred to as the following:
1. Method used by a business in keeping its books and records for the purpose of completing income and to determine taxable income.
2. A method that includes not only the overall accounting procedure, but also the accounting treatment of any item like long-term contracts, stock movement for sale, etc.

## accounting period
It denotes the period of time at the end of which a summary of financial and costing information is prepared. Generally, this period is kept short to reveal variations in information so that remedial measures can be taken by the management.

## accounting procedure
The term is used for the tools which assist in day-to-day financial operations of a business. Procedures are meant to be used as guidelines or instructions for using the various accounting systems.

**Dictionary of Business**

## accounting rate of return

It implies a method of capital investment appraisal by which one can calculate the forecast average rate of annual profit from an investment, as a percentage of initial cash outlay.

## accounting records

It refers to the records kept by an organisation in compliance with the UK Companies Act, which requires organisations to keep accounting records to show and explain their transactions. Accounting records are kept in the form of manual or computerised ledgers and journals.

## accounting system

The term is used for a system that encompasses the means, including staff and equipment, by which an organisation produces its accounting information.

## account loading

It can be defined as buying and selling shares in the same stock exchange account. The account is settled by paying the difference of buying and selling, plus charges, taxes, etc.

## account number

It is the number allotted to a customer, vendor, employee, or a product for the identification. Though it may contain only numeric digits, yet these are defined and stored as a character field, also known as a strong or alphanumeric field.

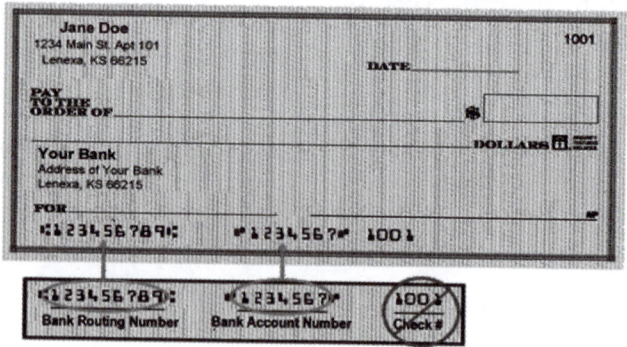

Account number

## account principles

These are generally accepted accounting principles. The term GAAP is used to denote the standard framework of guidelines for business accounting, used in any given jurisdiction, based on known accounting standards.

## accounts executive

It can be defined as the following:
1. An executive who maintains the accounts of and is in direct contact with company's clients.
2. A mediator between the company's interests and the clients' requirements.
3. A person in the advertising or marketing agency who is responsible for implementing a client's business which involves implementing the programme agreed between the agency and client.

## accounts payable

It is generally referred to as payables, i.e. the amount which is owed as the result of a purchase of goods or services on a credit basis. Although the firm making the purchase issues no written promise of payment, yet it enters the amount owed as a current liability in its accounts.

## accounts receivable

It means accounts on which monies are due from customers. Sometimes cash may be raised against accounts receivable by pledging them as collateral for a loan.

## accretion

It refers to growth of funds as a result of new contributions or interest received on capital investment.

## accruals

It means amounts as being owed for goods and services before their inclusion in the Balance Sheet.

## accrued basis

It is a system of accounting based on accrual principle under which revenue is recorded when earned and expenses are recognised when incurred. Totals of revenues and expenses are shown in the financial statements which are prepared at the end of an accounting period, usually the financial year. It is also called accrual method of accounting.

**Dictionary of Business**

## accrued benefits
The term refers to benefits due under a defined benefit pension scheme in respect of service up to given time. Accrued benefits may be calculated in relation to current earnings or protected final earnings.

## accumulated dividend
It is a dividend that has not been paid to a holder of cumulative preference shares and is carried forward to the next accounting period. It represents a liability to the company.

## accumulated depreciation
It is the total amount of depreciation on a tangible asset accumulated up to a specified period of time. The amount is deducted from the original cost/initial cost of the item being depreciated to arrive at its book value. This amount represents only the expired value of an asset.

## accumulated profits
It denotes the amount showing in the appropriation of profits account that can be carried forward to the next year's accounts, i.e. after paying dividends, taxes, and keeping some reserve.

## accumulation factor
It can be defined as the difference between the present cash value and the terminal value of an asset, etc.

## accumulation unit
It refers to a unit in a unit trust or an investment trust (in UK) in which dividends are ploughed back into the trust, after deducting income tax which enables the value of the unit to increase. It is generally linked to a life assurance policy.

## accuracy
In business, it is the degree of exactness, usually expressed as a range when used in connection with cost and time estimates.

## achievement analysis
The term is used for evaluation of progress in the different stages of a project.

## acid test ratio
The term implies the ratio of total cash, debtors, and market value of saleable investments to current liabilities of a company. This ratio acts as a guide to know the creditworthiness of a

company and for credit rating.

## acquisition
It can be described as follows: (a) taking custody of records; (b) taking possession of an asset by purchase; and (c) taking control of a firm or company by purchasing 51 per cent or more of its shares to expand the operations.

## acquisition evaluation
The term refers to review and analysis of responses for determining supplier's ability to perform the work as requested. This activity usually includes an evaluation of supplier's financial resources, ability to meet technical requirements and delivery schedules, satisfactory record of performance and eligibility for award, among other attributes.

## acquisition negotiations
It means contracting without formal advertising. This method offers more flexible procedures and allows for bargaining. It also provides an opportunity to prospective suppliers to revise their offers for the award.

## acquisition process
It denotes the process of acquiring personnel, good and/or services for new or existing contracts, requiring an offer and acceptance, the amount to be paid, lawful subject matter, and competent parties.

## acquisition programme
It refers to a directed, funded effort designed to provide a new, improved, or continuing system in response to a validated operational need.

## active file
Hard copy or electronic file containing documents used in the daily operations of a company. The file contains active records.

## active item
It refers to any inventory item that has been used or sold within a given period. It is common for some retailers to have 1,00,000 items in their items master register, but only 10,000 'active' items.

## active money
The term is used for money in circulation or being used in business transactions.

## activity
In business management, it is

# activity analysis

an element of work performed during the course of a project. An activity normally has an expected duration, expected cost and expected resource requirements. Activities are often subdivided into tasks.

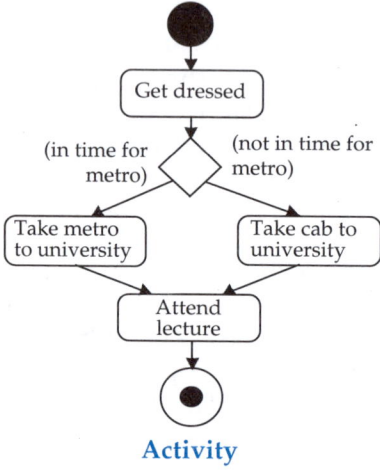

Activity

## activity analysis

It refers to the identification and description of activities in an enterprise. Each department will determine the key activities, and what resources are needed to perform the activities.

## activity based cost (ABC)

It is an information system that maintains and processes data on a firm's activities and products. It identifies the activities performed, traces cost to these activities and then uses various cost drivers to relate the cost of activities to products. Such cost drivers include the number of persons performing work, the number of set-ups required per product marketing, etc. By costing the various activities performed, it is possible to pinpoint changes in resource requirements for each activity if the firm changed its process or procedure.

## activity calendar

In computer scheduling, it is the calendar that defines the working and non-working patterns for an activity. The activity calendar is normally overridden by the project calendar.

## act of God

The term is used for some natural event that is not caused by any human action and cannot be predicted. Insurance policies covering homes include acts of God. In fact, they cover such natural events as storms, floods, etc. However, some contracts exclude liability for damages arising from acts of God.
In business, an act of God can

be interpreted as an implied defence under the rule of impossibility such as the promise is discharged due to unforeseen, naturally occurring events, which were unavoidable and which would result in an insurmountable delay and for which the parties involved in the contract cannot be held responsible.

### actual cost
It is the amount actually paid for an asset, not its market value, insurable value, or residual value. Generally, it includes freight and installation cost, but not interest on the debt, if any, to acquire it.

### actual damages
Also known as compensatory damages, these are injuries or losses suffered as a direct result of an act, or failure to an act, and for which the injured or aggrieved party has a right to compensation, etc.

### actual direct costs
These are costs specifically identified with a contract or project, based upon the contractor's cost identification and accumulation method.

### actual finish date (AFD)
The term is used for date that work actually ended on an activity. It must be prior to, or at least equal to the data date. The remaining duration of activity after this date is zero.

### actual market volume
It is the sum total of supplier's sales made at a given price or in a given price range to specific market segment.

### actual product
The term is used for design, features, brand name, and other attributes that combine to deliver a product with specified benefits.

### actuals
These are commodities that are physically available and are bought and sold immediately, e.g. at spot markets. These are distinct from markets in futures where trading is in contracts for future delivery.

### actuarial return
It is the return on a project or enterprise as measured by discounted cash flow techniques.

### actuary
It refers to a person trained in the application of statistics

and probability theory and capable of answering the questions of commercial risk. Actuaries are employed by insurance companies to calculate probable lengths of life and to advise insurers on the amounts that should be kept aside to pay claims and the amount of premium to be charged for each type of risk.

### adaptive control
The term is used for a method of computer control of industrial processes in which the computer makes calculations based on past experience to change the plant settings in order to improve its performance.

### adaptive customisation
It is the provision of the same basic product to all customers, who have the capability to filter out or alter various qualities of the item. It is often used with Internet software.

### added value
It is the addition of some worthwhile quality or performance improvement due to some action taken, which may or may not have been part of the original agreement or contract.

### adjusted basis
It is a net cost of an asset after adjusting for various tax-related items. It can be defined as a base price of an asset and deductions taken on or improvements to an asset, used to compete the gain or loss when the asset is sold.

### adjuster
The term is used for insurance company employee who evaluates claims and advises on policy liabilities and losses incurred. His/her role is to research into major claims and ensure that settlements are fair and reasonable.

### adjusting entries
These are journal entries that are made at the end of the accounting period, to adjust expenses and revenues to the accounting period where they actually occurred. They are adjustments based on a reality, not on a source document.

### administration costs
These are indirect costs charged to a department, factory, or unit as its share of general administration costs for the organisation as a whole, over and above indirect costs attributable

solely to the department or factory.

## administrative change
It is a unilateral contract modification, in writing, that does not affect the substantive rights of the parties, e.g. a change in the mailing address.

## administrative expense
Also known as administrative cost, it is the cost of all the administrative activities, i.e. managements, accounting and general office personnel and supplies that cannot be directly linked with manufacturing cost. It includes salaries and related benefits, including fringe benefits of those employees who perform clerical or administrative, i.e. non-technical activities.

## ADMOS
It is acronym of Automatic Device for Mechanical Order Selection which is a card-activated machine for checking stock availability, selecting quantities of goods required, recording stock balances and conveying items direct to the despatch department.

## adoptions of innovations
The consumers who accept an innovation fall into the five groups, understanding each of which should help a company in devising effective marketing strategies. The groups are as follows:
1. *Innovators* – The first to buy and use new products. They keep the innovation in high priority to create the image of being venturesome.
2. *Early adopters* – Those who adopt new ideas early but carefully.
3. *Early majority* – People regarded as being deliberate in their decisions, who are rarely leaders.
4. *Late of majority* – Sceptres who only adopt an innovation after most other people have tried it.
5. *Laggards* – Those who are suspicious of changes and innovations. They tend only to adopt the innovation when it has become widely accepted.

## ad valorem
It describes a tax, duty or fee which varies in proportion to the value of the goods or services on which it is levied.

**Dictionary of Business**

## advance

It can be defined as an increase in the interest rates or in the market price of a commodity, good or property. It is also known as advance payment.

## advanced planning and scheduling (APS)

The term refers to a manufacturing planning and scheduling system that is normally used to supplement 'infinite planning' systems based on MRP logic. An APS can create detailed schedules for orders, while traditional MRP systems create very crude plans based on fixed planned lead times.

## advanced shipment notification (ASN)

It is a type of notification used to inform a customer of a shipment. ASNs often include PO numbers, SKU numbers, quantity lot, number pallet or container number, and sometimes carton number. ASNs may be paper-based, but electronic notifications are preferred. Advanced shipment notification systems are normally combined with bar-coded compliance labelling which enables the customer to receive the shipment into inventory with the use of bar-code scanners and automated data collection systems.

## adventure

In business, the term is used for commercial undertaking of a speculative nature. It is often associated with overseas trading.

## adverse opinion

It refers to an opinion expressed in an auditor's report that the financial statements do not reflect true and fair view of the organisation activities. This situation arises when there is a disagreement between the auditor and the directors, and the auditor considers the effect of the disagreement to be so material that he thinks that the financial statements are seriously misleading.

## advertising

It is a generic term for presentation and publication of information or opinions on goods, services, institutions, etc. with a view to attracting purchases or to building up a corporate image or prestige among the public. It denotes any means by which a company tries to influence people to promote its ideas, sales, and goodwill. Advertisement is intended to persuade people about products. The two basic aspects of advertising are the message and the medium. The media carrying advertising range from the press, television, cinema, radio, and posters to company logos on apparel. It is believed that advertising creates awareness of a product; extensive advertising creates confidence in the product, and good advertising creates a desire to buy the product.

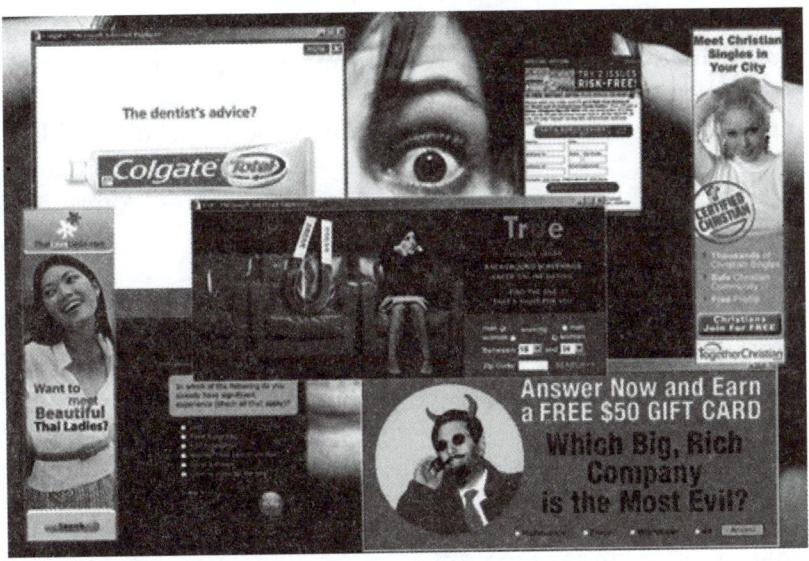

Advertising

## affective component

It is one of three main components of the attitudes, a person can have regarding an object. This component is related to the customer's emotional reaction and involves such questions as: Is this brand good or bad? Is it useful? It also involves such judgements as: 'I love Toyota', 'The Japanese are competent to make luxury cars', etc.

## affiliate

An organisation in which another organisation has a minority interest. In other words, a company which is related to another company in some way, such as through ownership, working agreement, etc., may be called its affiliate.

## affirmative action
It can be referred to as policies that take factors which include race, colour, religion, sex, or national origin into consideration in order to benefit an under-represented group.

## after date
These are words used in a bill of exchange to indicate that the period of the bill should commence from the date inserted on the bill, viz. "90 days after date, we promise to pay....s".

## aftermarket
Also known as replacement market or secondary market, it supplies accessories, second-hand equipment, spare parts and other goods and services used in repair and maintenance. Some aftermarkets like those of wheels, parts, tyres, etc. are very large.

## after-sales service
It refers to maintenance of products by the manufacturers or their agents after purchase by the customers. This often takes the form of a guarantee, which is effective for a stated period during which the service is free in respect of both parts and labour, followed by a maintenance contract for which the buyer of the product has to pay a certain sum of money. Efficient and effective after-sales service is key to good marketing policy, especially for such consumer durables as cars, computers, laptops, washing machines, ACs, etc.

## after tax
The amount obtained after taxes have been subtracted. Profit after tax is profit after taxes due on it have been deducted from it.

## age analysis
It is a count normally produced monthly, which analyses the age of the debts by splitting them into such categories as up to one month old, two months old, and more than two months old.

## agent
A person or a firm that has expressed (oral or written) or implied authority to act as a

Dictionary of Business

representative for another (the principal), e.g. a company sales representative or an insurance agent.

The ownership of any goods handled by an agent does not pass, even though the agent may carry stock, and the entire profit, after deduction of expenses approved and a commission on the gross proceeds of sale, is accountable to the person appointing the agent.

### agent di cambio

The term is used for stockbrokers trading on the floors of the Italian stock exchanges. They are also authorised non-bidding dealers, who may buy and sell securities but not through trading floor biddings.

### aggregate

An aggregate is a collection of information or items that are gathered together to form a total quantity.

### aggregate inventory management

It consists of tools that are used in group items and to manage each group with policies, key performance indicators, targets, etc. A particular group of items for example might share carrying charge parameters, turnover targets and have a fixed space allocation.

### aggregate planning

It is the process of translating the annual business and marketing plans into a production plan. It is also called the production plan. Aggregate planning is difficult for firms with seasonal products. An aggregate measure is particularly useful if the production plan includes many dissimilar products.

### aggregate supply

It is the total supply of all the goods and services in an economy. It was the noted economist J.M. Keynes who made aggregate demand the focus of macroeconomics. However, since the 1970s, many economists have questioned the importance of aggregate demand in determining the health of an economy, suggesting instead that governments should concentrate on creating conditions to encourage the supply of goods and services.

### agio

It is the proportional

**Dictionary of Business**

# agribusiness

difference between current market prices and the payment-settled inventory value plus last payment.

## agribusiness

It can be described as follows:
1. Various businesses that involve food production including farming and contract farming, seed supply, farm machinery, etc.
2. Production, processing, storage, transportation, and distribution of farming suppliers and producers.

## AIDA

It is an abbreviation for attention, interest, desire, and action which are the four key requirements in successful selling. It is used as a basis for many sales training for programs.

## air freight

It refers to the charges of transport of goods by aircraft, either in a scheduled airliner or in a freight plane. Air cargo usually consists of goods that have a high value compared to their weight.

Agribusiness

## air waybill

It refers to document made out by a consignor of goods by air freight to facilitate swift delivery of the goods to the consignee. It gives the name of the consignor and the loading airport, the consignee and the airport of destination, a description of the goods, as also the marks, number, and dimensions of the packages.

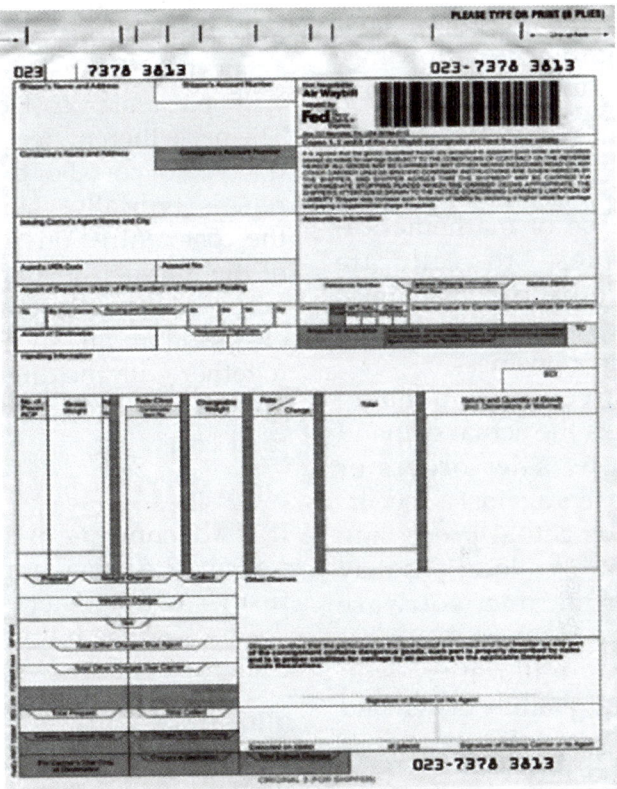

Air waybill

## all commodity volume

It is a market research and equal retail audit term for the turnover of all goods in a shop or shops. Such information is used, for example, in evaluating the significance of the turnover in the product being market researched or audited.

## allocation

It refers as follows:
1. The amount set aside for different products or prospects.
2. Fixation of the resources, like materials for the fabrication of various goods.
3. Assigning the allowance for the purchase of various goods and services, cost of manufactured products, through a formula.
4. The use of mathematical techniques to allocate available people, machines, and materials to get optimum results in a business.
5. In inventory management, it is the actual demand created by sales orders or work orders against a specific item. The actual processing that controls allocations may vary from one software system to another.
A standard allocation is an aggregate quantity of demand against a specific item in a specific facility.
A firm allocation is an allocation against specific units within a facility, such as an allocation against a specific location or serial number. Firm allocation is also known as specific allocation, frozen allocation, hard allocation, hard commitments, and reserved inventory.

## allocation of overheads

The term implies apportioning indirect costs and expenses, e.g. cleaning materials, lighting, heating and depreciation which cannot be directly identified with particular cost centres. The basis thereof depends on the type of cost. For example, rent is typically charged to the cost centres on the basis of the number of square feet occupied. The objective is to ensure that all such costs, together with the direct costs give a realistic picture of total costs.

## allonge

It is attachments to a bill of exchange to provide space for further endorsements when the back of the bill itself has been fully used.

## allotment

It is method of distributing previously unissued shares in a limited company in exchange for a contribution of capital. An application for such shares is usually made on the floatation of public company or on the privatisation of a state-owned industry.

Dictionary of Business

## allowance
It implies the following:
1. A sum set aside for an occurrence that may or may not come to pass such as an allowance made for bad debt.
2. An amount paid to employees as part of their salary package.
3. An acceptable increment or wastage included while estimating time or material for a production or other process.

## all-time demand
It refers to the total future requirements for an item. It is the sum of the demand up to the product termination date, and is used to determine the requirements for the final purchase or production run. It is sometimes called the 'all-time' or the 'lifetime' requirement.

## all-time order
It is the last order for a particular product in the last phase of its life-cycle. Such order should be so large that the stock provided satisfies all the expected future demand for the product concerned. It is also called a 'lifetime' buy.

## alpha stocks
The term is used for computerised classification of leading hundred or so stocks traded on the International Stock Exchange, London. Such stocks are selected because of the size of their market capitalisation.

## alternating shift
It denotes a system of shift working where workers are changed to a different shift periodically.

## amenity
A feature that adds value or perceived value to something. It adds to the comfort or pleasure provided to those employees who crossed a certain position.

## amortisation
It refer to the following:
1. The process of treating as an expense, the annual amount deemed to have been taken away from a fixed asset. The concept is particularly applied to leases, which are acquired for a given sum, for a specified term, at the end of which the lease would be without value. The common procedure is to divide the cost of the lease by the number of years of its term and treat the result as an annual charge against profit.

**Dictionary of Business**

2. It also refers to the repayment of debt by a borrower in a series of instalments over a period. Each payment includes interest and part repayment of the capital.

### analogous cost estimating

It is an estimating method, which determines the rough cost of a project by comparing it with an older, similar project for which the actual costs are available. A variety of top-down estimating is generally used in the early planning stages before a more accurate, bottoms-up approach can be generated.

### analyst

A person who analyses the organisation and design of businesses and non-profit organisations. He is a financial professional whose primary function is a deep examination of a specific area. Such professional expert is also known as financial analyst or a security analyst.

### anchor services

These are Internet service providers that form the basis of e-commerce websites by attracting traffic or providing credibility.

### annualiser

A professional employee whose job is to calculate data on a yearly basis, or to estimate data taking into consideration the fluctuations that occurred during the year.

### annual meeting

It is also known as annual general meeting (AGM). It is the gathering of the board of directors and stockholders (shareholders) at a meeting held each calendar year. In AGM, the main purpose is to comply with legal requirements like election of director, appointments of authorities for a new accounting year, etc.

### annual report

Also known as annual accounts, annual report is the presentation of a firm's audited accounts for the previous year. Besides, an annual report generally includes the following:
1. Management's review of the operations of the firm and its future planning.
2. Balance Sheet.

3. Income Statement (Profit and Loss Account).
4. Cash Flow statement.
5. Data for annual account, viz. the discharges for the inventory of the fortune as well as the report of the revision in prices, etc.

## annuity

It is not an insurance policy but a tax-shelter. It comprises a series of equal periodic payments or receipts. These are of two types, viz. ordinary annuity, where payments or receipts occur at the end of the period; and annual annuity, where payments or receipts are made at the beginning of the period.

## anomaly

In business, it is an opportunity for abnormal returns in financial markets. If markets are efficient, there should be no anomalies, and the assumption that this will really be the case setting the pricing of many financial obligations, particularly the derivatives.

## anticipation stock

It refers to the follows:
1. Materials, parts or finished goods, purchased or manufactured in advance of expected demand or in anticipation of rising costs and prices.
2. Inventory held in order to satisfy seasonal demand, a sudden spurt in demand, to cope with expected reduced capacity due to maintenance or anticipated strike or, to store seasonal supply for a demand level throughout the year.

## anti-pirating agreement

Also called anti-poaching agreement, it is a convention observed by employers in a particular industry or locality that they will not recruit each other's employees.

## antitrust legislation

It is a generic term for a number of laws concerned with preserving a competitive and open market. The first law was the Sherman Act of 1890 (in the US) which prohibited monopolies, conspiracies and combinations in restraint of trade. Subsequently, there were legislations, like the Clayton Act, the Federal Trade Commission Act, 1914, the Robinson Patmen Act, 1936, etc. and other laws for maintaining a free economy.

## A-plant
It is a type of plant wherein many components are assembled into just a few end items.

## application area
It comprises a category of projects that have a common element, not present in all projects. These are defined in terms of either the product of the project, i.e. by similar technologies or industry sectors, or the type of customer, viz. internal vs. external, government vs. commercial application areas which usually overlap each other.

## application service provider (ASP)
It is a system in which the software licenses are owned by the ASP and reside on their system while the client rents the rights to use the software manufacturer for a third party business. The advantages of using an ASP are lower upfront costs, quicker implementation and the reduction of the need for internal IS personnel and mainframe/server (hardware).

## applied cost
Cost that does not have to be based on actual costs incurred. It is the cost assigned to an activity, department or product on the basis of a pre-determined overhead rate.

## appreciation
It refers to the following:
1. An increase in the value of an asset through a rise in market price, or interest earned.
2. An increase in the value of a currency with a floating exchange rate, relative to another currency.
3. An increase in the prices of shares, etc.

## appropriation
The act of setting aside money for a specific purpose. An organisation or a government appropriates funds in order to delegate cash for the necessities of its business operations. It is also called capital allocation.

## approve
It simply means to accept as satisfactory. Approval implies that the item approved has the endorsement of the

approving authority. The approval, however, may require confirmation by somebody else, if there are levels of approval. In business management, there is an important distinction between approve and authorise.

## arbitrage

It refers to the following:
1. Utilisation of local or international evaluation differences of same securities or related values, whereby these are bought in the market with the lower price and sold at the market with the higher price, thus earning a profit.
2. Buying and selling of stocks and shares, currency, bills of exchange, etc. in different markets at virtually the same time in order to take advantage of different prices being quoted.

## area of project management application

It refer the environment in which a project takes place, with its own particular nomenclature and accepted practices, viz. facilities, products, services, systems of development projects, etc.

## arm's length transaction

It is a dealing between independent, unrelated and well-informed parties looking for their individual interests on the basis of determining fair market value. To qualify as an arm's length transaction, it is necessary that neither of the involved parties may have any interest in the consequences of transaction to the other party.

## arrears

Also called arrearage, these are the liabilities or obligations not met on due date. Loan payments are in arrears the day after they are due.

## arrow diagramming method (ADM)

It is a network diagramming technique in which various types of activities are represented by arrows. The tail of the arrow represents the start and the head represents the finish of the activity. Activities are also connected at points called nodes to illustrate the sequence in which these are expected to be performed.

**Dictionary of Business**

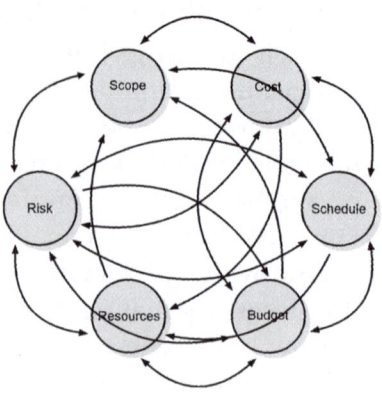

*Arrow diagramming method*

## articles of incorporation

Also known as articles of formation, articles of organisation, certificate of incorporation, corporate chapter or letters patent, it is the first document that needs to be filed with the appropriate government agency for the business entity to receive the legal recognition as a corporate. This document usually contains information regarding the company's name, business, purpose, address of the registered office, etc. It is required to be filed by both for-profit corporations and non-profit corporations.

## 'A' shares

These are shares which carry no vote, although they qualify for dividends in the same way as other ordinary shares.

## 'as is' goods

It is the condition of sale that a buyer will accept delivery of goods ordered as they come and without warranty.

## assemble to order

The term is used for a customer interface strategy that responds to a customer order by putting together standard components and modules for the customer. Customer lead-time is total of the assembly, packing and shipping time. This approach gives a large variety of final products within a relatively short customer lead-time.

## assembly

It implies number of parts or sub-assemblies or any combination thereof joined together to perform a specific function.

## assessment

It refers to the following:
1. The process of documentary which normally is measurable in terms of knowledge, attitudes, beliefs and skills.

Dictionary of Business

2. It is a process of setting a value on real or personal property, generally for the purpose of taxation.

## asset cover

It is a ratio that provides a measure of the solvency of a company. It is comprised of its net assets divided by its debt. Companies with high asset cover are considered more healthy and solvent.

## assets

These may be referred to as follows:
1. In financial accounting these are economic resources, viz. anything tangible or intangible that is capable of being owned of controlled to or produced value.
2. Anything that has value, which is a measure of strong points or abilities of a company, firm, or an individual.

## assign

It denotes the following:
1. To transfer ownership of a property or right, including shares, debts, etc. to another party by signing a document. The assignee is the person to whom the right or property is assigned. The assignor is the person who makes over or transfers the right or property.
2. To allot something for a specific purpose, e.g. to assign a date for a meeting, to assign a taste to an individual.

## assignment

The term can be defined as the transfer of ownership of a property or of benefits, interests, rights, liabilities, etc. under a contract by one party to another by signing a document known as the deed of assignment. Such a document usually needs to be stamped and registered.

## associated company

It refers to a company of which less than 50 per cent of the share capital is owned. The assets are not consolidated into the parent company accounts but are shown as trade investment.

## associate director

It refers to the title given to senior managers, viz. heads of major functions or divisions. It provides power, status, and recognition. However, associate directors under the UK Companies Act, are neither members of the board

**Dictionary of Business**

nor have the duties and responsibilities of directors.

## assurance
The term is used interchangeably with insurance in practice. But, technically, an assurance policy covers what is bound to happen but at an unknown time, e.g. death of a person, while an insurance policy is taken out against what may or may not happen, e.g. an earthquake or fire.

## at call
The term is used in context of money that has been lent on a short-term basis and must be repaid on demand. Discount houses are the main borrowers of money at call.

## at limit
It is an instruction to a broker to buy or sell shares, stocks, commodities, currencies, etc. as specified, at a stated limiting price. While issuing such instruction, the principal must state for how long the instruction stands, i.e. for a day or a week.

## at sight
The term is used in the context of negotiable instruments, particularly bills. For example, a bill at sight is payable immediately on presentation and does not first have to go through an acceptance procedure.

## atlas test specification
The term is used to define the test requirements for the unit under test, in a manner, which is independent of the test equipment used for its implementation. It is derived from the system/sub-system specification and contains the absolute values of the functional design performance parameters.

## attest
It means to affirm an act or event as genuine or true. Documents are legally attested when they are signed by the involved parties in the presence of a witness who also puts his signatures at the appropriate place.

## attribute comparisons
It denotes market research survey in which respondents are asked to choose which of a list of attributes is most appropriate to a particular brand or product.

## attributes
It refers to the qualitative data that can be counted for

recording and analysis. Examples include characteristics such as the presence of a required label and the installation of all required fasteners.

## attribution
It is defined as follows:
1. Loss of a material or resource due to spoilage or uselessness.
2. Uncontrollable and unpredictable, but normal reduction of workforce because of resignation, retirement, sickness or due to death.

## auction
It is a method of sale in which goods, securities, and rights are sold in public to the highest bidder. Auctions are used for any property for which there are likely to be a number of competing buyers such as houses, antiques, etc. as well as for certain commodities such as bristles, tea, wool, furs, etc., which must be sold as individual lots, rather than on the basis of a standard sample or grading procedure.

## audit
It refers to the following:
1. Systematic examination and verification of a firm's books of account, transaction records, physical inspection of inventory and other relevant documents by a qualified accountant called auditor.
2. Periodic onsite verification, by an authentic authority, to ascertain whether a document quality is being effectively implemented or not.
3. In onsite verification activity, audit is used to determine the effective implementation of a supplier's documented quality system.

## audit criteria
It refers to the set of procedures, or requirements used as a reference while conducting an audit.

## audit cycle
It refers to the period of time over which all sections of a company or organisation are under auditing by rotation.

## auditing
It records the sequence of activities that occur on any given file or body of content within a content management system. An audit trail is often used by content auditors to

determine how and why content was changed.

### audit resolution process
The term is used for the process by which the department determines whether costs in an audit report are actually allowable or not. If costs are identified as not being allowable, the department has to take appropriate action.

### automated storage and retrieval system (ASRS)
It refers to a system of rows of racks with each row having a dedicated retrieval unit that moves vertically and horizontally along the rack picking and putting away loads.

### automatic competition
In business, the term is used for pure and direct competition, without government intervention in the working of the market.

### automatic vending
It denotes sale of goods, particularly foodstuffs, etc. installed at places like malls, markets, cinema halls, etc. and in coin-in-the-slot machines.

### autonomous bargaining
It refers to bargaining where local bargaining has been established as a matter of policy rather than where it happens due to lack of the power of trade unions and/or employers' associations.

### autonomous maintenance
It is a principle in which each worker is responsible for both maintaining and operating a machine. Maintenance activities include cleaning, doing adjusting, lubricating, inspecting, and repair.

### available-to-promise (ATP)
The uncommitted portion of a company's inventory and planned production, maintained in the master schedule to support customer order promising. The ATP quantity is the uncommitted inventory balance in the first period, and is usually calculated for each period in which a receipt is scheduled.

### average adjuster
It is a term for insurance official skilled in assessing average, viz. the value of damage or loss to goods at sea, during shipment, etc.

## average cost
Also called unit cost, it is the production cost per unit of output computed by dividing the total of fixed costs and variable by the number of total unit produced.

## average cost method
In business, it is favourable utilisation of exchange rate fluctuations. It sets on the advantage of regular payments, whereby with same monthly deposits the investor thus acquires more with low issue prices and with higher issue prices of fewer portions. The investor thereby achieves a more favourable average cost price on a long-term basis, than with the regular purchase of a given number of items or portions in the same period.

## average outgoing quality
Abbreviated as AOQ, it is average quality of outgoing product including all accepted lots, plus all rejected lots after the rejected lots have been effectively inspected and replaced by non-defectives.

## average outgoing quality limit
Abbreviated as AOQL, it is the maximum of the average outgoing qualities for all possible incoming qualities for a given sampling plan.

## avoidable costs
They are such costs as include any expenses that are not incurred if a new investment is made that would make the expenses unnecessary. For example, if a machine breaks down and must be fixed to operate the facility, there is a cost to fix the machine as well as the option to purchase a new one. If a new machine is purchased, there is no need for the repair expenses and hence, that expense was avoided.

## award fee
The term refers to a contract fee used to motivate a contractor to respond to issues that are assigned and measured periodically. The contract specifies award fee periods, usually a month to one year long. The award fee criteria are negotiated prior to the start of the award fee period, providing the buyer the flexibility to change the incentive emphasis as the project evolves.

**Dictionary of Business**

# B

## B2B
It is an abbreviation for business-to-business, implying direct connectivity between commercial organisations, especially via the Internet.

## B2b
It also means business-to-business, but denotes, a business selling to other businesses.

## B2C
It stands for business-to-consumer, viz. a business selling directly to consumers.

## backdate
It denotes the following:
1. To put an earlier date on a document than that on which it was prepared in order to make it effective from that earlier date.
2. To agree that salary increases settled in a pay award, should apply from a specified date in the recent past.

## back-end load
It is the final charge made by an investment trust, when an investor sells shares in the fund.

## backer
It refers to a person or enterprise that invests in a new company or project and may require a share in the equity of the company.

## backflush
It denotes method for issuing materials to a manufacturing order. With backflushing, the material is issued automatically when production is posted against an operation. The backflushing program uses the quantity completed to calculate quantities of the components used and reduce on-hand balances by this amount. There are options during the backflush process to report scrap.

## back freight
It refers to the cost of shipping goods back to the port of destination if they have been overcarried. In case the master overcarried the goods

40

for reasons beyond his control, the shipowner may be responsible for paying the back freight. If delivery was not accepted in the given time at the port of destination and the master sent them back to the port of shipment, the back freight is the responsibility of the cargo owner.

## back order

It is the customer demand for which no stock is available and where the customer is prepared to wait for the item to arrive in the stock. If a firm cannot immediately satisfy a customer order, the customer is asked to wait. Such an order is called a 'back order' and is usually filled as soon as the items become available.

## back-selling

It is an indirect form of sales promotion by stimulating the sales of a product or service further along the sales chain. Thus, in a sales chain comprising manufacturer, wholesaler, retailer and consumer, back-selling by the manufacturer might consist of sales promotion among retailers to stimulate demand back along the chain through the wholesalers.

## back to back credit

It is a type of credit given to an exporter by a finance house or bank, acting as a go-between with a buyer in an export market.

## backward/back loading

It denotes the method that plans backwards from the due date to determine the start date. The word 'loading' implies that we are not creating a detailed schedule. Backward loading might continue until the capacity is fully utilised.

## backwardation

It denotes the following:
1. The situation in which the spot price of a commodity, including any costs thereon, is higher than the forward price.
2. A situation in a stock exchange when a market maker quotes a buying price for a share that is lower than the selling price quoted by another market maker.

## backward pass

It is the calculation of late finish dates and late start dates for the uncompleted portions of all network activities. It is determined by working backwards through the network logic from the project's end date. The end date is calculated in a forward pass or set by the customer or sponsor.

### backward scheduling
It implies a scheduling method that plans backwards from the due date to determine the start date. As against backward loading, backward scheduling creates a detailed schedule for each operation based on the planned available capacity.

### backwash effect
It refers to divergence in productivity between the developed countries' exports consisting mainly of manufactured goods, and those of the developing countries consisting largely of agricultural commodities.

### bad debt
An amount owed by a debtor that is unlikely to be recovered, e.g. amount due to a company going into liquidation. The full amount should be written off and a provision for bad debts should be made as per prudential norms. Bad debts subsequently recovered either in part or in full should be written back to the provision account.

### bailment
It refers to delivery of goods from the bailor, i.e. the owner of the goods, on the condition that the goods will ultimately be returned to the former. The goods hired, lent, pledged, or deposited for safe custody are said to be bailed. A delivery of this nature is also the subject of some contract.

### balanced scorecard system
It refers to a method of measuring performance of a firm beyond the typical financial measures. It connects corporate goals and direct performance measures in a framework specific to a firm and is the method of measuring the impact of knowledge management.

### balance of payments
Abbreviated as BoPs, these are accounts setting out a country's transactions with all other countries. They are divided into various sub-accounts, notably the current account and the capital account. The former includes the trade account, which records the balance of imports

and exports. Favourable BoPs denote more exports from the countries than imports into it, whereas a negative BoP implies more imports than exports.

## balance sheet

Statement of a company's financial position at a particular date, normally at the last date of financial year, viz. 31st March, balancing assets against liabilities and showing the sources and applications of funds. Earlier balance sheets were produced with liabilities shown on the left and assets on the right. Now they are often produced in vertical form showing Fixed Assets and Net Current Assets (described together as capital employed) and then showing capital ownership. The complementary statement of financial accounting is the profit and loss account showing company's performance over a particular period of time, viz. a year or a half year.

## bank

It can be defined as a commercial institution that takes deposits and extends loans. Banks are concerned mainly with making and receiving payments on behalf of their customers, accepting deposits, and making short-term loans to private individuals, companies, and other organisations. These days, banks have increased their range of services to include ATM facilities, collection of income tax, receipt of bills, etc.

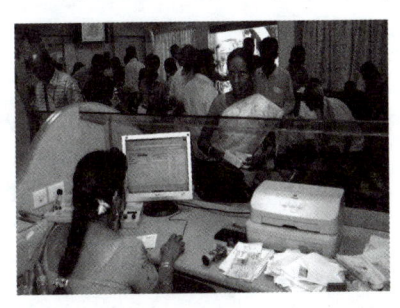

**Bank**

## bank guarantee

It refers to an undertaking given by a bank to settle a debt in case the debtor fails to do so. A bank guarantee can be used as a security for a loan but the banks themselves will require good cover in cash or counter-guarantee before they issue such a guarantee. A guarantee is in writing and legally binding. It often contains indemnity clauses, which place a direct onus on the guarantor.

### bankruptcy
It denotes the following:
1. A situation where a person is unable to pay creditors in full.
2. A condition where an individual or corporate debtor is judged legally insolvent. Any remaining property is administered for the creditors.

### bargaining range
It refers to the range within which a wage claim is likely to be settled, keeping what the employees claim and the employers are willing to offer.

### baseline review
It implies a customer review conducted to determine with a limited sampling that a contractor is continuing to use the previously accepted performance system.

### base stock
A certain volume of stock, assumed to be constant and below which stock level is not allowed to fall. When the stock is valued, this proportion of the stock is valued at its original cost.

### basic product
It refers to the product marketed not to the public or consumer, but to industry as a component or constituent part in other products.

### BASIS
It is abbreviation for Booking and Sampling for Indirect Standards.

### basis of assessment
It is the basis upon which personal income or business profits are assessed in India for each income tax schedule identifying the profits or income to be assessed in that year.

### basle-II
It refers to an accord, implemented in 2004, that supplants the Basle Convergence Accord of 1988. It established a new framework for defining risk capital and weightings, based to greater extent than previously on credit ratings and internal models. It also gave a supervisory process to ensure that banks have adequate internal systems to understand and establish their capital at risks and assess their adequacy.

## batch picking
The term is used for order picking method where orders are grouped into small batches. It is associated with pickers with multi-tiered picking carts moving up and down aisles picking batches of generally 6 to 12 orders. Batch picking is also very common while working with automated material handling equipments.

## batch processing
It denotes the following:
1. A method of processing data, using a computer, in which the programs to be executed are collected together into groups, or batches for processing. All the required information to execute the programs is loaded into the computer so that it can work without further intervention.
2. Manufacture of a quantity of a product but not in conditions of continuous or standardised production.

## batch production
It implies a manufacturing process in which medium to high volumes of similar items are made in batches, rather than continuously, with the product moving from process to process in batches.

## bear
The term is used for a dealer on a stock exchange, currency market, or commodity market who expects prices to fall. A bear market is one in which a dealer is more likely to sell securities, etc. than to buy them. A bear may even sell securities, currency, or goods without having them. This is known as short selling bear position. The bear hopes to cover such a short position by buying at a lower price, the amount of securities, currency, or goods already sold, so that he/she earns a profit.

## behaviour study
It is a market research statistical technique for assessing the behaviour pattern and the opportunities existing in a particular market.

## below-the-line item
In accounting, it refers to non-recurring expenditure or gain, which may be added or deductable adjustment to attributable net profit.

## below-the-line promotion
It is a marketing term for sales

promotion in such forms as reduced price offers, premiums and point-of-sale displays.

## benefit segmentation
The process of dividing a market according to the specific benefits which the consumers seek from a product. For example, some car buyers want comfort and reliability from their car, while others look for style and speed. A car manufacturer, therefore, has to decide which benefits to offer. This will depend on the target buyers.

## bid
It refers to the following:
1. The price at which a buyer is willing to close a deal. If the seller has made an offer that the buyer considers too high, the buyer may make a bid at a lower price or on more advantageous terms.
2. The price or yield at which a buyer indicates that he or she is willing to take a financial obligation.
3. An approach by one company to buy the share capital of another.

## bid cost considerations
It is the consideration of supplier's approach and reasonableness of cost, the forecast economic factors affecting cost and cost risks used in the cost proposal.

## bid evaluation
It refers to review and analysis of response to determine the supplier's ability to perform the work as requested. This activity usually includes an evaluation of supplier's financial resources, ability to comply with technical criteria, meeting delivery schedules, satisfactory record of performance and eligibility for award, among other things.

## bid qualifications
It is a list of qualifiers that the supplier attaches to the submitted bid. Such bid is usually contingent upon these requirements being met.

## bid response
These are communications, positive or negative, from prosecutive suppliers in response to the invitation to bid.

## bid technical consideration
The term is used for supplier's technical competency, understanding of the

technical requirements and capability to produce technically acceptable goods or services.

### bidder
It refers to anyone who responds to a request for proposal, i.e. one who submits a bid.

### bidders source selection
It refers the pre-selection of qualified bidders from a given speciality. Tender invitations are only distributed to those listed. If the list is large, bidders may be chosen in rotation.

### bidding strategy
It is the manner in which bids are to be obtained. Options vary from the stage of development of the project's definition to the manner in which the work is divided and the timing in the marketplace, given the degree of existing competition.

### bill of entry
It is a detailed statement of the nature and value of a consignment of goods prepared by the shipper of the consignment for customs entry.

### bill of exchange
It is defined as an unconditional order in writing, by one person to whom it is addressed to pay on demand, or at a fixed or determinable future time, a certain sum of money to a specified person. A bill of exchange can be negotiated,

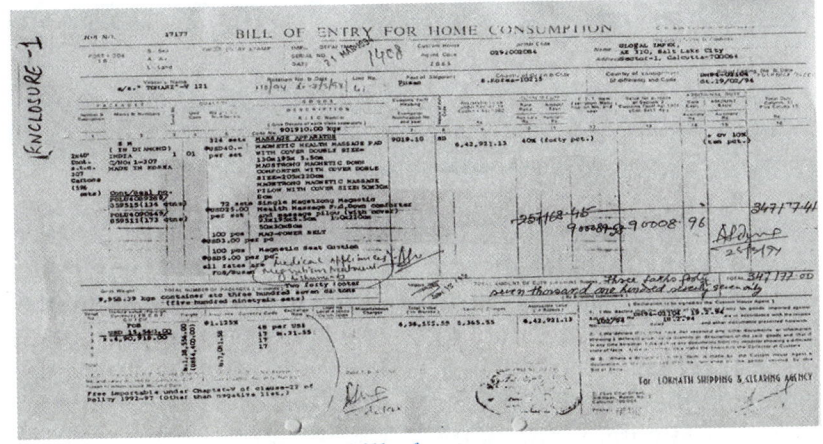

Bill of entry

# bill of material

i.e. used in lieu of cash or as evidence of ability to meet obligations elsewhere. It can be discounted through a discount house which purchases the bill of exchange immediately for an agreed sum which is less than the sum it will be worth when it matures. It can also be used as security for and advance made by a bank or an acceptance house.

# bill of lading

It refers to the following:
1. A consignment of goods transported by ship, copies being sent ahead of the shipment to give proof of title to the consignor. Copies are also held by the exporter and sent with the goods.
2. It is a document used to acknowledge the receipt of products.

Bill of lading

# bill of material

Abbreviated as BOM, it is a listing of components, parts and other items needed to manufacture a product, showing the quantity of each intermediate item. The BOM is generally drawn as 'tree structure' with the end items at the top. This bill is similar to a list of parts except that it usually shows how the product is fabricated and assembled.

## bills payable
It denotes the following:
1. The amounts owed by a business to its creditors such as trade suppliers.
2. An item that may appear in a firm's accounts under current liabilities, detailing the bills of exchange being held, which will have to be paid when they mature.

## bills receivable
It refers to the following:
1. The amounts owed to a business by its debtors, viz. its customers.
2. An item that may appear in a firm's accounts under current assets, detailing the bills of exchange being held until the bills mature and funds become available.

## bimodal distribution
It refers to a distribution with two identifiable curves within it, indicating a mixing of two sets of workers such as different shifts, machines and workers.

## blacking
The term is issued for employees who during industrial action, refuse to work on goods or components that they consider are being processed or supplied by employers in a way which evades the industrial action.

## black-leg
It refers to a worker who continues working during a strike.

## black market
The term is used for an illegal market for a particular good or service. It can occur when regulations control a particular trade or a particular period.

## blanket order
It refers to a standing order to supply certain products and/or services over time or against which specific quantities can be called for as required.

## blanket purchase order
It is an agreement with a supplier that specifies the price, minimum quantity and maximum quantity purchased over a defined time period. Purchase orders are placed against the blanket order to define the quantity due for the specific order. The advantage of such purchase orders for both parties is that they lock in the price and the parties only have to negotiate once every year or so.

**Dictionary of Business**

### blind counts
It describes a method used in cycle counting and physical inventories where you provide your counters with their item number and location but no quantity information.

### blind test
It is a test of consumer's views of a product without revealing the identity of the product.

### blocking
In business management, production is considered 'blocked' when a process is not allowed to continue when the output storage area is full. Blocking is good for non-bottleneck process.

### blue-collar worker
The term is used for manual worker, normally one working on the shop floor, as opposed to an office worker, who is known as a white-collar worker.

### bond
It is an I owe you (IOU) issued by a borrower to a lender. Bonds are normally in the form of fixed interest securities issued by governments, banks, local authorities, or companies. They come in many forms, viz. with fixed or variable rates of interest; redeemable or irredeemable; short or long-term; secured or unsecured; and marketable or non-marketable. Bonds are generally sold against loans, mortgages, credit-card income, etc. as marketable securities.

**Bond**

### bonded warehouse
A warehouse in which goods intended for re-export are deposited in the custody of customs officers immediately on importation in case the importer wishes to avoid payment of customs duty or other taxes.

### bonus
It denotes the following:
1. An extra payment made to employees by management,

to compensate for something or to share out the profits of a good year.
2. An extra amount of money additional to the proceeds, which is distributed to policyholder by an insurer.
3. Any extra or unexpected payment.

## bonus shares

It refers to shares issued to the existing shareholders in proportion to their holdings, when a company has built up considerable capital reserves in relation to the size of its nominal capital, and its board of directors decides to capitalise its reserves through a scrip issue. The number of bonus shares received depends on the number of shares held prior to the bonus issue. The number of bonus shares is usually one share for a specified number of shares held before the issue. For example, if the specified number is two this would be denoted as a 1:2 bonus issue. It is also possible to have a 1:1 bonus, when one share is issued for one share held.

## book

In business, it refers to the following:

1. The totality of the purchases and sales that make up the position of a trader on financial markets. The terms long book, short book, and open book are used synonymously with long position, short position and open position, respectively.
2. To record an item in the accounts, usually a sale.
3. Also, short for book value.

## book inventories

These are theoretical levels of stocks or inventories based on records of existing stocks plus incoming goods less outgoing goods. Matching of book inventories with physical stocks will reveal errors, pilferage, etc.

## book value

It is the value of a company calculated as its total assets less intangible assets and liabilities. The information required to calculate the book value is mentioned in the balance sheet. However, it can be very misleading to measure value on this basis, as assets (stocks, machinery, buildings, land, etc.) are historical accounting figures. The book value of a company is often compared to its

*Dictionary of Business*

market value, particularly as a means of valuing intangible assets like goodwill, brand name, etc.

Book value is usually the written down value of the assets, taking into account original cost less accumulated depreciation.

## boom

It is a situation in an economy where prices rise faster than real incomes. The boom comes as firms reach a crescendo of competition for limited resources of labour and materials, pushing up costs, money, incomes, profits, and prices.

## bootstrap financing

The term is used for any method of generating cash flow without resource to external sources. It includes converting fixed assets into cash, reducing overhead costs, seeking bigger discounts on raw materials, etc.

## boycott

It denotes refusal to participate in an activity or not to use a product or service.

## brain drain

The term is used for loss of skilled labour force from a country due to emigration in large number.

## brainstorming

It can be defined as putting a large number of ideas before small groups of people, virtually bombarding their brains, who will suggest solutions to various problems without inhibition. These groups sometimes produce breakthrough ideas that otherwise may not have occurred. In business management, brainstorming is used for such purposes as technological forecasting.

## breakdown structure

It refers to a hierarchical structure by which project elements are broken down into parts or segments.

## break-even analysis

It is the system or method of determining break-even points and the relationships between costs, output, sales revenue, profit margin, etc.

## break-even chart

It is a business management, tool for identifying the relationship between costs, output volume, revenue, profit, etc. The chart shows the break-even point. It also shows fixed costs and variable costs.

## break-even point

It refers to the following:
1. The point where an enterprise's sales revenue is equal to its total costs, fixed as well as variable.
2. The point where all the money invested in a project or enterprise, including initial and cumulative running costs, has been recovered and the cumulative value of cash flow is zero. The period until break-even is achieved is called the payout period. The extent to which target and/or actual performance exceeds the break-even point constitutes the margin of safety.

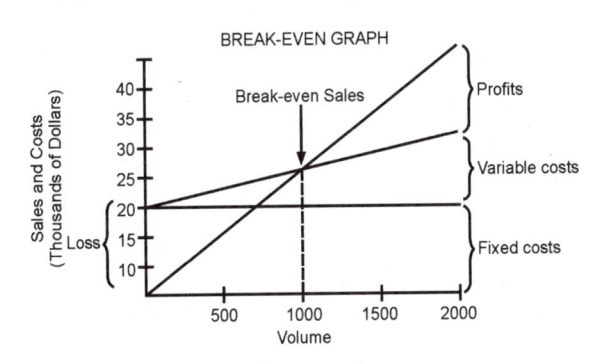

BREAK-EVEN GRAPH

Break-even chart

## brick-by-brick forecasting

It is a forecasting used in market and sales where it is an unsophisticated averaging out of views and opinions expressed by sales people and customers taken from various sections of society.

## broad money

It is an informal name for M3 or any wide definition of the money supply. It affects demand, and thus prices.

## brokerage

It refers to payment made to a broker by his principal for carrying out buying or selling of goods, shares, etc.

## brokers' contract notes

These are confirmations by brokers to their principals that their instructions for buying and/or selling have been carried out.

## bubble

The term is used to express a situation in which asset prices are seriously inflated. The unstable boom thus created may lead to a market crash. The most infamous examples are: the South Sea Bubble of 1720, which led to the collapse of the British share market and the bankruptcy of many investors; the 'dot com bubble' of 1999-2000, in which the share prices of Internet start-up companies rose to mind-boggling levels before collapsing amidst panic selling; the recession of 1929-31 and the subprime bubble in 2008 in the US which led to a worldwide recession.

## budgeted cost of work performed

Abbreviated as BCWP, it is the sum of the approved cost estimates for activities completed during a given period.

## budgetary control

It is a term for ways and means of controlling future levels of activity and expressing these in monetary terms.

## built-in obsolescence

It is the inclusion of factors in a product's design which ensure that it will need to be replaced after a certain period of time. It may be built-in by use of materials of limited durability or by technologic changes in later models. The application of built-in obsolescence is peculiar to certain consumer durables like cars, TVs, cameras, washing machines. Built-in obsolescence is sometimes known as planned obsolescence though this term implies greater precision and control than usual.

## bulk buying

It refers to the buying of products or commodities in sufficiently large quantities to take advantage of bulk discounts or other quantity discounts.

## bullion

It is a term for gold, silver, or some other precious metal used in bulk, i.e. in the form of bars or ingots rather than in coins. Central banks use gold bullion in the settlement of international debts.

## bundling

It is the marketing ploy of

giving away a relatively cheap product with a relatively expensive one to attract customers, e.g. giving a bar of chocolate with a jar of fruit jam.

### burn rate
In business, it is the rate at which funds or man hours are being expended on a project.

### business case
It refers to a structured proposal for business improvement that functions as a decision package for decision-makers in an organisation. A business case includes an analysis of business process needs or problems, assumptions, constraints and risk-adjusted cost-benefit analysis.

### business criterion
It is a management technique in public administration in terms of commercial criterion.

### business data
It is the data about people, places, things, business rules and events, used to operate a business.

### business game
The term is used for enactment by students or trainees of business situations, based on presentation of skilfully selected information, followed by progressive decision-making, leading to assessment of profitability and other crucial factors.

### business impact analysis
It is an analysis that identifies project constraints, alternatives and related assumptions as they apply to the initiation phase.

### business indicators
It is a generic term for statistical data on factors likely to influence the level of business activity. They are of different types: Indicators with a forecasting value are called leaders; those contemporaneous with the business activity are termed as coincident, whereas those that only become apparent after the activity are mere laggers.

### business manager
On a large project or program it is the person responsible for managing the project's business functions such as contracting, sub-contracting, planning, budgeting, human resources, legal matters, etc.

## business name
It refers to name under which a person or organisation trades.

## business objectives
It refers to the business goals which the project's product is designed to satisfy.

## business planning
It is a planning based on the objectives of all aspects of a company's business in order to determine research and development, manufacturing, marketing and acquisition programmes considered indispensable to achieve the objectives, and the financial and manpower resources required to carry out the programs.

## business problem
It refers to a question, issue or situation, pertaining to the business, which needs to be answered or resolved.

## business process redesign
It is an examination of key business processes in order to identify radical changes for improving production and getting better results.

## business process reengineering
It denotes a systematic disciplined improvement approach, particularly the internal approach that critically examines, rethinks and redesigns mission, i.e. delivery processes and sub-processes within a process management approach. In a political environment, the approach achieves radical mission performance gains.

## business promotion
It refers to sales promotion designed to generate business leadership, stimulate purchase, reward business customers, and motivate the marketing team.

## business requirements planning
Abbreviated as BRP, it refers to a conceptual model showing how business planning, master planning, materials planning and capacity planning processes work.

## business segments
It implies the separately identifiable parts of the business operations of a company or group whose

activities, assets, and results can be clearly identified. It is mandatory for companies to disclose in their annual report and accounts, certain financial information relating to business segment.

## business structure
It is the formal structure of a business. At the simplest level is a sole proprietor, a small business run by a single owner. Then, there is partnership which is a business owned and controlled by two or more persons through a partnership agreement. A private limited company is one in which the liability of the owners is restricted to their shareholdings and the shares are not available to a wider public. A public limited company (plc), on the other hand, offers its shares for sale to the public and often has a very diverse ownership. Finally, there is co-operative which is a business in which the ownership and control is held equally by its worker members.

## business system
It denotes the distinctive system of a nation's business organisations. In India, business systems acquired their distinctive characteristics at an early stage of the industrialisation process after Independence. They have subsequently developed and adopted to their environment since then.

## business transaction
The term is used for a unit of work acted upon by a data capture system to create, modify or delete business data. Each transaction represents a single valued fact about a single business event.

## business unit
It refers to any segment of an organisation or an entire business organisation, which is not divided into further segments.

## business vision
It denotes a description of what senior management wants to achieve in the organisation in the future. A business vision normally addresses a medium to long-term period, and is expressed in terms of a series of objectives.

## buyer credit
It refers to credit allowed by

a bank, financial institution, etc. to enable an individual or company to purchase goods or services.

## buying behaviour
It is the way in which a buyer behaves when deciding whether or not to buy a product or service and the factors that determine the behaviour.

## by-product
It is the product which is not the main purpose or product for which a business or process is operated but is produced to optimise the total operation and/or take advantage of what would otherwise be waste material. For example, paraffin is the by-product in petrochemical industry.

## by-product pricing
It refers to setting the price for by-products in order to make the price of the main product more competitive.

# C

## call
It refers to the following:
1. Demand from a company to its shareholders to pay a specified sum on a specified date in respect of their partly paid shares.
2. A notification that redeemable shares or bonds should be presented for repayment.

## callable bonds
These are fixed-rate bonds, usually convertible, in which the issuer has the right, but not the obligations, to redeem, i.e. to call the bond during the life of the bond.

## call off
In business, it means to request delivery or part of an order as and when the goods are required.

## cancellation
It denotes the following:
1. The right to cancel a commercial contract after it has been entered into. Such right exists generally for contracts concluded at a distance, viz. mail order, and Internet sales, when the contract is with a consumer, especially in such sectors as time-shares sales and consumer credit.
2. Also, the act of cancellation of an order, etc.

## cannibalisation
It refers to a market situation in which increased sales of one brand leads to decreased sales of another brand within the same product line, generally because there is little differentiation between them. For instance, two cold drinks marketed by the same manufacturer and packaged in almost the same colour, e.g. Thumps up and Coke could cause increased sales of one to be achieved at the expense of decreased sales of the other.

## cantilever rack
It is the racking system in which the shelving supports are connected to vertical supports at the rear of the rack. There are no vertical supports on the face of the rack allowing for storage of

very long pieces of material like piping lumber, piping, glass, etc.

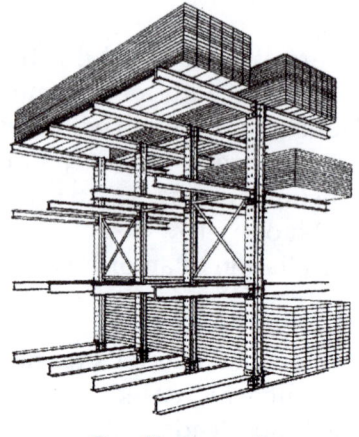

*Cantilever rack*

## capability maturity model

Abbreviated as CMM, the term is used for the stages through which software organisations evolve as they define, implement measures, control and improve their software processes. It is a guide for selecting the process improvement strategies by facilitating the determination of current capabilities.

## capacity

It can be defined as the rate of output for a process, measured in units of output per unit of time. The unit of time may be of any length, i.e. a session, a day, a shift or a minute. Capacity can be of the following types:

1. *Demonstrated capacity:* It is the capacity that the process has actually been able to sustain over a long period.
2. *The theoretical capacity:* It is the maximum production rate based on mathematical or engineering calculations, which do not consider all relevant variables, and therefore, it is quite possible that the capacity can be greater than or less than the theoretical value.
3. *The optimal capacity:* It is that capacity which minimises the total relevant cost, which is the sum of the capacity and waiting cost.

## capacity requirements planning

It refers to the process for determining the amount of machine and labour resources required to meet production.

## capital

It can be defined as stock of money or goods used in a business enterprise. Such goods are either fixed capital, e.g. land, buildings, plant and machinery, or working capital or circulating capital goods consisting of raw materials, semi-finished goods, components, finished goods in store, etc.

## capital cost
It refers to the total expenditure made for acquiring an asset. It constitutes the sum of all money spent on a project and transferred to the capital account of an organisation, generally upon completion.

## capital turnover
It is the ratio of the sales of a company to its capital employed, i.e. its assets less current liabilities. It is presumed that the higher this ratio, the better the use that is being made of the assets in generating sales.

## carat
It denotes the following:
1. A measure of the purity of gold. Pure gold is defined as 24 carat; 18 carat fine gold contains 75% pure gold, the remainder generally being copper.
2. A unit for measuring the weight of a diamond or other gemstones, equal to 0.2 gram.

## cargo insurance
An insurance covering cargoes carried by ships, aircraft, or other forms of transport. In a free on board (fob) contract, the responsibility for insuring the goods for the voyage rests with the buyer. The seller's responsibility ends once the goods have been loaded. In a cost and freight (cf) contract, the buyer is likewise responsible for insurance, even though the seller arranges the shipment and pays the freight. If it is specified that the seller pays for insurance, this is a cost insurance and freight (cif) contract.

## carousel
It is an automated material handling equipment generally used for high-volume small parts order-picking operations. Horizontal carousels are the versions of the same equipment used by dry cleaners to store and retrieve clothing. They have racks hanging from them that can be configured to accommodate storage bins of various size. Vertical carousels comprise a series of horizontal trays on a vertical carousel. They are frequently used in laboratories and some manufacturing operations.

## carrier
A firm that carries goods or people from place to place, usually under a contract and for a fee. Such a carrier must carry goods (within certain restrictions) on regular routes. It charges a reasonable rate, and is liable for all loss or damage to goods in transit.

## carrying charge
It is a rate parameter that is used in applying managerial economics for operations decision-making with respect to inventory. The rate should be the sum of the weighted average cost of capital, a risk premium for obsolete inventory and a storage cost. Reasonable values are in the range of 20 to 40 per cent. This rate should only reflect costs that vary with the size of the inventory and should not include costs that vary with the number of inventory transactions.

## carrying costs
It denotes holding of items in stock, including interest on funds invested in stock, warehouse space, depreciation, obsolescence, insurance, etc.

## cartel
An association of independent companies formed to regulate the price and sales conditions of goods and/or services they offer. A cartel may be national or international, although some countries have legislation forbidding cartels to be formed on the grounds that they are monopolies that function against the public interest. Organisation of Petroleum Exporting Countries (OPEC) is an example of an international price-fixing cartel.

## cash and carry
It refers to wholesale outlet, or sometimes, a retail outlet, at which customers pay cash, rather than buying on credit. The term is also used for a wholesaler, who sells to retailers and others with business at discounted prices on the condition that they pay in cash, collect the goods themselves, and buy in bulk.

## cash book
The book of accounts in which are recorded receipts into and payments out of the enterprise's bank account. The cash book is also an

account as its balance shows the amount due to or from the bank.

### cash burn rate
It refers to the following:
1. How quickly the liquid assets are being spent.
2. The number of rupees of cash flow being lost each month or quarter.

### cash discount
It denotes the following:
1. Allowable reduction in price provided that payment is made in stipulated period.
2. A discount receivable or allowable for setting an invoice for cash. In the profit and loss account, discounts receivable are classified as revenue.

### cash flow
It refers to the following:
1. Flow of cash required to finance operating expenses on the daily basis.
2. Statement showing the sources of all cash receipts, the items on which cash was spent and the overall impact of these transactions on liquid cash resources.
3. A time-based record of income and expenditure, sometimes presented graphically.

### cash flow management
The term is used for the planning of project expenditure relative to income in such a way as to minimise the carrying cost of financing the project.

### casual labour
The term is used for workers not employed on a regular basis, but only as and when work is available. Such type of labour system is adopted in certain industries where the availability of work is uncertain. Casual labour makes for variations in wage payments from period to period, though these may be cushioned where a retainer is paid when there is no work.

### caveat emptor
It is common law principle which denotes that customers should beware when buying goods or services. They should check price, suitability, etc. before buying. If they subsequently suffer loss the law may not support their claim.

### cent
It is a monetary unit of several countries, including Antigua, Australia, the Bahamas, Barbados, Belau, Belize,

Bermuda, Brunei, Canada, East Timor, Ecuador, El Salvador, Fiji, Grenada, Guatemala, Guyana, Hong Kong, Jamaica, Kiribati, Liberia, Malaysia, Namibia, New Zealand, Puerto Rico, Saint Kitts and Nevis, Saint Lucia, Saint Vincent and the Grenadines, the Solomon Islands, Taiwan, Trinidad and Tobago, Tuvalu, the USA, the Virgin Islands, and Zimbabwe. It is worth one hundredth of a dollar.

### certificate of compliance
It is a document signed by an authorised party affirming that the supplier of a product or service has met the requirements of the relevant specifications, and contract of regulations.

### certificate of conformance
It is a certificate signed by a contractor or his representative that the supplies or services required by the contract have been furnished as per the requirements of the contract.

### certificate of damage
A certificate issued by a dock or wharfage company when it takes in damaged goods.

### certificate of incorporation
It is a document confirming that a company or corporation has been legally incorporated. In India, for example, it is issued by the Registrar of Companies, and in the USA by state officials.

### certificate of origin
It is a document sent with exported goods for the information of customs officers in order to establish any claim to preferential tariff rates by virtue of the country of origin of the goods being exported.

### certificate of quality
It is a certificate to provide proof that goods to be traded in a commodity market comply with the agreed standards.

### certification
It is the procedure and action of determining, verifying and attesting in writing, the qualifications of personnel, processes, procedures and/or items, in accordance with given requirements. Such certification is made by a duly authorised body.

## certiorari
It is court writ served on a lower court requesting a transcript of case proceedings so that the judgement and conduct of the case can be reviewed.

## *ceteris paribus*
It means that the given theory or model holds, provided that one or more variable factors remain constant.

## CGI
The term is used for a set of rules that describe how a web server communicates with another piece of software on the same computer and how the other piece of software talks to the web server.

## change control board (CCB)
It is a formally constituted group of stakeholders responsible for approving or rejecting changes to the project baselines.

## channel conflict
It implies contention between Internet players trying to sell to the same customers. Such conflict is not a new phenomenon with the Internet, but it has become more obvious with some disruptions caused by the Internet.

## channel partner
It refers to a firm that works with another firm to provide products and services to customers. Channel partners for a manufacturing firm normally include distributors, sales representatives, retailers, logistics firms, transportation firms, etc.

## charged coupled device (CCD)
The term describes a type of barcode scanner that acts like a small digital camera taking a digital image of the barcode as opposed to the standard barcode scanner that uses a laser.

## charter
It refers to a document prepared at the beginning of the project by the project participants. It includes a mission statement, high level objectives, assumptions and any cost or schedule objectives that are set.

## chartist
The term is used for analyst who uses charts of prices and volumes in an attempt to predict what will happen in

financial markets. Most of the chartist analyses are based on the assumption that history repeats itself and that the movements of share prices conform to a small number of repetitive patterns.

### chart of accounts
It denotes any numbering system used to monitor project costs by category. The project chart of accounts is based upon corporate chart of accounts of the primary performing organisation.

### chase strategy
It can be defined as a strategy in businesses that have seasonal approaches in meeting the demand. Such a strategy keeps finished goods inventory quite low and matches the production rate to the seasonal demand. The level strategy, on the other hand, maintains a constant production rate and builds inventory in the off-season to meet the demand in the peak season.

### checking
It refers to the process of verifying that an activity or object conforms to a given standard.

### checklist
It is a series of carefully prepared interrelated questions designed to aid analysis or appraisal of a specific subject. It provides guidelines for related tasks.

### check-off agreement
The term is used to denote a condition where an employer agrees to deduct trade union dues from trade union members' wages, handing the dues over to the trade union. This enables the union to ensure that dues are paid, and the loss of working time for the dues to be collected is avoided.

### check out
It is one of many exit points at self-service and supermarket stores where the value of goods purchased is checked, recorded and totalled and payment is made.

### chief information officer (CIO)
It denotes a senior position with strategic responsibility for information management and information technology.

### chief knowledge officer (CKO)
He/She is a senior position

with strategic responsibility for knowledge management.

## CIF
It refers to cost, insurance, and freight and implies that the seller of goods pays the freight and insurance charges to the named port.

## clarification contact
It is a contact with an applicant by a grant team member before the department makes a funding decision in order to obtain more detailed information about programmatic and budgetary items in an application.

## classification
It means the bringing together into classes the elements that are similar such as the grouping of costs, samples, tests, types of work, etc.

## classification of defects
It is defined as the enumeration of possible defects of the unit product, classified according to their seriousness. Defects are usually grouped into the classes of critical, minor or major. However, they may also be grouped into other classes or into sub-classes within these classes.

## clearance
It is an indication from a taxing authority that a certain provision does not apply to a particular transaction. The procedure is only available when specified by statute, e.g. on the increase of a company's share capital.

## client environment
It refers to the conditions under which a client operates, viz. the social factors found within the organisation.

## clocking-in
It refers to the recording by employees, of the times at which they start and leave work, usually by punching a card in a time clock.

## closed shop
It is a system whereby all workers must belong to a particular trade union. In the case of a pre-entry closed shop, an employee must be a member of the relevant trade union prior to employment.

## close-out
It means the completion of all work on a project. It may also refer to completion of a phase of the project.

**Dictionary of Business**

### cluster sampling
It is a method of selecting a sample in which the members of the sample are chosen from one or more groups, rather than from the population as a whole. The technique is used when random sampling from the whole population would be either impractical or expensive.

### co-branding
An arrangement between two or more companies in which they agree to display joint content and perform joint promotions using brand logos or banner advertisements. The objective of co-branding is to strengthen the brands by making them appear complementary to one another.

### cobweb theory
It is defined as supply and demand analysis where supply is reflection of demand for a previous period. For example, after a long industrial strike, many customers will have found alternative supplies and existing suppliers find it difficult to sell the same volume of goods as before the strike.

### cohort effect
It refers to the effect associated with being a member of a group born at roughly the same time and bonded by common life experiences. The effect is of great interest to advertisers and others involved in marketing.

### collaborative customisation
It can be defined as the tailoring of a product to meet a customer's unique requirements, based on a discourse between the seller and the customer.

### collateral
A guarantee or security given by a borrower as a safeguard for a loan. It can be either a guarantee by a third party, deposition of deeds to property or an undertaking to transfer particular stocks and shares if necessary.

### collective bargaining
Process or procedural rules for making agreement on wages, including conditions of employment, etc. between employers and employees collectively, the latter usually being represented by a trade union, or bargaining unit of

employees. There are various levels of collective bargaining such as industry-wide bargaining, factory agreement, plant bargaining, or workplace bargaining.

## collective contract
It is a type of workers' control based in the notion that a group of workers should be responsible for organising and supervising their own factory or shop in return for producing an agreed output.

## collision clause
It is an insurance clause indemnifying a shipowner against liability for damage caused to other ships in the collision.

## commercial criterion
Also called business criterion, it is public administration management technique in which some of the criteria of a commercial organisation or company are introduced. All inputs into a department or unit are charged at a market rate, whether they are purchased from outside or obtained from another part of the public service and, similarly, outputs are charged at a market rate.

## commercial paper (CP)
It is a relatively low-risk short-term form of borrowing. Some experts regard commercial paper as a reasonable substitute for treasury bills, certificates of deposit, etc. The main issuers have traditionally been large creditworthy institutions such as insurance companies, and pension funds. Recently, there has been a major growth in asset-backed commercial papers (ABCPs), in which the CP is secured against assets held by a structured investment vehicle.

## commission
It is the payment made for obtaining sales, orders, etc. sometimes on a percentage basis.

## commission agent
Agent paid on a commission basis for the business he or she brings, the principal then dealing with the customer directly.

## commitment fee
An amount charged by a bank to keep open a line of credit or to continue to make unused loan facilities to a potential borrower.

**Dictionary of Business**

## committed costs
These are costs to which the management of a project/enterprise are virtually irrevocably committed, once the project is under way. Such costs are different from managed costs which are those over which some degrees of management discretion remains throughout a project.

These costs will still be incurred even if the project is terminated.

## committed facility
It refers to an agreement between a bank and a customer to provide funds up to a specified maximum at a specified interest rate for a certain period. The total cost will be the interest rate plus the mandatory liquid asset costs.

## commodity
In inventory management, the term is defined as under:
1. Standard products commonly available from various sources, often called commodity items.
2. Specialised or custom products not widely available, or proprietary products only available from a small number of sources would not be considered commodity items.
3. The term commodity is also used to describe classifications of inventory, in which case, commodity codes are used to distinguish groups of inventory items to be used for reporting and analysis.
4. A generic term for goods or produce being transferred to manufacturer or consumer. The term is used particularly for foodstuff such as wheat, rice, coffee, tea, sugar, tobacco, and raw materials like zinc, copper, etc. Different types of commodity trading are actuals and futures.

**Commodity**

## commodity traded advisors
Abbreviated as CTAs, they

are groups that deal exclusively in futures and other derivatives. The majority of the CTAs pursue 'following a trend' strategy. The major reason being that there are temporary trends in the financial markets, and they make profits both from falling and rising markets.

## common cost
It refers to cost incurred generally and not attributable to particular activities or departments.

## common external tariff
It refers to customs duty or tariff charged in common by the member states of a common trading area and customs union on goods imported from non-member states.

## common law
It is the English system of law which is based on court decisions, the doctrine underlying them being custom and usage, rather than statutes or codified, written laws.

## communications management
It implies the proper organisation and control of information transmitted by any available means to satisfy the needs of the project. It may include the processes of transmitting, filtering, receiving, and interpreting information, using appropriate skills.

## communities of interest
These are networks of people who share a common interest in a particular topic, either related to work or peripheral to work and who come together informally to share knowledge on that topic, area or field.

## commutation
It refers to the right to receive an immediate cash sum in return for accepting smaller annual payments at some time in the future. For example, some life insurance policyholders can, on retirement, take a sum from the pension fund immediately and thereby, a reduced annual pension.

## company seal
A seal with the company's name engraved on it in legible characters. It is used to authenticate share certificates and other important documents issued by the

**Dictionary of Business**

company or affixed to contracts.

*Company seal*

## compensating rest
It refers to time off granted to an employee to recover from particularly arduous work. It may be under an agreement in writing or based on mutual understanding.

## compensation
It is another term for all forms of remuneration. It not only includes pay but all types of fringe benefits that may accrue to employees such as stock options, pensions, insurance, and bonus payments, etc.

## compensation and evaluation
It is the measurement of an individual's performance and the financial payment provided to employees as a reward for their performance and as a motivation for future performance.

## competitive exclusion
It is diversion of online traffic, away from competitors by companies, holding exclusive partnership deals with popular websites on the Internet.

## competitiveness
It can be defined as the ability of an economy to supply increasing aggregate demand and maintain exports. A loss of competitiveness is usually signalled by increasing imports and falling exports. It is also the ability of an enterprise to successfully complete with its competitors. For example, if the yen-dollar exchange rate remains constant, but prices rise faster in Japan than in the US, Japanese goods will become relatively more expensive, reflecting a loss in competitiveness; and this may lead to a falling demand for exports.

## completion date
It is the date by which the project could finish following careful estimating, planning and risk analysis taking into

account resource limitations and contingency.

## complexity
It implies an affirmative indication or judgement that the supplier of a product and/or service has met all the requirements of the desired specifications, agreed contract or regulations.

## compliance labels
These are standardised label formats used by trading partners. Compliance labels are used as shipping labels, container or pallet labels, and carton labels and contain bar codes. Many barcode labelling software products now have more common compliance label standards set up as templates.

## component
It refers to the following:
1. Any raw material, substance, piece, part, software, labelling or assembly which is intended to be included as part of the finished, packaged and labelled device.
2. In banking, the term 'component' is used to denote the subsidy given by the government for loans granted to certain poor classes of borrowers.

## compulsory liquidation
It refers to the compulsory winding up of a company. A petition must be presented at both the court and the registered office of the company. The grounds on which a company may be wound up by the court include a special resolution of the company that it be wound up by the court, and that the number of members is reduced below two, etc.

## computer hardware
These are devices capable of accepting and storing computer data, executing a systematic sequence of operations on computer data

Computer hardware

or performing several functions like substantial interpretation, computation, communication, control, among other things.

### computer numerical control

Abbreviated as CNC, it is a type of controller that is found on machining centres and other machine tools. CNCs control process part programs in the form of M and G codes that describe tool paths required to machine production parts. Robots that are not machine tools are not considered CNC.

### computer program

It is defined as a combination of computer instructions and data definitions that enable computer hardware to perform computational or control functions.

### computer software component (CSC)

It is a logically distinct part of a computer software configuration item. Such components may be top level or low level.

### computer software configuration item

It is a software item, which is identified for configuration management. It is essentially an aggregation of software that satisfies an end-use function and designated for separate configuration management.

### concept of execution

The term represents the dynamic relationships of the components and may include such descriptions as flow of execution control, data flow, state transition diagrams, timing diagrams, and priorities among units.

### concept phase

It is the first of four sequential phases in the generic project life-cycle. It is also known as idea, economics, feasibility or prefeasibility phase.

### concept study

It implies consideration of an idea that includes a review of its practicality, suitability, cost-effectiveness, etc. It is generally followed by a recommendation, whether or not to proceed with the project.

### concession

It refers to permission to use or release a product that does not conform to specified requirements.

### concurrency
It refers to a requirement that development and the extension of infrastructure takes place at the same time. It is used to prevent sprawling development in areas that do not have infrastructure in place as also to ensure that there is too heavy financial burden on the localities that build it.

### concurrent delays
It denotes two or more delays that occur or overlap during the same period, either of which taking place alone would have affected the fixed completion date.

### conditional sale agreement
It refers to a contract of sale under which the price is payable by instalments and ownership does not pass to the buyer who is in possession of the goods, until all the specified conditions relating to the payment have been fulfilled.

### confidence level
In business, it is stated as a percentage for a budget or schedule estimate. The higher the confidence level, the lower the risk.

### configuration
It refers to the functional and physical characteristics of hardware/software as set forth in technical documentation and achieved in a product.

### configuration control
The term is used for systematic evaluation, co-ordination, approval and dissemination of proposed changes and implementation of all desired changes in the configuration of any item after formal establishment of its configuration baseline.

### configuration control board
A board composed of technical and administrative representatives which approves or disapproves proposed engineering changes to an approved baseline.

### configuration documentation
It is the sum of all the documents that define the physical and functional characteristics of a system, sub-system, or designated

equipment, e.g. specifications and designs documents source code listings.

### configuration identification
It refers to the conditionally approved technical documentation for a configuration item as set forth in specifications, drawings, associated lists, etc. and documents referred therein.

### configuration item (CI)
It is an aggregation of hardware or software that satisfies an end-use function.

### configuration management (CM)
It can be defined as a formal discipline among team members and customers with processes, methods for product development to establish baselines, control and track status and audit the product.

### configure-to-order
Abbreviated as CTO, it is comprised of a system in which a firm sells standard products that require that certain parameters, adjustments or modules be added in response to a customer order. Selecting the language option for a software package is an example.

### conformance
It implies the following:
1. An affirmative indication or judgement that a product or service has met all the requirements of the relevant specifications, contract, etc.
2. Also the state of meeting the requirements.

### conformance quality
It is the degree to which the product or service design specifications are met. Conformance quality is usually the yield rate, i.e. the percentage of units started that have to be discarded because they are defective.

### consensus decision process
It is comprised of group decisions resulting from members engaging in full and open discussion and then reaching a consensus.

### conservation easements
These are voluntary, legally binding agreements for landowners that limit parcels of land or pieces of property to certain uses.

**Dictionary of Business**

## consideration

It refers to the following:
1. A tangible benefit that is exchanged as part of a contract. It usually comprises a promise to do, not to do something, or to pay a sum of money.
2. The money value of a contract for the purchase or sale of securities on the stock exchange before deducting commissions, charges, stamp duty and any other expenses.

## consignment

It denotes the following:
1. A shipment or delivery of goods sent at one time.
2. Goods sent on consignment by a principal (consignor) to an agent (consignee) for sale, either at an agreed price or at the best market price.

## consignment account

The term is used for sale when goods are distributed through agents, the ownership remaining vested in the seller, while the transaction is said to be on consignment. A consignment account is prepared for such goods. As the goods are no longer in the seller's possession, he or she cannot have them in stock. As they have not been sold by the agent, they cannot be classed as sales. They are therefore termed as goods on consignment. The agent, while accounting to his/her principal, will submit an account sales so that the goods may then be recorded as sold.

## consignment stock

It refers to the stock held by one party but legally owned by another. The dealer has the right to sell the stock or to return it unsold to its legal owner.

The term is specially used for the inventory held by a customer that is owned by the supplier. Payment is made only when stock is sold by the customer.

## consignor

It refers to the following:
1. Any person or company that sends goods to a consignee.
2. A principal who sells goods on consignment through an agent usually in a foreign country.

## consolidated goodwill

It is the difference between the fair value of the consideration given by an

**Dictionary of Business**

acquiring company when buying a business, and the aggregate of the fair values of the separable net assets acquired. Goodwill is a positive amount and is shown as an asset in the balance sheet. It is often called a fictitious asset.

### construction manager

It is a position in a project team. Construction management is responsible to the project manager for directing within the construction of a project within authority and responsibility limits, usually established by an agreed contract. On smaller projects, a construction contractor may assign this role to a superintendent.

### construction stage

It refers to a part of a project life-cycle during which the construction work is still carried out.

### consular invoice

It is an invoice for export order which carries an endorsement by the importer's consul in the exporting country.

### consumable

It is defined as a type of product that is used up in the process, e.g. paper, petrol, tape, oil, grease, etc. Many firms make more money selling consumable products than they do in selling capital goods or other products.

### consumer

It refers to purchaser of consumer goods and/or services for immediate use and consumption.

### consumer acceptance test

It is a market research test for making a product or service available under controlled conditions. Its aim is to discover how much the product is acceptable to consumers.

### consumer action

It denotes an action through consumers or groups representing their interests, who confront manufacturers, suppliers and government departments in direct action to seek improvement or desired changes in products and/or services. Consumer action has become common in most advanced societies. It was pioneered by Ralph Nader of the USA.

### consumer credit

It is a short-term loan to the public for the purchase of

goods. The most common forms of consumer credit are credit accounts at retail outlets, personal loans from banks and finance houses, hire purchase and credit cards.

## consumer goods
These are products sold to

*Consumer goods*

non-business end-users, etc. Clothes, eatables, etc. are examples of consumer goods.

## consumer promotion
A sales promotion aimed directly at the consumer or ultimate customer through discount offers, coupons, trading stamps, etc. Promotions aimed at distributors are called trade promotions.

## consumer's risk
It refers to the risk of receiving a shipment of poor quality product and believing that it is of good quality.

## consumer's sovereignty
It is a concept that in a competitive society the consumer is the 'king' and spends money on the goods he/she prefers. To remain competitive and ensure a place in the market, the producer must always keep in mind the consumer's demand, behaviour, preference and taste.

## containerisation
It is the system of transportation and distribution of goods in standard size container loads in order to avoid the handling of individual goods or each pack, packet or carton. Such a system is applicable to rail, road, air and sea travel, and gives benefits in terms of labour and space economy at major transit points like railheads, airports and docks.

## contemplated change notice
It is a form issued to a construction contractor requesting its quotation for a

proposed change in the scope of work that would be a part of managing its contract.

## contingencies
In business, it refers to the specific provision for unforeseeable elements of cost within the defined project scope. It is particularly important where previous experience relating to estimates and actual costs has shown that unforeseeable events which will increase costs are likely to take place. When an allowance for escalation is included in the contingency, it is kept as a separate item, determined to fit expected escalation conditions for the project.

## continental shift system
A type of shift working in which workers change shifts frequently, possibly two or three times a week.

## contingency allowance
An additional sum given for tasks a worker has to undertake occasionally in addition to the work allotted to him/her.

## contingency insurance
An insurance policy covering financial losses occurring as a result of a specified event happening. The risks covered by policies of this kind are unusual such as a missing file, indemnity, etc.

## contingency plan
It refers to a plan that identifies key assumptions beyond the project manager's control and their probability of occurrence. It is an alternative strategy for achieving project success.
Contingency planning means to prepare in advance, what course of action will be adopted in case some abnormal incidents happen.

## contingent gain
A gain that depends upon the outcome of some contingency. For instance, if a company wins a legal battle against another company, it has a contingent gain.

## contingent liability
It denotes the following:
1. An obligation that may arise from past events, whose existence will be confirmed only by the occurrence of one or more uncertain future events.
2. A present obligation that arises from past events in which either the amount of

the obligation cannot be measured reliably, or it is not probable immediately to transfer economic benefits to settle the obligations.

## contingent worker
A type of worker who has a conditional arrangement with an employer such as a temporary agency or casual worker. Contingent workers tend to be employed by organisations when they have temporary need for a particular service at a particular time and place.

## continuation option
The term describes the right of an insured person ceasing membership of a life assurance scheme, etc. during his/her working life to obtain endowment assurance, whole life assurance, up to the amounts for which he/she is covered under the scheme.

## continuous flow manufacturing
It is an integration of production systems, normally through computerisation, to optimise manufacturing and minimise operational stock levels.

## contract breakdown
It is the breakdown of a contract into measurable packages and activities like units of work performed or milestones, verifiable by corresponding checklists.

## contract change
It refers to an authorised modification to some terms of the contract. It may involve any of the following:
1. A change in the volume or conditions of the work involved.
2. The quality of the work or units.
3. The number of units to be produced.
4. The costs involved.
5. The time for delivery and/ consequences thereof.

## contract closeout
It is the completion and settlement of the contract, including resolution of all outstanding items.

## contract costing
It refers to a costing technique applied to long-term contracts such as civil engineering projects in which the costs are collected by contract. A particular problem of long-term projects is that of determining the annual

profits to be taken to the profit and loss account when the contract is not yet complete.

## contract, cost plus a percentage of cost
It is a form of contract which provides for a fee or profit at a specified percentage of the contractor's actual cost of accomplishing the work. No public contract is however given on the basis of cost plus a percentage of cost.

## contract dispute
It implies a disagreement between the parties. It may crop up during contract execution or at completion, and may include misinterpretation of technical requirements and any terms and conditions, etc.

## contract elements
These are elements which, to be legally enforceable, must include an offer, an acceptance, consideration, execution by competent parties, legality or purpose, and clear terms and conditions.

## contract for services
The term refers to a contract by which a person undertakes to perform certain services for an employer, but not as an employee. Such a contract generally involves payment of a fee, rather than a salary, and does not carry the employment protection rights, etc.

## contract guarantee
It is a legally enforceable assurance of performance of a contract by the contractor.

## contract line item number
It denotes an identifier used in request for proposals to describe goods deliverable under the contract.

## contract negotiation
It refers to a method of procurement where a contract results from bid, which may be changed through bargaining.

## contract note
It denotes the following:
1. A document containing details of a contract sent from one counterparty to the contract, to the other.
2. A document sent by a stockbroker or to a client confirming that the broker has bought securities or commodities in accordance with the client's instructions.

## contract of manufacturing
A joint venture in which a company contracts with a manufacturer, usually in a foreign market, to produce a particular product for the company to sell.

## contractor
The term is used for an individual, partnership, company, corporation, association or other service, having a contract with an acquirer for the design, development, manufacture, modification or supply of items under the terms of a contract.

## contractor evaluation
It refers to the collection of background, past performance and current capabilities of potential contractors for purposes of getting bids from qualified contractors.

## contractor shortlisting
It implies a method through which a short list of contractors is assembled and designated for receipt of an invitation to bid. It helps avoiding dealing with proposals by contractors who are not qualified to do so.

## contract/procurement management
It is defined as the function through which resources such as people, plant, equipment and materials are acquired for the project generally through some form of formal contract in order to produce the end product. It includes the processes of establishing strategy, identifying sources, instituting information systems, selecting, conducting proposal or tendering invitation and award and administering the resulting contract.

## contract quality requirements
These are technical requirements in the contract regarding the quality of the product or service and those contract clauses that prescribe inspection and other quality controls incumbent on the contractor. The purpose is to ensure that the product or service fully conforms to the contractual requirements.

## contract requirements
These include requirements defined in the statement of work, specifications, standards and related documents. Such

**Dictionary of Business**

requirements also list management systems and contract terms and conditions.

## contract risk

The term is used for the potential and consideration of risk in procurement actions. The forces of supply and demand determine who should have the maximum risk of contract performance. Usually, the objective is to place on the supplier the maximum performance risk while maintaining an incentive for efficient performance.

## contract warehouse

It is a business that handles shipping, receiving and storage of products on a contract basis. Generally, warehouses require a client to commit to a specific period of time for the services. Contracts may require clients to purchase or subsidise storage and material-handling equipment. Fee for contract warehouses may be transaction storage, etc. or it may be fixed costs plus other charges.

## contract work breakdown structure

Abbreviated as CWBS, it is a customer-prepared breakout or subdivision of a project, which subdivides the project into all its major hardware, software and other elements. It also integrates the customer and contractor effort, and provides a framework for the planning, control and reporting.

## contract, cost plus a fixed fee

It is a cost-reimbursement type contract that provides for the payment of a fixed fee to the contractor. Once the fixed fee, etc. is negotiated, it does not vary with the actual cost, but may be adjusted as a result of any subsequent changes in the scope of work and/or services to be performed under the contract.

## contributed value

The term is defined by Peter Drucker as follows:
"The difference between the gross revenue received by a company from the sale of its products or services, and the amount paid out by it for the purchase of raw materials and for services rendered by outside suppliers. It accounts for all the resources the business itself contributes to the final product and the

Dictionary of Business

appraisal of the efforts by the market."

## contribution

It denotes the following:
1. The amount that a given transaction produces to cover fixed overheads and to provide profit. The unit contribution is normally taken to be the selling price of a given unit of merchandise, less the variable costs of producing it.
2. Also the sharing of claim payments between two or more insurers who find themselves insuring the same item, against the same risks, for the same person.

## contribution pricing

It means setting price at such levels that they at least cover variable costs and ideally contribute towards fixed costs and profits.

## contributory

The term is used for a person who is liable to contribute towards the assets of a company on liquidation. The list of contributories will be settled by the liquidator or by the court and will include all shareholders, although those who hold fully paid-up shares will not be liable to pay any more amount.

## control account point (CAP)

It refers to the management control unit in which the earned value performance measurement takes place.

## control cycle

The stages of a cycle that include planning, measuring, monitoring and taking corrective action, based on the results of the monitoring.

## control item

It is a project element that is considered a unit for the purpose of change and configuration management. It includes such items as software modules, versions of software systems, the project design documents, the project plans, and so forth.

## controllable costs

These are identified costs as being controllable and therefore able to be affected by a particular level of management. Information about those costs is thus directed to the concerned management personnel.

## controllable variables

These are decision variables that can be changed and manipulated by a decision maker, like quantity to produce, amount of resources to allocate, etc.

## control limit

It denotes a line on a control chart used as a basis for judging the significance of the variation from one subgroup to the other. Variation beyond a control limit indicates special causes that are affecting the process. These limits are calculated from process data and should not be confused with engineering specifications.

## construction management (CM)

It is the process by which a potential owner of a capital engages a professional agent, to coordinate, communicate and direct the entire process of construction from the project planning stage to design, procurement, construction and also in terms of scope, quality, time and cost.

## construction work

It denotes the construction, rehabilitation, alteration, extension, demolition or repair of buildings, highways, pavements, etc. or other changes or improvements to real property, including facilities providing utility services. It also includes the supervision, inspection and other onsite functions incidental to the actual construction.

## convenor

Senior shop steward in a plant, who, in some countries like UK, is elected by the plant's joint shop stewards committee.

## conversion cost

It is the cost incurred in a production process as a result of which raw material is converted into finished goods. It usually includes direct labour and manufacturing overheads, but excludes the costs of direct material itself.

## convertible term assurance

It is a term assurance that gives the policyholder the option to widen the policy to become a whole life policy or an endowment assurance policy, without having to provide any further evidence of good health.

## cooling-off period

The term is used for

**Dictionary of Business**

postponement of a strike or other industrial action to give time to the parties to the dispute in which they must reconsider the position.

## co-product

It denotes multiple items that are produced simultaneously during a production run. Co-products are used to increase yields in cutting operations such as die-cutting or sawing, when it is found that scrap can be reduced by combining multiple-sized products in a single production run. They are also used to reduce the frequency of machine set-ups of operations. Co-products are also called by-products. The concept of such products appears simple, but the programming logic required to provide for planning and processing thereof is very complicated. That is why most off-the-shelf manufacturing software has problems with co-product processing.

## copyright

It can be defined as the exclusive right to reproduce particular written or illustrative material. It normally belongs originally to the author who may assign it to someone else such as a publisher, though the situation is a little more complex for some types of material like music, photographs, etc.

## core processes

They are defined as processes that have clear dependencies and that require the same order on most projects.

## corner

In business, it refers to the situation in which an individual or organisation succeeds in establishing a controlling influence over the supply of a particular good or service. It will then force the price up until further supplies or substitutes can be found. However, this practice is now generally prohibited by government restrictions on monopolies and antitrust laws.

## corporate anorexia

It can be defined as a melody that affects businesses after a severe cost-cutting phase. The firm's ability to expand production to maintain its competitive position in the market may, for instance, be compromised by a misguided pressure to bring costs down by downsizing, which may result in the layoff of those who made a long-term contribution to the company's viability.

## corporate planning system

It is normally a model-driven decision support system based upon a financial model that assists in planning decisions that cut across organisations, units and involve all of an organisation's functions, including production, finance, marketing, HRD operations, etc.

## cost

It can be defined as the sum of money or equivalent expended in terms of raw material, labour, use of equipment, rent, etc. to produce a good or service. It is different from the price asked for the product or service and from the value of the product or service to the purchaser.

## cost account manager

He is a member of a functional organisation, responsible for cost account performance as well as for the management of resources to accomplish the given tasks.

## cost accumulation methods

The term is used for various ways in which the entries in a set of cost accounts may be aggregated to provide different perspectives on the information.

## cost and schedule impact analysis (CSIA)

It defines a process followed to determine the cost and schedule impact of a specific change in a project.

## cost analysis

In business, it is the analysis of the cost-elements of proposal or an ongoing work. It includes verification of cost data and evaluation of all elements of costs.

## cost and freight (c&f)

It is an export sale term under which the supplier of goods pays for their shipment to the country of the purchaser, though the latter is normally responsible for their insurance on board the ship.

## cost applications

The term refers to the processes of applying cost data to other techniques that have not been described in the other processes.

Dictionary of Business

### cost avoidance
It implies an action taken in the present designed to decrease costs in the future.

### cost benefit
It denotes the comparison of the cost versus the benefit, expected generally for purposes of evaluating alternative forms of investment.

### cost breakdown structure
Abbreviated as CBS, the term denotes a hierarchical structure that rolls budgeted resources into elements of costs, labour, materials and other direct costs.

### cost centre
The term is used for a department, unit or geographical location for which costs including those for direct materials, labour expenses, etc. can be ascertained and allocated to enable effective control of costs.

### cost control point
It is the point within a programme at which costs are entered and controlled. Mostly, such point is either the cost account or the work package.

### cost control system
It implies a system of keeping costs within the bounds of budgets or standards based upon work actually performed. Cost control is characteristically a level in the budget element breakdown structure.

### cost distribution
The term is used for the distribution of overhead costs on some logical basis, viz. the time or cost of all associated direct cost activities.

### cost driver
In a system of activity-based costing, it refers to any factor such as number of units, number of transactions or duration of transactions, that drives the costs arising from a particular activity. When such factors can be clearly identified and measured, they are used as a basis for allocating costs to cost objects.

### cost-effectiveness
It is a systematic quantitative method for comparing the costs of alternative means of achieving the same stream of benefits or a given objective.

### cost envelop
It denotes the area bounded

by a cost curve based on early start dates of activities and a cost curve based on late start dates of activities.

### cost estimating
It means estimating the cost of the resources needed to complete project activities.

### cost estimating relationship
It is defined as a technique adopted to particular cost or price by using an established relationship with an independent variable.

### cost forecasting
It is a term for any activity of predicting future trends and costs within the project duration. Such activities are usually marketing-oriented. However, items such as sales volume, price and operating costs can affect the projected profitability analysis. The items that affect the cost management functions include predicted time/cost, salvage value, etc.

### cost growth
In business, it is the net change of an estimated or actual amount over a base figure previously established.

### costing
In business, it is the process of determining actual costs from actual expenditures. Large costs are estimated initially and the way the money is actually spent as the project develops is recorded.

### costing systems
These are systems established to determine current costs and their trends up or down so that appropriate management action can be taken.

### cost of goods sold
Abbreviated as COGS, it is an accounting term used to describe the total value of products sold during a specific time period. Since inventory is an asset, it is not expensed when it is purchased or produced. When product is sold, the value of the product, viz. the cost, not the selling price is transferred from the asset account to an expense account called cost of goods sold.

### cost of quality
It can be described as the total cost of ensuring good quality. There are four such major costs:
1. *Appraisal costs:* These include the costs of inspecting

parts from suppliers, testing products in manufacture, and performing quality audits.

2. *External failure costs:* These are the costs incurred when the customer receives a poor quality product, e.g. investigating complaints of replacing products returned by the customer, and warranty charges.

3. *Internal failure costs:* These are the costs incurred when a product does not conform to quality standards such as costs of scrap, repairs to defective products, etc.

4. *Prevention costs:* These are the costs incurred in preventing mistakes through quality planning, process controls, and market research.

## cost overrun
It is the amount by which actual costs exceed the baseline or approved costs.

## cost performance measurement baseline
It is a formulation of budget costs, measurable goals, for the purposes of comparisons, analysis and forecasting future costs.

## cost plan
It refers to a plan that sub-divides the total project budget into meaningful cost classes, each with its own related outline specification or scope. It gives the first principal frame of reference required for a valid cost control system.

## cost plus contract
It is a form of contract wherein the contractor is reimbursed for the costs he/she incurs in performing the work plus a lump sum or percentage fee, hence it is called cost plus. Such contract is favoured where the scope of the work is indeterminate or highly uncertain and the types of labour, material and equipment needed are also uncertain.

## cost plus fixed fee contract
It refers to reimbursement of allowable cost plus a fixed fee, which is paid proportionately as the contract progresses.

## cost plus incentive fee contract
A contract that provides the supplier for cost of delivered performance, plus a pre-

**Dictionary of Business**

determined fee as a bonus for superior performance.

## cost plus percentage of cost contract (CPPC)

It is a contract that provides reimbursement of allowable cost of services performed plus a previously agreed percentage of the estimated cost as profit.

## cost plus pricing

It implies calculation of prices by adding a percentage to the estimate of cost. It is the cost used in contract involving large work. It is difficult to anticipate. A cruder approach than techniques such as product analysis pricing.

## cost-price squeeze

It is a tough situation where there is pressure of increasing costs at a time when competition or other pressures make it difficult to push up prices, so that there is virtually no margin for profit.

## counter-purchasing

In international trade, it refers to the placement of an order by a purchaser with a supplier in another country on the condition that goods to an equal or specified value are sold in the opposite direction between the two countries.

## cost reduction plan

It is a type of incentive in which cost savings above an agreed level are shared between the employer and the employee in previously agreed proportions.

## cost reimbursement

It implies payment of direct costs and directly associated overhead costs, but without any allowance for profit.

## cost reimbursable contract

In business, it is a contract that provides for payment of allowable incurred costs, to the extent prescribed in the contract. Such contracts establish an estimate of total cost for the purpose of obligating funds and establishing a ceiling that the contractor may not exceed without the approval of the contracting officer.

## cost reimbursement type contract

It is a category of contract based on payments to a contractor for allowable estimated costs, usually requiring a high performance standard from the contractor.

## cost reviews
These are planned and systematic reassessments of the estimated cost at the completion of the scope of work in a cost category. Every design review should be accompanied by a re-forecasting of cost.

## costs incurred
These are costs identified through the use of the accrued method of accounting or costs actually paid. Such costs usually include direct labour, direct materials and all allowable indirect costs.

## cost sharing contract
It is a contract that provides payment for only a share of allowable costs. Such contracts are often awarded to motivate development of new technologies.

## cost study
It is the critical examination of the major ingredients or subheads. It studies the total cost of a product or service.

## cost unit
A unit of production for which the management of an organisation wishes to collect the costs incurred. In some cases, the cost unit may be the final item produced, for example, a table or a switch, but in other more complex products the cost unit may be a sub-assembly, for example, a car engine part.

## cost variance
It denotes any difference between the estimated cost of an activity and the actual cost of such activity.

## country of origin
It refers to the country from which goods are being exported in a particular transaction. Such goods may not have been produced there and may have been imported into that country, wholly or in part, under previous transactions. Exports of goods or commodities that have been produced within the country of origin are called domestic exports.

## coupon
The term denotes several dated slips attached to a bond, which must be presented to the agents of the issuer or the company to obtain an interest payment or dividend. There are discount coupons which entitle the holder to just a

specified discount in the purchase of an item.

Coupon

## coverage analysis
It is a technique for finding what would be an ideal stock level which both minimises the amount of capital tied up in stock and yet meets a given level of service.

## craft union
Trade union whose members are skilled craftsmen who have served an apprenticeship. In other words, it is a union for general workers and white collar workers.

## crashing
It means taking action to decrease the total project duration by analysing several alternatives to determine how to get the maximum duration compression for the least cost.

It can be defined as the action to decrease the duration of an activity or project by increasing the expenditure of resources.

## Crawford small parts dexterity test
It is a test for psychomotor skill, that originated in the USA. The first part involves the use of tweezers-type instruments to place small pins in holes and then to place collars over the pins. The second part of the test involves screwing down small screws as quickly as possible.

## create value
It denotes the following:
1. Make a better product or service.
2. To increase a customer's perception of usefulness of something.

## credit card
It is a plastic card issued by a bank to enable holders to obtain credit in malls, shops, hotels, restaurants, petrol stations, etc. The retailer or trader receives monthly payments from the credit card issuing company equal to its total sales in the month by

means of that credit card, less a service charge. Credit cards may also be used to obtain cash either at a bank or its ATMs.

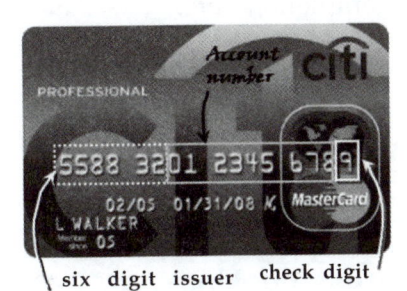

*Credit card*

## credit factoring
It refers to financial services normally offering a ready cash for the face value of goods invoiced to customers.

## credit insurance
It is a sort of guarantee or insurance that a supplier of goods or services will receive payment even if the customer does not himself make the payment.

## creditor
One who is owed money by company or individual, either as a result of making a loan or receiving a product or service. The company or individual owing the money is the debtor.

## credit sale
Allowance by the seller to the purchaser to purchase particular goods or services. Though the customer is not immediately making payment, the goods become his/her property at the time of the purchase, and thus the credit sale differs from hire purchase. In other words, the vendor is, in effect, making a short-term loan.

## creeping takeover
It refers to the accumulation of a company's shares, by purchasing them openly over a period of time on a stock exchange, as a preliminary step to a takeover. There are regulations governing the process and stipulating the maximum number of shares that can be acquired before formal notification must be made for takeover.

## criterion test
It refers to the test to measure terminal behaviour of a trainee after training and thus, to establish the extent to which he/she has achieved criterion behaviour and objectives of training.

## critical activity
The term is used for any

**Dictionary of Business**

activity on a critical path. It is generally determined by using the critical path method. Some activities are termed as critical without being on the critical path because of some other factors like expected change legislation.

## critical incidents technique

The term is used for a method for identifying the underlying dimensions of customer satisfaction. It involves collecting a large number of customer complaints and complements and analysing each of these to identify the underlying quality dimension. This method is also used to identify the key dimensions of service quality on a customer satisfaction survey. The technique is used mainly for quality improvement.

## critical path method (CPM)

It is a network analysis technique used to predict project duration by analysing which sequence of activities has the least amount of scheduling flexibility. Early dates are calculated through a forward pass method using a specified start date. Late dates are calculated by means of a backward pass method starting from a specified completion date.

## critical path network

It refers to a plan for the execution of a project, which consists of activities and their logical relationships to one another.

## cross-booking

It is the practice by employees on piece work, or on a combination of piece work and day work, not to book the actual time taken in each job but instead, book shorter than actual time in some jobs and complementary longer than actual time on other jobs in order to benefit or smooth out piece work earnings. Cross-booking may also involve a worker manipulating the time by booking longer than actual time on certain jobs in order to be able to book shorter than actual time on any later jobs that have tight rates.

## cross-docking

It can be defined as the action of unloading materials from an incoming trailer or rail car and immediately loading these materials in outbound trailers, etc. thus eliminating the need for cross-docking. Many cross-docking operations require large staging areas where inbound materials are sorted, consolidated, and stored until the outbound shipment is ready for ship. These stages may take days or even weeks in which case the 'staging area' is, for all intents and purpose, a warehouse.

## cross selling
It refers to the practice of selling related products and services to existing customers. For example, a car dealer may also offer its customers servicing of the vehicle, wheel aligning and re-upholstering. Companies often cross sell as part of their customer loyalty and retention strategy.

## currency option
It implies a contract giving the right, either to buy or to sell, a specified currency at a fixed exchange rate within a given period. The price agreed is sometimes called the strike price.

## current assets
These are most liquid assets and comprise all stocks, from raw materials to finished goods, accounts receivables short-term investments, and cash at bank and in hand. Current assets can be converted into cash in a short period of time.

## current ratio
It is the ratio of current assets to current liabilities. It gives a general indication of the adequacy of an organisation's working capital and its ability to meet day-to-day payment obligations. The current ratio is in order if its minimum value is 2 : 1.

## current yield
Yield or return of stocks or shares obtained by dividing annual interest or dividend payment by the current market price and converting it into a percentage.

## customer care
It can be defined as policies and techniques aimed at improving and maintaining efficient service to, and relations with not only external customers, but also internal customers or colleagues in the same organisation. External customers consist of

shoppers, clients, consumers, patients and passengers.

### customer/client personnel
These are individuals working for the organisation and will assume responsibility for the product made by the project when the project is complete.

### customer coalitions
These are comprised of customers working together to obtain preferential prices for specific goods or services or to ensure high quality service by the provider.

### customer expectations
It refers to the needs and wants of a customer that define quality in a specified product or service.

### customer relationship management
It is a business strategy based on selecting and managing the most valuable customer relationships. It usually needs customer-focused philosophy to support effective marketing, sales, and customer service processes.

### customisation flexibility
In business, it is the ability to provide a wider range of response to order products and still be profitable. This is sometimes called mass customisation.

### cut-off date
In business, it is the ending date in a reporting period. It also refers to a 'no later than' date for a deliverable.

### cutover
The term denotes the event or action that takes place when the product, service or project element contracted for by the client is placed in operation or turned over to the client. It is also known as the implementation date.

### cycle time
It is defined as the cumulative time required for a product from start to end, which can be measured as the completion time minus the start time. The term is used for manufacturing time and cycle time synonymously.

Dictionary of Business

# D

### daisy chain
It means buying and selling of the same items several times over, for example, stocks and shares. This is done to inflate trading activity as the sale of the same items is being included in the sales figure more than once.

### damages
It denotes the following:
1. In monetary form, a loss or injury, breach of contract, tort, or infringement of a right.
2. The term also refers to the compensation awarded for someone by some act of the company caused due to injury or loss.
The legal principle is that the award of damages is an attempt, as far as possible, to restore injured parties to the position they were in before the loss or injury was caused.

### data
It refers to the following:
1. Facts, observations and data points.
2. A set of facts, concepts, or statistics that can be analysed.
3. A set of information on a subject.

### data application
It is the development of a database of risk factors both for the current project and as a matter of historic record.

### data capture
It refers to the insertion of information into a computerised system. For example, information about the sale of an item, the sales price, and discount given, date and location of sale, etc. is taken into the accounting system either at the point of sale in a retail organisation by an electronic system or by key-boarding in to the systems when the invoice is prepared.

### data item description
It is a complete document that defines the data required from a supplier. The document specifically defines the data content, format, and intended use.

### date of acceptance
In business, it is the date on

which the client agrees to the final acceptance of the project. Commitments against the capital authorisation cease on this date.

## data refinements
It denotes redefinition of logic or data that may have previously been developed in the planning sub-function as required to properly input milestones, restraints, priorities, and resources, etc.

## data warehouse
It is a term for a database designed to support decision-making in an organisation. It is the batch updated and structured for answering rapid online queries and managerial summaries. Data warehouses contain large amounts of data, and are subject-oriented, integrated, time-variant, non-volatile collection of data in support of management's decision-making process.

## DC
It is a distribution centre, i.e. a location that is used to warehousing and shipping products.

## deactivation plan
It refers to the document that describes the approach and critical processes necessary to convert the project to the safe, deactivated or disposed state. Such plan includes methods of shutdown, disposition of records and hardware, security issues and transition to new or follow-on systems. Deactivation plan may include lessons learned, disposition of items of historical interest, environmentally sensitive and hazardous materials, etc.

## dead-cat bounce
It is a temporary recovery on a stock exchange, after a substantial fall. It does not indicate a reversal of the downward trend.

## dead freight
Freight charges incurred by a shipper for space reserved but not used.

## dead horse work
It implies work for which workers have been paid earlier or which it is agreed must be repeated, although it is not compulsory.

## deadline date
It refers to the date by which an applicant must mail a discretionary grant or

cooperative agreement application for it to be considered for funding by the authorities.

### dead stocks
Stocks for which there no longer appears to be a demand.

### dead time
It denotes the waiting time for workers. In most schemes, workers are paid day wage or an agreed fallback pay during dead time.

### deadweight cargo
Any cargo chemicals such as minerals, and coal, for

*Deadweight cargo*

which the freight is charged on the basis of weight rather than volume.

### dealer brand
Any product on which a middleman, usually a retailer, puts its own brand name.

### death-valley curve
It is a curve on a graph showing how the venture capital invested in a new company falls as the company meets its start-up expenses before it starts earning income of predicted levels.

### debriefing
In the procurement process in business, it refers to informing bidders about the strengths and weaknesses of their proposals.

### declaration of solvency
It refers to a declaration made by the directors of a company seeking voluntary liquidation, declaring that it will be able to pay its debts within a specified period, not exceeding 12 months from the date of the declaration. It must contain the latest statement of the company's assets and liabilities, and a copy must be sent to the Registrar of Companies.

### decline stage
It is the stage in a product life cycle when the sales of the product begin to fall, because of reduced popularity, obsolescence, changes in consumer behaviour, market saturation, etc.

### deed of arrangement
It refers to a document

**Dictionary of Business**

through which a person or company assigns or conveys his property to a trustee for the benefit of creditors.

### deed of partnership

A partnership agreement drawn up in the form of a deed. It covers the respective capital contributions of the partners, their entitlement to interest on their capital, their profit-sharing percentages, etc. All partners have a joint and several responsibilities.

### deed of variation

It is a written deed that identifies the specific provisions of a will to be varied. It must be signed by any person who would otherwise have benefited from the will as it was originally drawn. However, under the deed, no payment or inducement must pass between the beneficiaries so that they are encouraged to enter into the variation.

### de facto

The term denotes that something exists as a matter of fact rather than by right. For example, a respondent may have de facto control of a property. It is opposite to de jure, which denotes that something exists as a matter of legal right.

### default

It refers to the following:
1. Failure to do something that is required by law, especially failure to comply with the rules of legal procedure.
2. Failure to comply with the terms of a contract. A seller defaults by failing to supply the right quality goods contracted at the time. A buyer defaults by failing to pay for goods as per the terms of contact.
3. Failure to make required payments such as a mortgage default.

### defects per hundred units

It is the number of defective units divided by the total number of units of product, the quotient multiplied by one hundred.

### deferred asset

The term defines an amount receivable more than 12 months after the date of the balance sheet.

### deferred compensation

It denotes payments to be made by an organisation to its employees at some future time, particularly after normal retirement, e.g. pension.

## deferred pricing
A situation in which a transaction is agreed upon before the price of the transaction is settled.

## deferred rebate
It is the rebate offered by a supplier of goods and/or services to customers on the understanding that further goods/services will be purchased from the same supplier. The rebate is usually paid periodically, once the supplier is ensured that he has the customer's continued support.

## deferred tax accounting
It implies making adequate provision for any anticipated future tax liabilities in the accounts of a company or organisation.

## definitive estimates
These are estimates prepared from well-defined data, specifications, drawings, etc. They cover all estimates that range from a minimum to maximum definitive type. Such estimates are used for bid proposals, bid evaluations, contract changes, extra work, legal claims, tenders, permits, and government approvals. Other terms associated with a definitive estimates check lump sum tender after contract changes, if any.

## delaying resource
The term is used for inadequate availability in resource scheduling of one or more resources. It may require that the completion of an activity be delayed beyond the date on which it could otherwise have been completed. Such resource is the first resource that causes the activity to be delayed.

## del credere agent
The term is used for an agent or distributor who, like a stocking agent, does not purchase the goods he/she handles, but accepts responsibility for ultimate payment and pays his/her principal if the customer fails to do so.

## deliverable
It refers to any measurable, tangible, verifiable outcome, result or item that must be produced to complete a project or part thereof. The term is also often used more narrowly in reference to an external deliverable, which

however, is subject to approval by the project sponsor or customer.

## delivery date
It is the day in the month that commodities on a futures contract have to be delivered. It also refers to the maturity date for foreign exchange in a forward exchange contract.

## delivery note
A document given to the consignee of goods when they are delivered to him. The consignee or his representative signs one copy of the delivery note as an evidence that the goods have been received.

## delivery order
It is a written document from the owner of goods to the holder of the goods instructing him to release the goods to the firm named on the delivery order or to the bearer. A delivery order backed by a dock or warehouse receipt may be accepted by a bank as security for a loan.

## demand
It can be defined as a want for which the necessary purchasing power exists. Without the purchasing power, the want remains merely a want or desire. There are two types of demand:
1. Final demand by the user needing a product for its end function, and complementary demand where two products are sold in conjunction and
2. Indirect demand for a product as a component to be incorporated in another product.

## demand filter
In business, it is a control tool for time series forecasting. When the forecast error is very large, an exception report is generated to warn the user. It is sent for test if the forecast error is larger than plus or minus three standard deviations of the forecast error.

## demand-pull inflation
It implies a rise in prices caused by an excess of demand over supply in the economy as a whole. When the labour force and all resources are fully employed, extra demand will only disappear as a result of rising prices and normal prices will return.

## demarketing
It is the process of

discouraging consumers from either buying or consuming a particular product such as cigarettes and alcohol. Demarketing may also be resorted to if a product is found to be faulty and the producers do not wish to risk their reputation by continuing to sell it.

## demerger
It is a business strategy in which a large company or group of companies splits up so that its activities are carried on by two or more independent companies. One of the main objectives for demerging is to improve the value of the company's shares, particularly if one part of a group's value can be better reflected by a separate share quotation.

## deming cycle
It refers to a model that describes the cyclical interaction of research, sales design and production as a continuous work flow, so that all functions are involved constantly in the endeavour to provide products and services that satisfy customers and contribute to improve quality.

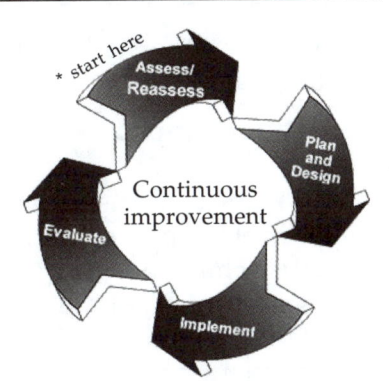

Deming cycle

## demonstration stoppage
The term is used for strike arising spontaneously as a demonstration of workers' feelings on a particular issue, rather than one started in the expectancy of a protracted struggle.

## demurrage
It refers to the following:
1. Damages payable under a charter party, at a specified daily rate for any days required for completing the loading or discharging of cargo after the given days, called lay days, have expired.
2. Damages to which a shipowner is entitled if, when no lay days are specified, the ship is detained for loading or unloading beyond a reasonable time.
3. Damages included in any contract to compensate one

party if the other is late in fulfilling his obligations.

## department improvement team

It is a team comprising all members of a department and usually chaired by the manager or supervisor. It is a vehicle for all employees to continuously participate in doing quality improvement activities.

## department store

A retail organisation that carries a wide variety of products such as clothing, home furnishings, and household goods. Each department in such store is managed by specialist buyers or merchandisers. Such department stores have occupied large multi-storey buildings in city centres these days.

Department store

## dependencies

These are the relationships between products or tasks. For example, one product may be made up of several other dependent products.

## deployment plan

It refers to the document that defines the approach to temporary system from the factory environment to the staging site or operational mode.

## deployment procedure

The term is used for the document that defines the step by step instructions for carrying out the deployment plan. It includes details of marking, packaging, shipping, transportation, unpacking, assembly and special risk management actions.

## depot bank

It is the bank, which is responsible for the fortune of a fund kept and for the expenditure and cancelling of the fund portions. Such a bank supervises the adherence to the regulations of the investment trust law and the fund folder by the fund line.

## depreciation

It refers to the following:

1. An amount by which the value of capital equipment decreases over a period of time as a result of business operations or technological innovation. It is virtually the gradual exhaustion of capital assets, including plant and machinery, employed in a business due to wear and tear, obsolescence, etc. Two common methods of depreciation are the straight line and reducing balance methods.

2. Depreciation is also defined as charge to current operations, which distributes the cost of a tangible capital asset, less estimated residual value, over the estimated useful life of the asset in a systematic and logical manner.

3. A fall in the value of a currency with a floating exchange rate relative to other currencies. It can refer both to day-to-day movements and to long-term realignments in value.

## depression

It can be defined as an extended or severe period of recession. The most recent occurred in the 1930s. The recession of 2008-09 was not a depression.

## depth interview

It is an unstructured interview that explores a marketing issue for purposes of marketing research. The interviewer, a specialist acting on behalf of a client, first compiles a topic guide that identifies the points to be explored, while the respondent is part of a sample chosen to match certain criteria. Such interview is conducted informally and the interviewer adopts a passive role encouraging the respondent to talk and ask questions, while ensuring that all the points on the topic are covered.

## deregulation

The term is used for removal of controls imposed by governments on the operation of markets. Many experts believe that in the latter half of 20th century, governments imposed controls over markets that had little or no justification. Since the 1980s, many governments have followed a deliberate policy of deregulation.

## descriptive research

It is marketing research aimed at providing good

**Dictionary of Business**

descriptions of marketing problems, situations, or markets. It explores the market potential for a product, the demographics of a market, and the attitudes of consumers.

### design
It refers to those characteristics of a system that are selected by the developer in response to the requirements such as definitions of all error messages. Other attributes include implementation such as decisions about what software units and logic to use to satisfy the requirements.

### design authority
It is an organisation responsible for the detailed design of material to approved specifications and authorised to sign certificates of design, etc.

### design development
It is the process of identifying and verifying technical solutions to meet the requirements of the conceptual design. It brings a conceptual design to the next level of detail. Depending on the size and nature of the project, it may be a separate stage in the project life-cycle.

### design failure mode and effects analysis
Abbreviated as DFMEA, it refers to an analytical technique used by a design engineer or team as a means to assure that potential failure modes and their associated causes, mechanisms, etc. have been considered and addressed.

### design for assembly (DFA)
It is a set of methodologies and principles used to guide the design process so that product assembly will have low cost, low assembly time, high labour productivity, low manufacturing cycle time and high conformance quality.

### design for disassembly (DFD)
It is a set of principles that can be used to guide designers in designing products that are relatively easy to disassemble for re-manufacturing and/or repair operations. Such design enables a product and its parts to be easily reused, after completing or recycled life. It is believed that DFD could make it possible to eliminate the need for landfills and incineration of

mixed waste. Products would be designed so as never to become waste, but instead become inputs into new products at the end of their useful lives.

## design for manufacturability and assembly (DMA)

It refers to a simultaneous engineering process designed to optimise the relationship between design function, manufacturability and ease of assembly.

## design management plan (DMP)

It implies a deliverable developed by the project manager, stating how the design phase will be managed, including known design constraints, trade-offs, approval processes, roles and responsibilities, among other things.

## design of experiment

The term describes the planning of an experiment to minimise the cost of data obtained and maximise the validity range of the results. There are some requirements for a good experiment, which include clear treatment comparisons, controlled variables and maximum freedom from systematic error. The experiments should follow the scientific principles of statistical design and analysis. Each experiment should include three parts, viz. the experimental statement, the design, and the analysis.

## design records

They are comprised of all technical documentation necessary to define the designing, manufacturing, packaging, testing, installation and maintenance of the system and its elements.

## design to cost

It is a concept that establishes cost elements as management goals to achieve the best balance between life-cycle cost, acceptable performance and schedule. Under this, cost is a design, and development phase, and a management discipline throughout the acquisition and operation of the system.

## design validation

It means testing to ensure that product conforms to defined user needs and/or requirements. It follows successful design verification and is normally performed on the final product under specific operating conditions. Multiple validations are also performed if there are different intended uses.

### design verification

It refers to testing to ensure that all design outputs meet the design input requirements. Such verification may include activities like design review, performing alternate calculations, tests and demonstrations and review of design stage documents before release.

### detailed technical plan

It denotes a plan providing a detailed breakdown of selected major activities, e.g. system testing and produced as and when required. A detailed technical plan should be established on all the small projects.

### devaluation

It is defined as a reduction in the value of a currency relative to gold or to other currencies. Governments resort to devaluation when they feel that their currency has become overvalued, because of high rates of inflation making exports uncompetitive or due to a substantially adverse balance of trade. The belief is that devaluation will make exports cheaper and imports dearer, although the loss of confidence in an economy which is forced to devalue invariably has an adverse effect.

### deviation

The term implies any variation from planned performance. Such variation can be in terms of schedule, cost, performance, or scope of work.

### deviation permit

It is the written authorisation, prior to production or provision of a service, to depart from specified requirements for a specified quantity or for a specified time.

### dilutee

The term is used for a worker who has undergone shortened training and often experiences difficulty in gaining trade union acceptance as a semi-skilled worker on the grounds that this would dilute the level of skill in the workplace.

## direct advertising
It refers to the use of free-standing advertising materials such as leaflets, stickers and brochures, rather than advertisements carried in publications.

## direct costs
The term includes those labour, material and other direct costs that can be consistently related to work performed on a particular project. Such costs are in contrast with indirect costs that cannot be identified to a specified project.

## direct labour
It refers to the following:
1. Workforce directly involved in manufacturing production or the provisions of a service, as distinct from the ancillary work.
2. Use by a local authority or similar organisation of its own employees or directly employed labour on construction or other work instead of outsourcing or using a contracting firm and its labour.

## direct mail selling
It denotes sending specially prepared sales literature through the mail to specially selected prospective purchasers of a product or service, inviting them to place orders directly rather than through shops.

## direct materials
These are materials that are directly incorporated in the final product or cost unit of an organisation. For example, in the production of furniture, direct materials would include steel, glass, wood, glue, paint, etc.

## director
The term is used for a person appointed to carry out the day-to-day management of a company. A public company must have at least two directors and a private company at least one. The directors of a company, collectively known as the board of directors, usually act together.
The initial directors of a company are usually named in its Articles of Association or are appointed by the subscribers. They are required to give a signed undertaking

**Dictionary of Business**

to act in that capacity, which must be sent to the Registrar of Companies. Subsequent directors are appointed by the company at a general meeting, although in practice, they may be appointed by the other directors and the action is ratified in the general meeting.

## direct selling
It means actual selling and taking of orders for a company's goods and services by its sales force, etc. The term is normally used for selling to the public without use of a shop.

## dirty bill of lading
Also called a spurious bill of lading, it is bill of lading carrying a clause or endorsement by the master or mate of the ship in which goods are carried, to the effect that the goods or their packing, etc. arrived for lading in a damaged condition.

## discontinuous innovation
It refers to an entirely new product introduced to the market to perform a function that no previous product has performed. Such a product requires new consumption or usage patterns to be developed.

## discount
It refers to the following:
1. Deduction of a specified amount or percentage from a price or cost.
2. Purchase or sell a bill of exchange after deducting a sum equivalent to the amount of interest that will accumulate, before its maturity.
3. Reduction in cost, value, or quantity.
4. To advance money on a bill which is not due for immediate payment, after deducting a sum.

## discounted payback method
It is a method of capital budgeting in which managers calculate the time required before the forecast discounted cash inflows from an investment will equal the initial investment expenditure.

## discrete activity
It describes a task that has a deliverable, is measurable and has a definite start and finish. An item on the work breakdown structure is an example of a discrete activity.

**Dictionary of Business**

## discrete manufacturing
The term describes manufacturing of distinct items like a pencil, a light bulb, a cell-phone, a bicycle, fuel pump, etc. It is opposite to process manufacturing.

## discrimination
In business, it refers to the requirements imposed on the organisation and the procedures implemented by the organisation to assure fairness in hiring and promotion practices.

## disintermediation
It means displacing a distributor in the channel. For example, a manufacturing firm may replace its distributors with a website to sell directly to its customers which implies that it has disintermediated its distributors. A wholesale distributor is an intermediary between manufacturers and customers. If you remove the distributor, you have disintermediation.

## displaced plant
It denotes a plant made obsolete or taken out of commission earlier than had been expected at the time of its commissioning. This may happen when a newer, more technologically advanced process is introduced, or when new materials or components are introduced, requiring important changes in the process.

## display
It is a pictorial, written or verbal tabulated or graphical means of transmitting findings or results.

Display

## disposable income
It refers to the following:
1. The income of a person available to spend after payment of taxes, insurance, EMIs and other deductions such as pension contributions.
2. In national income accounts, the total value of income of individuals and households available for consumer expenditure and savings, after deducting income tax, etc.

**Dictionary of Business**

## dispute benefit
It is the payment made by trade unions to workers on strike to compensate for loss of their normal wages.

## distributed data processing
It means effecting input, processing and retrieval of information from remote locations.

## distribution planning
A planning to determine the optimum methods of distribution and prepare and implement programs to put these methods into effect. This involves (i) selecting the best channels of distribution; (ii) evaluating the costs of alternative methods of distribution; (iii) deciding on most suitable locations for warehouses and depots; and (iv) integrating transportation, storage and production flow to provide an efficient product flow from the supplier to the customer.

## distribution requirements planning (DRP)
It refers to the following:
1. Process for determining inventory requirements in multiple plant/warehouse environment. It may be used for both distribution and manufacturing. In manufacturing, DRP will work directly with MRP.
2. DRP may also be defined as distribution resource planning, which also includes determining labour, equipment, and space requirements for warehouse.

## distribution statement
It is a statement used in marking a technical document to denote the extent of its availability for distribution release and disclosure without the need for additional approvals or authorisations from the controlling agency.

## distributor
It refers to a middleman to whom a manufacturer has granted an exclusive right to buy and re-sell a specific range of products and/or services in specific markets or geographical areas.

## diversification
It refers to the company policy to market a wider range of products and/or services, usually in order to avoid overdependence on too few products, services or markets.

## division of labour
It refers to the breaking of tasks down into operations so that employees specialise in one area of activity.

## documentary bill
It denotes a bill of exchange to which the payee attaches documents showing that he has sent the goods involved in the contract or sale so that the drawee will accept the bill.

## documentary credit
It is a type of credit arrangement opened at a bank by an importer in favour of a person or company supplying goods from another country. The supplier receives credit on presentation of specified documents.

## dog
It is a pejorative for business or product which is unprofitable and needs drastic action, either to revive or discontinue it.

## doomsday strike
It is a type of strike likely to occur towards the end of the period covered by a wage agreement and when a fresh agreement has therefore to be negotiated quickly.

## double declining balance
It is received book value multiplied by a fixed rate, often double the straight-line rate. Initially, the asset's cost is the book value. For subsequent periods, the book value at the end of one period becomes the next period's beginning book value. Once the book value is reduced to the expected salvage value, depreciation may not be recognised.

## doubtful debts
The term refers to money owed to an organisation, which it is not likely to receive. A provision for doubtful debts may be created, which may be based on specific debts or on the general assumption that a certain percentage of debtors' amounts is doubtful. As the doubtful debt becomes a bad debt, it may be written off to the provision for doubtful debts.

## downer
It refers to a short strike or stoppage intended to draw attention to a particular grievance. It usually involves workers in downing tools, but not leaving the factory

premises. It is a form of demonstration strike.

## downstream
It refers to the following:
1. To borrow funds for use by a subsidiary company at the better rates appropriate to the parent company, which would not have been available to the subsidiary company.
2. The respondent bank, viz. downstream bank in an arrangement with a correspondent bank.
3. A later stage in the production process or value chain.

## dragon markets
It is a colloquial term for those markets and economies in the Pacific basin that developed rapidly in the 1990s such as Indonesia, Malaysia, the Philippines, and Thailand.

## drawback
A system where an exporter is repaid or credited for customs duties paid on imported goods which are then re-exported either in their original form or as component parts of manufactured goods.

## drawdown
It refers to the following:

1. The drawing of funds against a credit line.
2. The movement of a customer's funds from one account to another account, which may be in another bank.

## dropship
In business, when a distributor makes a supplier send an order directly to a customer, it is said to be dropshipped to the customer. It reduces the customer's lead time, but usually increases the distribution cost for the system.

## drum-handling attachments
The term describes the various designs of lift-truck attachment used to handle 55 gallon drums. Some are

Drum-handling attachments

smaller versions of a paper role clamp, while others may engage the upper rim of the drum attachments rings. Yet some other drum attachments are capable of picking up multiple drums at the same time.

## dual unionism

It is a situation where two or more trade unions represent similar types of workers in the same bargaining unit. Usually the unions concerned are in a state of peaceful co-existence. Where they are more competitive, the term rival unionism is more applicable.

## dumping

It means selling goods in an export market at prices below those for the same goods in the exporter's home market. The exporter thus dumps his excess production in a manner making for unfair competition with producers based in the export market itself.

## duopoly

It is defined as a market in which there are only two producers or sellers of a particular product or service and many buyers. The profits are less than could be achieved if the two suppliers merged to form a monopoly, but more than, if the two allowed competition to force them into marginal costing.

## duration compression

It is a term for shortening the project schedule without reducing the project scope. Such compression is not always possible and often requires an increase in project cost.

## dyadic product test

It is a market research term for a product test based on the paired comparison principle. In it, the informants are asked for comparative reactions to two products at a time. A ranking for a number of products, packs, etc. can then be built up.

**Dictionary of Business**

# E

### earliest feasible date
It is the earliest date on which the activity could be scheduled to start on the basis of scheduled dates of all its processes, but in the absence of any resource constraints on the activity itself. Such date is calculated by resource scheduling.

### earliest finish
It is the earliest day that the work item can finish if it starts on its earliest start date and is completed in its expected time.

### earliest start
It denotes the earliest day that the work item can start, provided every preceding work item starts at its earliest start day and is completed in its expected time.

### early finish date
It is the earliest possible point in time on which the uncompleted portions of an activity can finish, based on the network logic and any schedule constraints. Early finish dates can change as the project progresses and changes are made to the project plan.

### early suppression fast response
Abbreviated as ESFR, it is sprinkler system technology that works faster and with a substantially greater volume of water. ESFR sprinklers obviate the need for in-rack sprinkler systems in many warehouses, thus reducing the cost of installation and, more importantly, the risk of water damage caused by damage to in-rack sprinklers.

### earned income
It includes the following types of income:
1. Income from employment.
2. Income from trades, professions, and vocations.
3. Foreign business profits.
4. Patent and copyright income received by the creator.
5. A proportion of the annuity or bonus paid to a retired partner.

## earned value management

It is a business management technique that relates resource planning to schedules and to technical cost and schedule requirements. All work is planned, budgeted, and scheduled in time-phased increments forming a cost and schedule measurement baseline.

## earnings

It refers for the following:
1. Wages or salary.
2. Profits of a company available for distribution to shareholders after payment of tax and any dividend to shareholders.

## earnings drift

It is the extent to which wages or earnings rise above national rates through the influence of such factors as local rates, overtime, bargaining, etc. called wage drift. It happens most in conditions of full employment, etc.

## earnings per share

It refers to the amount of profit after allowing for tax but before any extraordinary items due to the shareholders have been issued.

## earn-out agreement

It is an agreement to purchase a company in which the purchaser pays a lump sum at the time of the acquisition. It is usually accompanied by a promise to pay a more contingent consideration if certain criteria, usually specified earnings levels, are met for a specified number of years.

## EBITDA

It is the abbreviation for earnings before interest, taxation, depreciation, and amortisation. The EBITDA figure is frequently cited by investment analysts since it represents a cash flow vision of return to shareholders.

## e-commerce

The use of the Internet to buy and sell goods and services. In it, each company has a website that provides details of its products, including prices and contact media.

## economic environment

It constitutes the factors that affect the buying power and spending patterns of consumers. Such factors include income distribution,

**Dictionary of Business**

changes in purchasing power due to inflation, the state of the country's economy, substitutes available, etc. Since the economic environment can be influenced extensively by government activity, companies need to monitor these changes to predict their sales estimates, and plan accordingly.

## economic evaluation
It is the process of establishing the value of a project in relation to other corporate benchmarks, like project profitability, financing, interest rates, general market conditions and acceptance.

## economic growth
It can be defined as the annual rate at which a nation or other community's real income or national income, or flow of goods and services increases. Five broad stages of national economic growth in a developing economy are traditional society, pre-take-off, take-off, drive to maturity and maturity.
It can also be termed as the expansion of the output of an economy, expressed in terms of the increase of national income. Different nations experience different rates of economic growth because of demography, available resources, growth, investment and technical progress.

## economic life
It denotes the period of time over which the benefits to be gained from a project may reasonably be expected to accrue.

## economic manufacturing quantity
Abbreviated as EMQ, it is a term for the optimum size of production run for a particular product, in particular conditions, arrived at by techniques such as economic batch determination.

## economic order quantity
Abbreviated as EOQ, it refers to the following:
1. The optimal order quantity that minimises the sum of the carrying and ordering cost. The equation for the total incremental cost is,
$TIC = (D/Q)S + (Q/2)ic$
where D is the annual demand, Q is the order quantity, S is the order cost, i is the carrying charge and c is the unit cost.

2. The result of a calculation that determines the most cost effective quantity to order the manufacture items. The formula finds the point at which the combination cost is the least.

### economic union

A situation where two or more countries unite their economies at least to the extent of permitting a free flow of capital, goods, labour, services and movement between them.

### economic value

It refers to the value of project in terms of its expected financial returns from the perspective of the enterprise's overall commercial strategic objectives.

### economies of scale

It denotes reductions in the average cost of production, and hence in the unit costs, when output is increased. If the average costs of production rise with output, this is known as diseconomies of scale. The economies can enable a producer to offer his product at more competitive prices and thus to capture a large share of the market. These are of two types: (i) Internal economies of scale occur when better use is made of the factors of production and by using the increased output to pay for a higher proportion of the costs of marketing, financing, and development, etc. and (ii) The external economies of scale are comprised of market conditions, technological advancement and infrastructure which help the enterprises.

### economies of scope

It is a concept from economics that denotes the cost per unit will decline as the variety of products increases. Economies of scope arise from synergies in the production of similar goods. A firm with economies of scope can reduce its cost per unit by having a wide variety of products that share resources.

### effective capacity

It is the capacity of a system in units per time, taking into account such factors as staffing decisions, i.e. whether to run 24 hours a day, 7 days a week or take some breaks in between.

### efficient consumer response (ECR)

It refers to a consumer goods

initiative aimed at reducing inefficient practices and waste in the supply chain.

## efficient markets hypothesis

A theory of modern finance which states that transactors in financial markets cannot make abnormal returns on the basis of exploiting information, since market prices incorporate all available information.

## effort

It can be denoted as the number of labour units required to complete an activity or other project

*Effort*

element. It is normally expressed as staff hours, staff days or staff weeks.

## elapsed time

It refers to the total number of calendar days that are needed to complete an activity. It gives the idea how long an activity is scheduled to take for completion.

## electronic data interchange (EDI)

It is a system that firms can use to communicate routine business transactions between computers without human intervention. EDI transactions information can include information for inquiries, planning, purchasing, acknowledgements, scheduling, test results, shipping and receiving, invoices, payments and financial reporting.

## electronic mail (e-mail)

It is the transmission of documents and messages between computer terminals electronically. It can be transmitted at one time for reception or reading later. A central facility may store messages for further later transmission.

It uses Internet technologies to send messages and documents to and from computers around the world in a matter of seconds. Sending or receiving e-mail requires Internet access and an email address.

**Dictionary of Business**

## electronic signature
It is an item of data incorporated that fulfils the function of a written signature. There is a distinction between an electronic signature and a digital signature, as the latter is simply an authentication code to verify the source of a document.

## embargo
It refers to ban on some or all of the trade with one or more countries. A trade embargo is a form of economic sanction. Prominent examples include the US sanctions against Iran.

## e-meetings
The term is used for a meeting supported by full-motion video, audio and web meetings tools. One or more participants in the meeting participate remotely in the meeting. It is also possible that all participants are in different physical locations.

## emerging markets
The term is used for countries particularly in Asia, Eastern Europe and Latin America, which are developing rapidly, and whose national economies have not yet achieved western standards. They are also called threshold markets. India, China, Brazil, South Africa are the examples of emerging markets.

## emoluments
It refer to the following:
1. Income received from office or employment.
2. Payment for services rendered.

## emotional appeal
It refers to an attempt by advertising to stir up negative or positive emotions to motivate a purchase. In it, marketing and advertising are geared to creating guilt, fear, love, pride, or joy in the potential customer, instead of evoking dispassionate appraisal on the basis of objective criteria.

## employee
A person who works for an employer, a firm, company, or organisation, in public or private sector, as distinct from a self-employed person working on his own account, or an unemployed person seeking employment.

## employee report
It is a simplified version of the statutory annual report and accounts of a company

prepared for the employees of the company.

## employer reference
An act by an employer seeking to use a dispute procedure or a grievance procedure.

## employers' association
It is a body of employers concerned with questions of employment and industrial relations instead of the commercial and kindred matters that are the concern of trade associations, though some employers' associations may also have a trade association function.

## employment agency
An agency concerned with introducing office staff and unskilled or semi-skilled manual staff to prospective employers who pay to the agency a fee if they employ someone introduced in this way.

## employment costs
The term is used for wages or salary paid to an employee plus the related payments for insurance, pensions, etc. that have to be met by the employer.

## employment training
It denotes training and work experience for those unemployed through placements in employing organisations.

## end stage assessment
It is a mandatory business management control at the end of each stage of the project. Work may not proceed on the next stage until the project board has approved current status and future resource plans and technical plans assessment.

## end-item
It is a deliverable item, which is formally accepted by the acquirer in accordance with requirements of detail specification.

## engineering change order
Abbreviated as ECO, it refers to a change made in the product design. The timing for an ECO can be dependent on the current inventory. This is a major opportunity for improvement for many firms, given that ECOs are inclined to be error-prone and the timing is complicated by documentation, training and other processes.

## engineering management

It refers to the management of the engineering and technical effort to transform a conceptual requirement into an operational system. It manages the system performances parameters and preferred system configuration to satisfy the requirement, planning and control of technical program tasks.

## engineering query note

It is a document used in communication between manufacturing and design departments, especially when dealing with production difficulties.

## engineering specialty integration

It is the timely and appropriate intermeshing of engineering efforts and disciplines such as maintainability, logistics engineering, safety value engineering, standardisation and transportability, among others, to ensure their influence on system design.

## enquiry

An initial request from a potential purchaser for information regarding the quality, price, delivery date, after sale service, etc. of a particular product.

## enterprise program management (EPM)

It is a methodology based on Information Technology Investment Management (ITIM) which enables to manage programmes and projects of significance to the enterprise. It focuses on the management of multiple related programs and projects that individually support the same mission or ongoing activity.

## enterprise resources planning (ERP)

It is comprised of integrated applications software that helps manufacturing corporations run their business. ERP systems include accounts payable, accounts receivable, general ledger, payroll, MRP and many other interrelated systems.

## enterprise technology programme

It is a group-related IT project aggregated for management purposes, which supports a defined enterprise.

Dictionary of Business

## entrepreneur
It refers to the following:
1. A person taking initiatives to set up a business, etc.
2. Also a management role classification in which the manager seeks out and takes opportunities to initiate change.

## entry
A record made in a book of account, register, ledger, computer file, etc. of a financial transaction, event, proceeding, etc.

## environment project
It refers to the combined internal and external forces, both individual and collective which assist in the attainment of the project objectives. These may be business- or project-related, or may be due to political, economic, technological, or regulatory conditions.

## E & OE
Abbreviation for errors and omissions accepted, printed on invoice forms to protect the sender from the consequences of any clerical of accounting errors in the preparation of the invoice.

## e-procurement
It is a web-based information system that improves corporate purchasing operations by handling the specification, authorisation, competitive bidding and acquisition of products and services through catalogues, auctions, request for proposals and quotes, etc.

## equitable interest
An interest in, or ownership of, property that is recognised by equity but not by the common law. For example, a beneficiary under a trust has an equitable interest. Any disposal of an equitable interest must be in writing. Some equitable interests in land must be registered or they will be lost if the legal title to the land is sold.

## equity
It refers to the following:
1. The ordinary shares in a company or the value of its assets after allowance has been made for all liabilities other than those to shareholders themselves.
2. Risk capital or venture capital.
3. Branch of law providing legal remedies and justice for problems not covered by common law.
4. Something that is fair and impartial.

Dictionary of Business

## escalation
It is an anticipated rise in uncommitted costs of resources, i.e. labour, material, equipment, etc. over a period of time, due to reduced purchasing power of money. The allowance for escalation is a component within the anticipated award cost of a cost class.

## escalation clause
It is a clause in a commercial contract agreeing to an increase in price in the event of an increase in costs such as wages or raw materials.

## essential characteristics
These are minimum operational, functional, performance, reliability and safety requirements, which must be fulfilled to meet the needs of the user. To these characteristics, may be added maintenance, which sometimes requires a separate contract called annual maintenance contract.

## estate
It refers to the following:
1. The sum of total of a person's assets less his liabilities, usually as measured on his death for the purposes of distribution among legal heirs.
2. A substantial piece of land, generally attached to a large house.

## estimate
It denotes an assessment of the likely quantitative result, and is generally applied to project costs and durations. It should always include some indication of accuracy (e.g. +/−x per cent). It is normally used with a preliminary conceptual feasibility.

## estimate at completion (EAC)
It is the expected total cost of an activity, a group of activities of the project when the defined scope of work has been completed. Most techniques for forecasting EAC provide for some adjustment of the original cost estimate, based on the project performance to date.

## estimate class c
This estimate is used only in preliminary discussion of feasibility having a precision variance of 50 per cent or more. It is not used for making commitments.

## estimate class d
It is an estimate based on a comprehensive statement of requirements in mission terms and an outline solution.

## estimated cost to complete (ECC)

It is the remaining cost to be be incurred to satisfy the complete scope of a project at a specific data date. It constitutes the difference between the cost to date and the forecast final cost.

## estoppel

A rule of evidence by which a person is prevented (estopped) from denying that a certain state of affairs exists, having previously asserted that it does.

## eternal loans

These are obligations without specific date of maturity. Such loans carry regular interest payments out. However, they never erase the nominal amount, and in order to get the capital back, an investor must sell such obligations at the stock exchange.

## euro

It is the currency unit of the European Union's eurozone, divided into 100 cents. It was adopted for all purposes except cash transactions by Austria, Belgium, Finland, France, Germany, Ireland, Italy, Luxembourg, The Netherlands, Portugal, Spain, and Greece. Euro-denominated notes and coins were issued in January 2002 and the national currencies were withdrawn after a short period of dual circulation.

Euro

Slovenia adopted the euro in 2007 and Cyprus and Malta on 1 January 2008. The euro is also legal tender in some other countries.

## eurocurrency

It refers to the currency held in a European country which is not the country of origin of that currency. For example, US dollars deposited in the Bank of England are eurodollars.

## event of default

A specified occurrence that will make the loan repayable immediately. The breaching of any covenant clause will be one such event of default. Events of default also include failure to pay, failure to perform other duties and obligations, misrepresentation, adverse material change, bankruptcy, alienation of assets, etc.

## ex post
It implies after the event. This term is used to refer to the collection of financial data for transactions after the same have been affected.

## ex works
It is a clause in a contract to supply goods, which states that the buyer has to meet the cost of collection or carriage of the goods from the works or warehouse.

## examination
In business management, it is an element of inspection consisting of investigation, without the use of special laboratory appliances or procedures of supplies and services, in order to determine conformance to those specified requirements, which can be determined by such investigations. It is generally non-destructive and includes, visual, auditory, olfactory, and other investigations.

## exception reporting
It implies the process of documenting those situations where there are significant deviations in a project. The assumption here is that the project will be developed within established boundaries. When the process falls outside of those boundaries, a report is made on why this deviation occurred.

## excess reserves
The term is used for higher reserves than required, held by banks. This state is normally undesirable and occurs as a result of poor demand for loans or high interest rates.

## exchange control
It is a type of control introduced by a country over the ways in which its currency may be exchanged for other currencies. Exchange control is used where a country seeks to influence the internationally recognised value of its currency.

## exchange rate
Rate at which a currency may be exchanged for other currencies.

## exchange risk
It is the risk that future business will be affected by changes in the exchange rate.

**Dictionary of Business**

### excise duty
It refers to the tax levied on certain goods and services in their country of origin or manufacture.

### excusable compensable delays
These are delays caused by the owner's actions or inactions. The contractor is entitled to a time extension and damage compensation for extra costs associated with this delay.

### execution phase
It is the period within the project life-cycle during which the actual work of creating the project's deliverable is carried out.

### executive authority
It is the individual or collective body representing the source of project management authority. Such authority may be channelled through a project sponsor or project director.

### executive control point
It refers to a point between different project stages when top management can review the project status, the plan for the ensuing stage, verify its consistency with their latest business objectives and give or withhold, approval to proceed further.

### executive information systems (EIS)
It denotes the following:
1. A computerised system intended to provide latest and appropriate information to support executive decision-making for managers using a networked workstation. The focus is on graphical displays and an easy-to-use interface that present information from the corporate database.
2. They are tools to provide reports or briefing books to top-level executives. These systems offer strong reporting and drill-down capabilities.

### exempt supplies
These are supplies of goods or services in the categories of items that are identified as exempt from value added tax. The main categories are land rent, insurance and financial services, postal services, sports, charities activities, education, health care, etc.

### expenditure
It is the conversion of cash into real assets by a company or organisation. The opposite process, revenue, is the

conversion of real assets into cash, and the differences between the two, is its profit or loss.

## expense
It is a sum spent for goods or services, which therefore reduces the cash or bank balance of the purchasing organisation. Examples are normally shown as charge against profit in the profit and loss account.

## experience curve
It is a learning curve but also takes into account on-the-job improvement after the end of formal training.

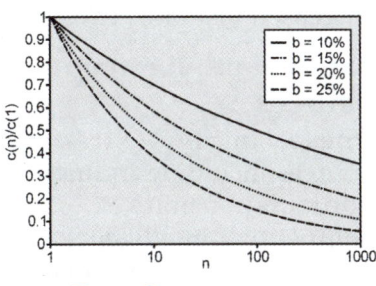

Experience curve

## expiry date
It refers to the following:
1. The date on which a contract expires.
2. The last day on which an option expires.
3. A date after which the use of a product will not give as much benefit as before expiry or may even prove harmful.

## explosion-proof lift trucks
These are lift trucks designed to work in hazardous environments where highly combustible materials may be handled. Such trucks are designed to avoid sparks. In it, components which can resist combustible temperatures and special electrical systems and materials are used.

## exports
It is a generic term for goods and/or services sold to foreign countries. Export selling may be achieved by using international marketing middlemen or by a company's own overseas branch or sales outlets, representatives or by the company's agents abroad.

## exposure
It is the degree of risk involved in holding a particular position on a financial market.

## extension risk
It refers to the risk associated with an agreement that permits one of the partners to extend its term, so that payments take place later than expected.

## external audit
An audit of a company carried out by an auditor who is external to, and independent of, the organisation. Such audit is conducted by professional auditors.

## external costs
These are costs, which are not contained in the market prices, since they are not carried by the actuals as external costs designated. To this category belong the costs of the forest dwindling, health damage, building and material damages, climate change, etc.

## external environment
It is a term for the institutions and people outside a business organisation that affect its activities. These include national and local governments, trade unions, competitors, customers, suppliers, etc. The external environment is taken into account in designing an organisation.

## external growth
It refers to the factors, activities, etc. that help a business grow, i.e. by merger, takeover, or joint ventures, rather than by growing organically through its own internal development. Such route of growth is widely used by companies as it can offer greater speed in achieving its corporate objectives than internal development. The firms can increase their market share by merging with or taking over a competitor in the same field.

## externality
It is a cost or benefit to an economic agent that is not matched by a compensating financial flow. For example, siting a metro station close to a shop represents an externality to the shopkeeper. It is an external economy if the shopkeeper benefits from increased visitors, etc.

## external procurement sources
These imply extra-firm sources including industries, contacts, market data, competitive intelligence and legal regulatory information which could aid procurement decision-making.

## extinction
It refers to the end of all activity on a project, usually before meeting its stated objectives. The end results of a project terminated by extinction are not terminated by inclusion or integration.

**Dictionary of Business**

# F

### face value
Also called par value, it is the nominal value of a share as opposed to its market value.

### facsimile
It is the process of scanning an image and converting it into signals which can be transmitted to another location where the receiver can get a copy of the original.

*Facsimile*

### FACT assembly test
Mechanical comprehension test of ability to visualise how mechanical parts, etc. fit together.

### fact book
It is a file containing information on the history of a product, e.g. data on sales, distribution, competition, relevant marketing research undertaken as well as a detailed record of the product's performance in relation to the marketing effort made on its behalf.

### factor
It refers to an individual or firm that acts as an agent in some trades, receiving a factorage, i.e. commission based on the amount of sales effected. Contrary to some other forms of agent, a factor takes possession of the goods and sells them in his own name.

### factorial sample design
It refers to a survey to obtain data on a number of factors influencing a product's impact and to show which these factors has the greatest influence. Factors tested may, inter alia, include purchasers' preferences, regional preferences, cultural influences, relative success in different types of retail outlet and volume of sales on different days of the week.

### factoring company
It refers to the following:

133

1. A firm that does not manufacture goods itself but acts either as a wholesaler or as an agent.
2. Finance house that buys invoice debts from firms, assuming responsibility for all credit control, sales accounting, and debt collection. Rather than buying debts at a discount, some factors undertake collection for their clients, at the same time ensuring them a constant flow of payments.

## factor prices
These are a type of performance measurement. Factor prices are given by relating physical input measures to value input measures. For example, wages per worker is the average wage rate, while material bill per tonne of material is the average price per tonne.

## factor proportions
These are also a type of management ratios or performances measurement. In it, relating either physical or value measures for one input to those of another gives factor proportions such as capital per employee.

## factor rating
It is a performance appraisal and job evaluation technique used in business management in which managers are ranked in order for each of certain factors selected to know the extent to which they have qualities which are considered desirable. Free report, forced choice approach, ranking system, task-based appraisal, etc. are other management appraisal techniques being used.

## factor rating and comparison
It is a method of reporting in performance appraisal procedures, etc. on the performance of staff, using multiple step scales or linear scales against a series of features. Factor rating is sometimes weakened by subjective judgements and is being less used as management appraisal systems have given way to management by objectives given by Peter Drucker.

## factors of production
These are resources required to produce economic goods. Land, labour, capital,

entrepreneurial ability and the willingness are the major factors of production. For each of these factors there is a price, i.e. rent for land, wages for labour, interest for capital, and profit for entrepreneurship.

## factory

It can be defined as any premises in which, or in precincts of which, persons are employed in manual labour in manufacturing or related processes, by way of trade or for purposes of gain.

Factory

## factory agreement

An agreement reached after collective bargaining on behalf of employees from the whole of a factory, as different from workplace bargaining on behalf of a smaller group or larger scale bargaining such as for company agreements, industry-wide agreements, etc.

## factory profit

It is the sales value of goods produced minus the full cost of production.

## fair trade

It is a generic term that calls for fair trade with cooperative attitude. It covers prices, guaranteed minimum wages for female workers as well as long-term trade relations, among other things. However, the enterprises cultivate their products in accordance with strict guidelines and thereby ensure a high quality.

## fair value

It is the amount of money for which it is assumed an asset or liability could be exchanged between informed and willing parties.

## fall-back pay

It refers to the guaranteed minimum level of pay written into a payment-by-results scheme, etc.

## family group

It refers to a reference group brought together for the purpose of examining consumer buying motives. It is a form of membership group in the sense that the

**Dictionary of Business**

individuals concerned belong naturally to the groups, values, and tastes preferences.

## fast-moving consumer goods

Abbreviated as FMCGs, the term is used for the products that move off the shelves of retail shops quickly, which therefore require constant replenishing. These include standard groceries, etc. sold in supermarkets, stores and malls as well as CDs sold in music shops.

## feasibility study

It is an assessment to determine which of a range of decisions is likely to give a satisfactory return in a financial appraisal or economic appraisal of the alternatives.

## Federal Reserve Bank

It refers to any of the 12 banks that together form the Federal Reserve System in the USA. They are situated in New York, Boston, Philadelphia, Cleveland, Atlanta, Richmond, Chicago, St. Louis, Minneapolis, Dallas, Kansas City and San Francisco. They provide central bank services and are involved with the Federal Reserve Board of Governors in developing and enacting monetary policy, as well as regulating local commercial banks. Each Federal Reserve Bank is owned by the local banks in its district. After the global recession 2008-09 Federal Reserve Bank has been given the role of maintaining financial stability.

## fiat money

It denotes money that government has declared to be legal tender, although it has no intrinsic value and is not backed by reserves.

## fictitious assets

These are items which must appear in the balance sheet for accounting reasons but which may not have value and could not actually be realised. They include goodwill, patent, etc.

## fidelity insurance

It is a type of insurance policy in some countries, taken out by an employer against the possibility of a cashier, sales person or other employee embezzling funds, etc.

## fiduciary

The term is used for a person who holds property in trust for someone else, or as an executor. Persons acting in a

## fiduciary issue

fiduciary capacity do so to safeguard the interests of some other person.

## fiduciary issue

It refers to notes or paper money, not backed by gold or silver.

## field research

It is a research consisting of visits, interviews, etc. to collect fresh information. It is opposed to desk research, which is based on published or other existing information.

## FIFO

The term applies to a method of costing or valuing stocks or inventories. It stands for first in first out and presupposes that the first items purchased or produced are the first items sold.

## fill rate (unit, line order)

It is the per cent of the units filled immediately from stock. It is of various types. The line fill rate is the per cent of lines on purchase orders that are filled immediately from stock. Such rate is generally of a lower number than the others and therefore is a more difficult fill rate to satisfy.

## final assembly schedule

Abbreviated as FAS, it refers to a schedule for the assemble-to-order portion of a manufacturing process. The firm will use MRP to plan the production of all major components and then use the FAS to schedule the final assembly for specific customer orders after those orders arrive.

## final salary pension scheme

It is a scheme under which pension is calculated in relation to the final salary, being expressed as a fraction of final salary for each year of service with the employer. This scheme has many attractions for the individual employee, compared with the average salary pension scheme, since the final salary is generally the highest salary and will be least eroded by inflation.

## financial accounting

It is defined as preparing and presenting an organisation's accounts for the internal information of management but particularly for reporting to shareholders. The two basic tools of financial accounting are the balance sheet, showing the company's financial entrepreneur or, more specifically, a partnership.

### first-hand distribution
It refers to the method of selling by wholesale distribution in very large consignments. The trading can either be straightforward wholesaling or on consignments account.

### first-line supervisor
Also called frontline supervisor, he/she is a supervisor with direct and immediate responsibility for the management and work of shop floor workers.

### fiscal drag
It implies the deflationary impact on a country's economy of a steady increase in tax revenues. Since most developed countries have progressive rates of taxation, the proportion of national income paid in taxes increases as national income grows.

### fiscal policy
A policy regarding the use of government spending and taxation to influence macroeconomic conditions. Fiscal policy is actively pursued by the government to sustain full employment.

### fiscal year
It refers to financial year used for the purposes of a government's fiscal or tax policy. This varies from country to country. In India, the fiscal year is from 1st April to 31st March; in the UK, the fiscal year runs from 6th April to 5th April, while in the USA, it is from 1st July to 30th June.

### five s (5s)
In business management, 5s is a methodology for simplifying organising, cleaning, developing and sustaining a productive work environment. This methodology originated in Japan and is based on the simple idea that the foundation of a good production system is a clean and safe work environment. It has been translated from Japanese words that begin with an 'S', of which the closest English equivalents are:
1. Sort—get rid of clutter:
2. Set in order—organise the work area:
3. Shine—clean the work area:
4. Standardise—use standard methods to keep sort, set in order and shine at a high level.

## financial statements
These are annual statements summarising a company's activities over the previous year. They mainly consist of the profit and loss account and balance sheet.

## finished goods
The term denotes stocks of manufactured products, and farming stock ready for sale to customers. Other forms of stock include raw materials stock, bought out goods and work-in-progress.

## finite element analysis
It is the computerised method of forecasting and analysing the performance of a component.

## finite scheduling
It means creating a sequence of activities with associated times so that no resource, viz. person, machine or tool is assigned to work more than the time available. It is of different types:
1. A due-date feasible finite schedule will satisfy all due date requirements for all tasks orders.
2. A start-date feasible schedule will start after the current time, as opposed to the situation where you should have started 2 weeks in order to get done on time. The opposite of finite scheduling is infinite planning which ignores capacity constraints when a schedule is created. While many ERP systems and project management tools have finite scheduling capabilities, infinite planning is mostly used for both ERP and project management.

## fink
It refers to a trade unionist who acts as an informer on union affairs to his or her employer.

## firewall
It refers to the following:
1. In a conglomerate, it denotes a barrier created between the organisation, funding and ownership of one business entity and those of other entities in the group.
2. A system usually inserted between a local area network (LAN) and the Internet to filter incoming traffic to try to eliminate viral infection, and to restrict the access of hackers to the system.

## firm
The term is loosely used to describe any business,

entrepreneur or, more specifically, a partnership.

## first-hand distribution
It refers to the method of selling by wholesale distribution in very large consignments. The trading can either be straightforward wholesaling or on consignments account.

## first-line supervisor
Also called frontline supervisor, he/she is a supervisor with direct and immediate responsibility for the management and work of shop floor workers.

## fiscal drag
It implies the deflationary impact on a country's economy of a steady increase in tax revenues. Since most developed countries have progressive rates of taxation, the proportion of national income paid in taxes increases as national income grows.

## fiscal policy
A policy regarding the use of government spending and taxation to influence macroeconomic conditions. Fiscal policy is actively pursued by the government to sustain full employment.

## fiscal year
It refers to financial year used for the purposes of a government's fiscal or tax policy. This varies from country to country. In India, the fiscal year is from 1st April to 31st March; in the UK, the fiscal year runs from 6th April to 5th April, while in the USA, it is from 1st July to 30th June.

## five s (5s)
In business management, 5s is a methodology for simplifying organising, cleaning, developing and sustaining a productive work environment. This methodology originated in Japan and is based on the simple idea that the foundation of a good production system is a clean and safe work environment. It has been translated from Japanese words that begin with an 'S', of which the closest English equivalents are:
1. Sort—get rid of clutter:
2. Set in order—organise the work area:
3. Shine—clean the work area:
4. Standardise—use standard methods to keep sort, set in order and shine at a high level.

5. **Sustain**—maintain through empowerment, commitment, and discipline. There are several benefits of 5s programme which include improved safety, reduced waste, high morale, ownership of workspace, higher productivity, better quality, improved maintenance and a good reputation among customers.

## fixed charge
It implies the part of an expense that remains unchanged, irrespective of the amount of the commodity or service used or consumed.

## fixed cost
It implies a cost that remains constant, whatever the level of business activity, e.g. rent. A cost that remains constant until a particular new level of activity is reached and then changes to a new constant cost is called a stepped cost, e.g. if the production level is increased. It is distinct from a variable cost that varies virtually with the level of activity and may be constant per unit of volume.

## fixed exchange rate
It is the exchange rate of a country which lays down an official exchange rate for its currency with other currencies instead of having a floating exchange rate.

## flexible firm
The term is used for a firm that has four categories of employees:
1. A core group of full-time, permanent, career employees having skills particularly needed by the company.
2. A first peripheral group who are also full-time but with less job security and career opportunities.
3. A second peripheral group to supplement the numerical flexibility of the first group of peripheral workers and with some functional flexibility. They work on an overlaid shift, or in a job sharing arrangement.
4. External groups sub-contracting specialist services known as outsourcing.

## flexible manufacturing system (FMS)
It is an integrated set of machines that have automated materials handling between them as well as an integrated information system in place.

## flexible time
It refers to flexible working hours for the periods during the day when each employee can choose his or her own working hours. The rest of the day is core time when all employees are expected to be present.

## flexing
It is the process of adjusting the budget in relation to changes in volumes of production or sales.

## flexi-worker
The term is used for a worker employed temporarily, i.e. hired from a temporary help service, during peak time under flexible manning.

## float
It refers to the following:
1. The amount of leeway in the time allowed for a particular activity or, in network terms, arrow. If an activity uses up more than its float time, the network has to be re-balanced.
2. The amount of time by which an activity may be delayed from its early start without delaying the project finish date. It is a mathematical calculation and can change as the project progresses and changes are made to the project plan.
3. Money created as a result of a delay in processing cheques, e.g. when one account is credited before the paying bank's account has been debited.
4. Money set aside as a contingency fund or an advance to be reimbursed.

## floating charge
It is the property rights surrendered as security or collateral on a loan, not restricting use of the property if the terms of the loan are met.

## floating exchange rate
It is a policy in which a country does not have an official exchange rate for its currency with other currencies but allows its currency to float or find a natural exchange rate. This can virtually be a devaluation.

## floatation
It is the process of launching a public company for the first time by inviting the public to subscribe in its shares. It applies both to private and to previously nationalised share issues, and can be carried out through introduction, issue by tender, offer for sale, or a public issue.

**Dictionary of Business**

## floating labour
The term is used for workers who tend to change their jobs and/or job locations from time to time.

## flow chart
It is a diagrammatic representation of inter-relationships between stages, activities and achievements in a system or method of operation, etc.

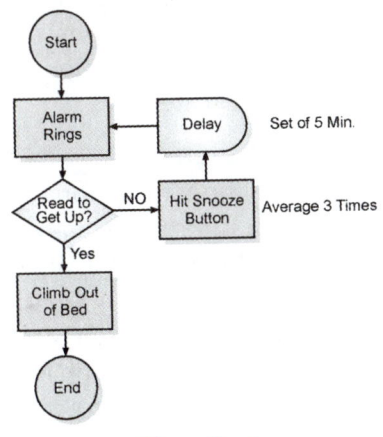

Flow chart

## flow line production
It is a method of production in which successive operations on a product are carried out in such a way that work flows in a single direction through the factory or workshop, the product being passed from worker to worker or from section to section for doing further work on it. Assembly line production is also a type of a flow line production.

## flow process chart
It is a work study chart showing the order of operations in an activity or process, with an indication of timings, transportations and distances.

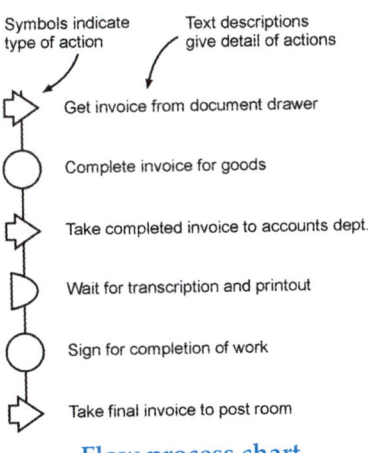

Flow process chart

## fluctuating price contract
It is an agreement in which it is specified that the price may be varied according to fluctuations in costs and/or other factors.

## focused factory process
It refers to a process that is aligned with its market and therefore requires a limited range of operations objectives. A factory focused

**Dictionary of Business**

on making high production of standard goods at low cost is likely to have minimum wage workers, fairly automated processes, maximum retail price (MRP) systems, etc. A focused factory reduces the variability of the requirements in the process and thus helps the process achieve its stated operations objectives.

### forbearance
It is a position taken by a lender who chooses not to exercise his/her legal right of foreclosure when a borrower defaults.

### force majeure
An event outside the control of either party to a contract, e.g. a strike, riot, act of God, or even a new legislation that may excuse either party from fulfilling his contractual obligations in certain circumstances, provided that the contract has a force majeure clause.

### forced sale
It defines a sale that has to take place because it has been ordered by a court or because it is necessary to raise funds to avoid bankruptcy or liquidation.

### forced saving
It is a government measure imposed on an economy for increasing savings and reducing expenditure on consumer goods. It is generally implemented by raising taxes, increasing interest rates, or raising prices.

### forced scale
In marketing research, it is a rating scale that does not include a 'no opinion' or 'no knowledge' category.

### forecast bias
It denotes the average forecast error over time. Such bias can be defined mathematically in different ways, but a simple recursive approach for handling this is to define $R_t = R_{t-1} + E_t$. The ideal forecast has a zero forecast bias.

### forecast consumption
It refers to the methods a company's inventory management software uses to reduce forecast demand by the actual demand that occurs during the forecast period. Wrongly set up forecast consumption parameters or lack of functionality related to forecast consumption may

put planning systems in jeopardy.

## forecasting

In business, it implies predicting the future of a variable. In a typical business context, the firm needs a forecast of the demand for its product without giving consideration to the firm's capacity supply. In response to this unconstrained demand forecast, the firm makes production and inventory plans. In some periods, the firm might plan to have inventory greater than the demand. In other periods, the firm might plan to have inventory well short of the demand.

## foreclosure

It can be defined as the legal right of a lender of money to recover the amount if the borrower fails to repay the money or part of it on the due date. The lender must apply to a court for permission to sell the property that has been held as security for the debt. The court will then order a new date for payment in an order called a foreclosure *nisi*. If the borrower again fails to pay, the lender may sell the property. This procedure can occur when a mortgagor fails to pay the mortgagee the instalments due.

## foreign investment

It implies investment in the domestic economy by foreign individuals or companies. Such investment takes the form of either direct investments (FDI) in productive enterprises, or investment in financial instruments such as a portfolio of shares. Foreign investment is said to sustain the markets in many countries including India.

## form

It is a generic term for the defined configuration of an item including the geometrically measured configuration, density and weight or other visual parameters which uniquely characterise a product, component or assembly. For software, form describes the language, language level, and media.

## formal testing

It is simply the process of conducting testing activities and reporting results in accordance with an approved test plan, at times making provision for customer involvement.

### forward buy
It denotes the practice of purchasing raw materials, components, etc. ahead of the need, generally in anticipation of a price increase.

### forward dealing
It means dealing in commodities, securities, currencies, freight, etc. for delivery at some future date, at a price agreed at the time the contract was made. It enables dealers and manufacturers to cover their future requirements by hedging their more immediate purchases. It differs from a futures contract in the sense that the former cannot be closed out by a matching transaction, whereas the latter can be and often is.

### forward integration
It is a policy wherein the manufacturer or main supplier of a product or service acquires or takes over certain customer or retail outlets in an endeavour to secure a further part of the market for the product or service.

### forward loading
It is a finite scheduling method that begins with the start date and plans forward in time, not violating the capacity constraints. The complete date is an output of the process.

### forward market
It refers to a market where there are dealings in promises to buy or sell commodities, foreign exchange or securities at a fixed price at a future date. Forward market is said to deal in futures. In contrast, a spot market deals with prices for immediate delivery.

### fractional bargaining
Also called fragmented bargaining, it is a type of collective bargaining on behalf of a minority of employees or to deal with a particular grievance. The term 'fragmented' is used, rather than as fractional, if the minority of employees carry out the negotiating for themselves.

### franc
The basic unit of currency in

**Dictionary of Business**

Switzerland.

**franc**

## franchise
It refers to the following:
1. A licence given to a manufacturer, trader, distributor, etc. to enable them to manufacture or sell a particular product or service in a specified area for a stated period. The holder of the licence (franchise) usually pays the grantor of the license (franchisor) a royalty on sales, often with a lump sum as an advance.
2. Also a clause in an insurance policy, usually a marine insurance policy, that excludes the payment of claims up to a specified level but agrees to pay in full all claims above it.
3. It also refers to the grant of a license to manufacture, market or distribute products or services. It includes the use of trade names, know-how in return for a continual share in the profitability of the activities covered by the franchise.

## free alongside ship
It is a clause in which the seller or supplier of goods is responsible for their delivery to the ship's side but the buyer is responsible for the cost of taking them on board ship. Under this clause, once the goods are within the reach of ship's crane, all costs and risks pass to the buyer. But the seller is responsible for arranging export documentation.

## free carrier
It is a clause in the transportation of goods where the seller or supplier of goods is responsible for the cost and administration of delivering them to a depot nominated by the buyer.

## free enterprise
The term is used where the ownership of the means of production and distribution are owned by private individuals or companies without government intervention, e.g. in a free economy or laissez-faire economy.

## free market
It denotes the following:
1. A market that is free from

government interference as the prices rise or fall in accordance with supply and demand.
2. A security that is widely traded on a stock exchange, as there is sufficient stock on offer and the price remains uninfluenced by availability.
3. Also a foreign exchange market that is free from influence on rates by government.

## free-market theory
A theory that the forces of supply and demand should be given free rein without any form of governmental intervention or direction such as in a laissez-faire economy.

## free on board (fob)
A clause where the seller or supplier of goods is responsible for the cost of delivering them to the ship.

## free on rail
It is a clause where the seller or supplier of goods is responsible for the cost and administration of delivering them to the railway for transportation.

## free port
It denotes the following:
1. Port in which imported goods can be held or processed before re-exporting free of any customs duties.
2. A harbour with port facilities open to all commercial vessels on equal terms.

## free ride
A situation in which an economic agent draws benefits from the expenditure of others without himself making a contribution. It is a type of externality and a source of market imperfection.

## free-rider
An employee who is not a trade union member but gets the benefits of a union's collective bargaining efforts by obtaining the same wages and terms and conditions of employment as union members.

## free trade
It implies the flow of goods and services across national frontiers without the interference of laws, tariffs, quotas, or other barriers. Under the World Trade Organisation (WTO), trade barriers have continuously fallen and free trade encouraged.

## free trade area
It refers to a trading area formed by two or more member states who have no tariffs on trade between them.

## freight release
It is an endorsement on a bill of lading made by a shipowner or his agent, stating that freight has been paid and the goods may be released on arrival. It may be a separate document providing the same authority.

## frequency distribution
It is a statistical term for method of condensing a large quantity of data by arranging it into various groups or classes which show the relative frequency with which members of the group have the various possible values, as shown below:

| salary | no. of employees |
|---|---|
| $ 10,000 | 40 |
| $ 11,000 – 20,000 | 25 |
| Over $ 20,000 | 9 |
| Total | 74 |

## frictional unemployment
It is a short-term unemployment arising from breaks in production caused by factors like seasonal fluctuations, random variations in sales, breakdown of supplies, etc.

## fringe benefits
These are rewards for employment, in addition to remuneration or payment of wages or salaries. Such benefits may include the use of a car, pension arrangements, insurance, subsidised meals, the provision of rent-free accommodation, short-term loans, and discounts on goods.

## front office—back office
It refers to those elements of an operating systems that are viewed by the customer. Those with which they can interact are known as front office, and those that are hidden from the customers are called back office. In the services sector, there is a trade-off between the benefits that accrue from close and open relationships with the customer and the greater ease with which operations can be controlled when they are out of sight.

## frustration of contract
It simply means the termination of a contract as a result of an unforeseen event

that makes its performance impossible.

## fulfilment

The term is used for the activity of processing customer shipments. Though most manufacturing and warehouse operations will process customer shipments, this term generally denotes operations that ship many small orders, e.g. parcels to end users, as opposed to operations that process larger shipments to other manufacturers, wholesalers or resellers. It also includes operations that process shipments for mail-order catalogues, Internet stores or repair parts.

## full employment

A situation where there is no general unemployment but only frictional unemployment so that virtually all those who are unemployed have either temporarily stopped to work or are in transit between jobs.

## function-specific decision support system

It describes a decision support system that has knowledge relevant for assisting in decisions about a specific function, which an organisation performs such as a marketing function and a production function.

## funding offer

In business, it is a situation when the concerned department proposes to a successful applicant, either orally or in writing, a level of funding less than what the applicant requested. It happens when the said department is either unwilling to accept certain items of cost in the applicant's original budget or it does not have a sufficient level of programs appropriations to fund all recommended projects at the requested level.

## fund manager

Also called investment manager, it is an employee of one of the larger institutions such as an insurance company, investment trust, mutual fund or pension fund, who manages its investment fund.

## funds flow analysis

It implies the analysis of the flow of purchasing power into and out of an organisation. Inward flows include sales

**Dictionary of Business**

revenue, sales of fixed assets and investments, and issue of debentures. Outward flows include purchases of fixed assets and investments, repayments of debt, payment of dividends and taxation on income earned during the year.

## fungibles

It denotes the following:
1. Interchangeable goods, securities, etc. that allow one to be replaced. Examples are bearer securities and banknotes.
2. Also perishable goods the quantity of which can be estimated by number or weight.

## fuzzy front end

It refers to the process for determining customer needs or taking advantage of market opportunities, generating ideas for new products, assessing necessary requirements, and developing product concepts so that a decision is made to go ahead with a development. This process is said to be the fuzzy front end as it is the least defined and most unstructured part of product development.

## gain sharing

It denotes the following:
1. A type of output-based incentive that operates at company or workplace level. Gain sharing has many forms, including the Scanlon and Rucker plans, and Improshare, but an attempt to link payment to a measure of value added is common to all. In it, the value added is calculated by removing labour costs and expenditure on raw materials, energy and support services from the income derived from the sale of the finished product. If value added increases above a target level, it is shared between workforce and company in accordance with a standard formula.
2. A plan in a bonus type scheme in which the worker receives a diminishing proportion of the value of the time saved as this time increases.

## Gaussian curve

It is a symmetrical curve which represents the normal frequency distribution when analysing natural or industrial phenomena, based on a large scale sample or population.

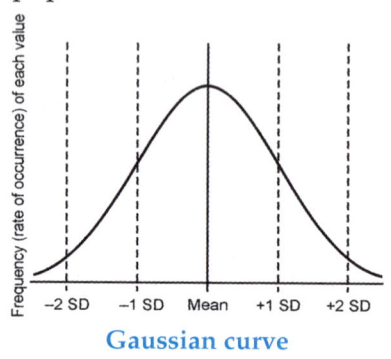

Gaussian curve

## GDP deflator

It can be defined as the factor by which the value of gross domestic product (GDP) at current prices must be reduced, i.e. deflated, to express it in terms of the prices of some base year. The GDP deflator is thus a measure of inflation.

## geared incentive scheme

It is a type of payment-by-results scheme in which incentive payments go up in stages rather than directly in proportion to output.

## gearing

Also known as leverage, it is the extent to which the money capital is divided between fixed interest or fixed dividend capital debentures such as preferences shares, and equity or ordinary shares that are not entitled to a guaranteed return or a minimum return. A company with a high proportion of fixed interest capital is said to be highly geared or highly leveraged.

## geld market funds

These are funds of investments trusts, which invest in short term, at fixed interest in certain currencies.

## GE matrix (McKinsey matrix)

It is a tool for analysing the relative strengths of brands or business units within a large diversified corporation. A range of measures are used to score items on each of two dimensions: (a) the attractiveness of the industry or market; and (b) the strength of the product or business.

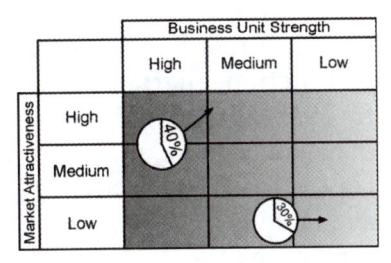

GE/McKinsey matrix

## general offer

It defines an offer of sale made to the general public rather than to a restricted number of people, e.g. an object displayed in a shop window with a price tag is a general offer. It must be sold to anyone willing to pay the price.

## generally accepted accounting practices

It is an extensive range of discounting and financial reporting standards issued by the US Accounting Standards Board in 1989 and is now widely accepted all over the world.

## generally accepted auditing standards (GAAS)

In some countries including the USA, it is the broad rules and guidelines set down by the Auditing Standards Board of the American Institute of Certified Public Accountants (AICPA).

## generally implied
It denotes customs or common practices for the organisation, its customers and other interested parties.

## geometric decay
It is a geometric series which is defined as
$$dt + 1 = rdt,$$
where r is the common ratio. For example, if the demand in period 1 is 50 and r=.8, then the demand in period 2 is .8(50) = 40. The demand in period T is dt+T = rTdt.

The geometric time series model is used to forecast demand for either a finite or an infinite number of periods into the future.

## Giles-Archer lantern test
It is a colour vision test used in some businesses in which the subject is presented with a number of lights of different colours and different degrees of brightness.

## gilt-edged securities
It is defined as fixed interest securities or stocks issued by the government in the form of bonds, etc. Gilts are among the safest of all investments, as the government is unlikely to default on interest or on principal repayments. They may be either irredeemable or redeemable.

However, most fixed-interest securities are sensitive not only to interest rates but also inflation rates.

Most gilts are issued in units of $ 1000. If they pay a high rate of interest, i.e. higher than the current rate a $ 1000 unit may be worth more than $ 1000 for a period of its life, even though it will only pay $ 1000 on redemption.

## global bond
It refers to the following:
1. A bond traded in a number of different markets.
2. A single bond for the total amount of a new issue of bonds, issued on a temporary basis to the bank that has responsibility for distributing the actual bonds to investors.

## global firm
The term defines an organisation that operates in more than one country. Global firms have research, production, marketing and financial advantages in terms of less costs and good reputation that are not available to purely domestic companies.

## globalisation
It can be defined as the process that has enabled investment in financial markets to be carried out on an international basis. It is the result of improvements in technology and openness of economies through deregulation. It can also be stated as the process by which the world economy has become dominated by powerful multinational enterprises operating across national and geographical barriers.

## goal divergence
It is the situation in which there is a disparity or conflict between the goals of those who should ideally be working together to achieve mutually beneficial outcomes. In business, goal divergence may arise between shareholders and managers, employers and workers, or between manufacturers or service providers and their marketing people.

## going-concern concept
It is the assumption that an enterprise will continue its operation for the foreseeable future, i.e. there is no possibility of its being liquidated or significantly curtailing the scale of its operation. The implication of this principle is that assets are shown at cost, or at cost less depreciation, and not at their break-up values.

The going-concern value of a business is higher than the value that would be achieved by disposing of its individual assets, since it is believed that the business has a continuing potential to earn profits.

## going public
It is a process by which a private company becomes a public company, offering shares for sale through a public issue, often with the advice of an issuing house or merchant bank.

## going-rate pricing
It refers to basing prices largely on competitors' prices with little attention being paid to the company's own costs or demand.

## golden handshake
It is a generic term for severance pay given to a senior executive on termination of his or her contract of employment or through voluntary retirement.

## goldilocks economy
It is a colloquial term for an economy that combines low inflation with steady economic growth. Such an economy is neither too good nor too bad, but just right.

## gold standard
It is a form of monetary system prevailing in earlier times, in which a country's currency unit was fixed in terms of gold. Under this system, a currency was freely convertible into gold and free import and export of gold was permitted. It formed the basis for stable prices, since it linked the money supply to the quantity of gold reserves in a country.

## good faith bargaining
It denotes a type of bargaining where business people are genuinely trying to achieve agreement and have a system of communication that can be expected to solve disputes. The concept is pursued in the USA where criteria of good faith bargaining are laid down by the National Labour Relations Board under the Wagnor Act and the Taft Hartley Act.

## goodwill
It can be described as excess value of a business or the net worth of its assets. It is built on technical know-how, location, regular customers and nature in the market. It is an intangible asset.

## go slow
It is a form of industrial action where, as in a work-to-rule, the workers do not strike or withdraw their labour, but instead slow down and obstruct the progress of work, due to some unfulfilled demand or grudge, etc.

## graded hourly rates
It is a method of payment employed under some forms of merit rating.

## gravity conveyors
In a manufacturing units, these are types of conveyors that use gravity to move materials. Skate-wheel conveyors and roller conveyors are the common types of gravity conveyors used.

Gravity conveyor

## gravity model
It is the model for retail store location. The retailers can locate one or more new retail stores, given that they know some basic information about their competitors in the area. The basic concept of the model is that large stores that are close to a set of customers have a high gravitational pull, i.e. attraction for the customers, and that stores that are smaller or farther away are not able to attract the customers in large number.

## gravy jobs
Jobs which are relatively easy or on which it is easy to earn bonus, etc. It is in contrast with lean work or stinker, which does not provide bonus easily.

## green pound
It is the national unit of currency for payments to farmers under the Common Agricultural Policy of the European Community.

Green pound

## green reporting
The term is used for a report by the directors of a company that attempts to quantify the costs and benefits of that company's operations in relation to the environment. It reflects the concerns of many investors, consumers, and other stakeholders about environment.

## grey market
It refers to the following:
1. Any market for goods that are in short supply. It differs from a black market, as it is legal.
2. A market in shares that have not been allocated, although they are due to be issued in a short time. Market makers will often deal with investors or speculators who are willing to trade in anticipation of receiving an allotment of these shares or are willing to cover their deals after floatation.

## gross investment
It is defined as the level of investment, or spending of current income on adding to stocks and to a fixed capital, before deducting the depreciation of equipment, etc.

**Dictionary of Business**

## gross profit
Also termed as margin, it is the amount by which sales revenue exceeds the factory cost of goods and services sold.

## ground rent
It refers to rent payable under a lease that has been granted or assigned for a capital sum. Long leases on offices, flats, etc. are usually granted for such a premium, payable when the lease is first granted. The leaseholder pays the landlord a relatively small annual ground rent, in addition to the rent.

## group discussion
In business, it is a marketing research technique that brings between eight and ten respondents together, for at least an hour, to discuss a marketing issue under the guidance of an interviewer. Once such a group is relaxed, it will fully explore issues in a manner that shows what is important to it, using its own rather than marketers' terminology.

## group incentives
These are incentive schemes in which the share of production plans is based on group and not individual worker performance.

## group technology
It is a management technique in which the operations and plant involved in the manufacture of a product are brought together in related groups with the possibility of job rotation or movement of workers between jobs. It is considered more economical and is better for workers' morale than the conventional sharp division of labour and conveyor belt-orientation of mass production and even batch production.

## group training methods
It refers to group training methods rather than individual methods of training, brainstorming, critical incident technique, case studies, expert witness, lectures and T-group training, etc.

## group training schemes
These are training arrangements common in small-or medium-sized firms that do not have the resources to provide other types of training.

## growth curve

It is a curve on a graph in which a variable is plotted as a function of time. The curve thus illustrates the growth of the variable.

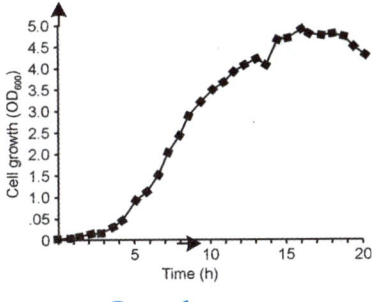

Growth curve

## growth rate

It is the amount of change over a period in some of the financial characteristics of a company such as sales revenue or profits. It is measured in percentage terms.

## guarantee company

It is a term for company in UK in which guarantors have undertaken to meet its debts to a certain level in the event of liquidation.

## guaranteed annual wage

It is a concept in collective bargaining aimed at achieving guaranteed job security at specific minimum wage.

## guaranteed working week

It is a full wages guarantee negotiated between employers and trade unions guaranteeing workers that they will be paid for a full working week, besides bonuses and other premium payments, even if there is insufficient work for a full week.

## guest worker

The term is used for a foreign national who is permitted to enter a country to work, but not settle there with his or her family. The term is used in the European Union for community workers from non-EU countries.

## guidance systems

These are systems used to guide automated guided vehicles through plants, guide lift trucks in very-narrow-aisle storage areas. Wire-guided and rail-guided systems are the most common guidance systems, but others such as laser and optical systems are also available these days.

**Dictionary of Business**

# H

### hacker
The term is used for someone who breaks into a computer information system or database dishonestly and illegally.

### half-life curve
It is a mathematical model that relates a performance metric like defects, costs per cent tardy or cycle time. The half-life concept suggests that the performance metric will be cut in half every so many periods. For example, if the half-life is 9 months and the defect rate is 10 per cent at time zero, at month six, the defect rate should be 7.5 per cent and at month twelve the defect rate should be 3.75 per cent.

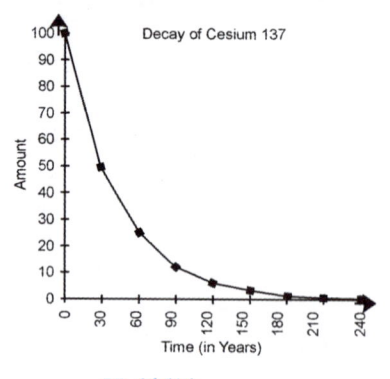

### hall test
It is a market research and sales promotion technique involving bringing together a number of people or informants for the purposes of testing their reactions to particular products.

### Halsey plan
It is a form of payment-by-results system in which the worker is paid a bonus for exceeding target production but not in proportion to the amount by which he/she exceeded the target.

### hard ball firm
It is a firm noted for its assertive or aggressive culture.

### hard currency
It refers to stable currency not subject to dramatic variations in the exchange rate.

### hardware configuration item
Abbreviated as HWCI, it refers to an aggregation of

**Half-life curve**

hardware that satisfies an end-use function and is designated for separate configuration management by the acquirer.

## hedge

It is a financial transaction or position designed to mitigate the risk of other transactions or positions. For example, a manufacturer may contract to sell a large quantity of a product for delivery over the next three or six months. If the product depends on a raw materials that fluctuate in price, and if the manufacturer does not have sufficient raw material in stock, an open position can be hedged by buying the raw material required on a futures contract.

## hedge fund

It is a unit trust that is subject to minimum regulation, e.g. a partnership or mutual fund that attempts to achieve large gains by exploiting the market conditions.

## hidden assets

These are assets not easily examined in the balance sheet. Examples include undervalued property which may be shown at historical cost, no longer realistic in present times, or higher depreciation on plant and machinery.

## high credit

It is the highest aggregate amount of credit that has been allowed to a customer at one time. It covers the total indebtedness.

## high-flier

The term is used for an employee, manager, etc. expected to be exceptionally successful.

## hire purchase

It is an instalment purchase, where the purchaser pays an initial deposit followed by regular instalments that cover the rest of the purchase price plus interest. The purchaser does not become the legal owner of the goods purchased until the last instalment has been paid.

## hired gun

In business management, it refers to a consultant with an expertise who may or may not have better knowledge than almost any employee.

## historic pricing

It is an accounting method in the fund business. The investor knows the net asset value of the fund at the time of the design/return.

**Dictionary of Business**

## hockey-stick phenomenon

In business, it is a pattern of sales or shipments that increase dramatically at the end of the week, month or quarter. This pattern looks like a hockey stick because it is low at the beginning of the period and high at the end. Such phenomenon is almost always a logical result of reward systems based on sales or shipments.

## home market

The term is used for the market for a product within the country in which it is manufactured, and therefore within the geographical area in which the product can be distributed without crossing a tariff barrier and without incurring custom duties.

## honeycombing

In business, the term refers to the unused pallet positions in high-density storage that occur when the number of unit loads for an item does not completely fill the storage lane.

## hostile bid

It is a takeover bid that is unwelcomed either to the board of directors of the target company or to its shareholders, as it is based on aggressive policies than on logic or basics.

## hot list

The term is used for most up-to-date names on a mail-order buyer or enquirer list. Hot lists are of great value in direct marketing.

## house claim

It defines a claim for more pay lodged on behalf of the employees of a single plant or company as the first move in plant bargaining or company bargaining. The term is especially used in the printing and publishing industries.

## hypothecation

It refers to the following:
1. An authority given by a borrower to the bank, usually as a letter of hypothecation, to enable the bank to sell goods that have been pledged in case of default.
2. A mortgage granted by a ship's master to secure the repayment with interest, on the safe arrival of the ship at its destination, of money borrowed during a voyage as a matter of necessity.

## idle capacity
It is the part of the budgeted capacity within an organisation that is unused. It is measured in hours using the same measure as production. Idle capacity can arise as a result of a number of causes like non-delivery of raw materials, shortage of skilled labour, lack of sales demand, etc.

## illegal contracts
These are certain types of contract which cannot be regarded as legally binding. These include the following:
1. Contracts in restraint of trade.
2. Agreements against the national interest.
3. Agreements to commit a criminal or civil wrong.
4. Agreements which hinder the administration of justice.

## illegal partnership
A partnership formed for an illegal purpose and therefore disallowed by law. A partnership of more than 20 partners is illegal, except in the case of certain professionals, e.g. accountants, doctors, educationists, researchers, solicitors and stock brokers.

## impact testing
Procedure for measuring the effect of an advertisement by discovering how much of it the people will recall while making purchases.

## import quota
It denotes an import restriction imposed on goods, to reduce the quantity of certain goods allowed into a country from a particular exporting country, in a specified period of time. It snacks of protectionism.

## import restrictions
These are restrictions imposed on goods and services imported into a country, which usually need to be paid for in the currency of the exporting country. These include tariffs, import quotas, currency restrictions, and prohibitions.

## imprest

It refers to the following:
1. An advance or loan.
2. Also a method of keeping petty cash float. The initial advance is made up again at the end of each accounting period against vouchers for expenditure incurred.

## improshare

It is a system which allows employees a cash bonus based on a percentage of their pay. This is determined by adding up the number of hours worked by all employees included in the plan, and then dividing that figure by the number of units produced by the company during the period.

## improvement curve

It refers to the following:
1. The learning curve of an employee.
2. Also the use of double logarithmic graph paper to plot the direct labour-hours spent on a given unit of output as a function of the cumulative number of units produced.

## imputed costs

The term is used for costs incurred, not in the trading transactions for which the company was established, but as inevitable costs of running a business.

## in-barrier option

It refers to an option that is eliminated if the price fails to pass a certain level. In such cases, the premium paid for the option is partly reimbursed.

## income

It denotes the following:
1. Any sum that a person or organisation receives either as a reward for effort or as a return on investments.
2. In economics, the flow of economic value attributed to an individual or group of individuals over a particular period.

## income and expenditure account

It is similar to profit and loss account, and is prepared by non-profit making organisations such as societies, which are concerned to show how income exceeds expenditure, or vice versa.

## income bonds

These are company or corporate bonds on which, though it is part of debt capital rather than contributed capital, interest is paid only if profit is made.

## income policy
It refers to the policy where a government intervenes in the free negotiation of rates of pay, normally in an attempt to restrict pay increases with the object of holding down inflation, especially cost-push inflation.

## income tax
It is tax on the income of an individual or company. It may be a flat-rate tax or a progressive tax and, if the latter, on either a slab scale or a slice scale. The rate of such tax rate and exemptions allowed vary from country to country.

## in-company training
Training for the employees of a company held in the company's own premises.

## incoterms
These are terms for use in international trade contracts drawn up by the International Chambers of Commerce (ICC). Incoterms include c and f, cif, fas, and fob.

## increasing returns
A situation when output expands more than proportionately to the increase in the variable input.

## incremental capital-output ratio
It denotes increase in capital stock divided by the increase in output of goods and services during a particular period. The ratio might be applied to an individual company, a complete industry, or an economy.

## incremental pricing
It refers to having a two-tier pricing system, one price covering full cost and the other being geared to the marginal cost of further production.

## incremental profitability
It means stepping up the profitability by such difficult-to-quantify measures as improving skills of workers or introducing more skilled workers.

## indemnity
It refers to the following:
1. An agreement by one party to make good the losses suffered by another, usually

by payment of money, repair, or replacement.
2. An undertaking by a bank's client who has lost a document that the bank will be held harmless against any consequences including claims, damages, of the document's absence if it proceeds to service the documents.

## indenture

It denotes the following:
1. A deed, especially one creating or transferring an estate in land.
2. A document establishing the terms and conditions of an equity issue.

## independent project oversight

It refers to a process that employs quality control, inspection, test measurement and other observation processes in order to ensure that project objectives are achieved in accordance with an approved plan. Such oversight is generally conducted by an independent entity trained or experienced in a variety of management and technical review methods.

## index number

The term is used for statistical measures giving an overall indication of change over time, particularly for prices, wage rates, imports, exports, etc. It is derived from detailed statistical data, an index number which typically covers a base year which is assigned the value 100, and subsequent changes reflect deviations from that value for each period measured.

## indifference curve

It is a curve which illustrates problems of choice between combinations of goods, etc. and indicates the ideal preferences of a decision maker. Each point on the curve represents a maximum combined utility or satisfaction, so that the buyer

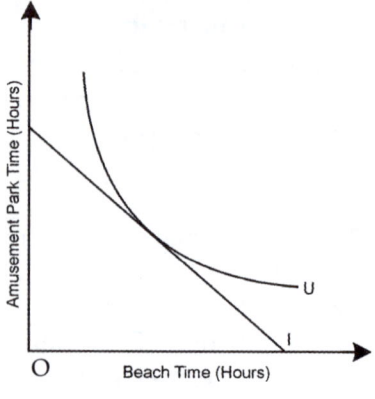

**Indifference curve**

is indifferent to the variations on one axis, provided that the variations on the other axis keep the resulting plot on the indifference curve.

## indirect costs

These are costs of a unit incurred for common or joint objectives, which cannot be readily and specifically identified with a particular project or other institutional activities.

## indirect materials

These are materials that do not feature in the final product but are necessary to carry out the production such as lubricants, cleaning materials, and consumable materials.

## indirect taxation

Taxation that is intended to be borne by persons or organisations other than those who pay the tax. The principal indirect tax is the value added tax (VAT), which is paid by traders as goods or services enter into the chain of production, but which is ultimately borne by the consumer of the goods or services.

## induction training

Training devised for new employees in a firm to familiarise them with company practices and procedures.

## industrial action

It refers to action taken by employees collectively to show either a grievance or a demand, usually on questions of pay and/or conditions of employment. Industrial action that resorts to withdrawal of labour or refusal to work is termed as strike. Action to limit the effectiveness of work, rather than refusal to do it, includes go-slow and work-to-do rule, and is sometimes called cut price industrial action. Industrial action by an employer of employees is a lockout which is intended to exclude workers from a factory during a dispute.

## industrial diseases

It refers to the diseases attributable to exposure to harmful or poisonous substances and rays at work. These diseases include toxic conditions such as poisoning by lead, phosphorus, arsenic or mercury; fibrosis of the lungs caused by silica or asbestos; skin ailments such as dermatitis; columnary obstructive pelvic disease (COPD) by smoke; and ulceration caused by chromic acid; etc.

## industrial dispute

Dispute between employers or their representatives and employees or their representatives over pay, working conditions, etc. An industrial dispute is sometimes regarded as confrontation between employers and employees that usually precedes industrial dispute as well as the industrial action itself. The UK Labour Office defines industrial dispute as a temporary stoppage of work wilfully, effected by a group of workers or by one or more employees with a view to enforcing a demand.

## industry

It refers to the following:
1. An organised activity in which capital and labour are utilised to produce goods.
2. The sector of an economy that is concerned with manufacture of various types of goods.

3. A group of firms that offer a product or class of products that are close substitutes for each other. The set of all sellers of a product or service, e.g. the textile industry, leather industry, or the banking industry.

## industry-based student

The term is used for college or university course sponsored by an employer who arranges his/her industrial training periods.

## industry-wide agreement

It denotes collective agreement or bargain between employers and trade unions on an industry-wide basis.

## inelastic demand

A market situation where the demand for a product or

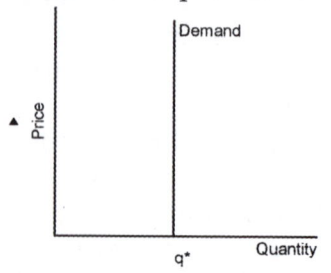

Inelastic demand

service changes only slightly, i.e. in response to changes in price.

**Dictionary of Business**

## inertia selling
It is a despicable sales approach under which goods are delivered to possible purchasers without their consent, these purchasers then being pressed to pay up rather than go to the trouble of returning the goods.

## inflation
It is a condition where the purchasing power of the community has increased beyond the level at which it can affect employment or real incomes, and has the effect of pushing up prices. In this situation, the money income flow expands faster than the supply of goods and services.

## information technology (IT)
It is a generic term for acquiring, processing, storing and disseminating information, whether in textual, numerical, graphical or vocal form, and using computers and telecommunications.

## information technology investments management
Abbreviated as ITIM, it implies an integrated approach to managing IT investments that provides for the continuous identification, selection, control, life-cycle management and evaluation of various IT investments. It uses structured processes to minimise risks and maximise return on IT investment (ROITI). Commonwealth's approach to technology management is based on ITIM.

## infrastructure
It is a term for power houses, roads, bridges, ports, airports, housing, hospitals, educational establishments, etc. which are a vital underpinning of industry and the economy and have an effect on economic growth of a country, viz. high industrial production.

Infrastructure

**Dictionary of Business**

## injection

In business, it refers to putting funds in the market, e.g. injecting purchasing power into the circular flow of income in an economy. Its opposite is a withdrawal, normally through savings, taxation, or imports.

## injunction

It can be defined as an order by a court that a person shall do, or refrain from doing a particular act. This is an equitable remedy that may be granted by the court wherever considered just and convenient. An interim injunction may be granted on the application of one party without the other being present if there is great urgency.

## inputs

It refers to the following:
1. Information and data fed into calculations such as in computer.
2. Value added tax term for the tax on the value of goods and services at the beginning of a particular stage in their production or distribution.
3. The materials and resources fed into a process of manufacturing.

## inscribed stock

The term is used for shares in loan stock, for which the names of the holders are kept in a register rather than by the issue of a certificate of ownership. On a transfer, a new name has to be registered, which makes them cumbersome and unpopular as a security.

## insider trading

The term is used for trading where directors, executives take advantage of their inside knowledge of a company to make profit from dealing in the company's shares before such knowledge becomes available to the public. In order to check insider training, the government has put restrictions to prevent directors, executives and others from dealing in shares when they are deemed to have sensitive information which could affect the share price, otherwise they may face heavy penalties.

## insolvency

It can be defined as inability to pay one's debts as and when they fall due. In the case of individuals, this may lead to bankruptcy and in the

**Dictionary of Business**

case of companies to liquidation. In both of these cases, the normal procedure is to appoint a trustee or liquidator to gather and dispose of the assets of the insolvent and to pay the creditors. Insolvency does not always lead to bankruptcy and liquidation, although it often does.

## inspection
It refers to the following:
1. The process of checking parts that have already been completed to make sure that they were done correctly. It can be done for either an accept/reject decision for a batch of parts, or to check to see if a process is still in control. Inspection is done at the source so that the process has immediate feedback and has a sense of ownership of quality.
2. Also the activities such as measuring, examining, testing the characteristics of a product or service and comparing these with specified requirements to determine conformity.

## institution
It is a stock exchange term for certain large organisations that have large shareholdings in various public companies and whose buying and selling of shares has a major influence on the stock market.

## insurance
The term is often used interchangeably with assurance but, technically, an insurance policy is taken out against what might happen, e.g. fire, riots, floods, etc. while an assurance policy covers what is bound to happen, e.g. death, and therefore, commit payment of life cover but at an unknown time.

## insurance company
It is a company that enters into contracts with individuals or with companies, organisations, etc. to pay compensation in specific circumstances in return for the regular and timely payment of insurance premiums.

## insured employment
It is an economist's term for labour force requirements, i.e. jobs available, or in times of scarcity, jobs taken.

## intangible asset
It refers to the following:

Dictionary of Business

1. The non-physical resources of an organisation. An example might be the goodwill of company. These assets are not generally accounted for in an organisation's financial statements.
2. Also the non-financial assets of an organisation which contribute to its success.

### integer programming

It is a mathematical programming technique that can be of more practical use than orthodox linear programming in some situations because it works to nearest whole numbers and does not leave management with the problem of rounding off different quantities.

### intellectual property

It is an intangible asset such as copyright, patent, trademark, or design right. Since intellectual property is an asset, it can be bought, sold, licensed, or exchanged.

### interchangeability

It refers to removal of demarcations between types of labour and jobs, having the advantage for employers of more economical use of employees.

### interest cover

It implies relationship between the amount of interest payable during a period, usually a financial year, and the amount of profit before interest and before tax.

### interest-sensitive

It describes an activity that is sensitive to changes in the general level of interest rates. For example, items bought on some form of hire-purchase basis is interest-sensitive because they cost more as interest rates rise.

### interference pay

It is payment made to employees on a payment-by-results scheme where they have to interrupt their work to carry out some other work the employer wants to be done.

### inter-firm comparison

The term is used for a method of checking company and management performance by comparing a wide range of data from firms with similar general characteristics in terms of production, sales, costs, etc. Such data may range across labour turnover, proportion of direct to indirect labour, stocks carried, variety of products, sales promotion, etc.

### intermediary
It denotes the following:
1. A third party linking the main parties to negotiations or a business deal.
2. Also a shareholder having nominee holdings or intermediary holdings.

### intermodal
In business, it is a transportation term describing the use of multiple modes of transportation for a shipment. A common example is ocean containers that are picked up by a truck, delivered to port, transported by ship, and then picked up by another truck.

### internal market
It refers to the following:
1. A market where a large organisation is broken down into a number of small units dealing with each other as customers.
2. As single market, it means a free market in trade, financial services, etc.

### internal rate of return (IRR)
It is a return on a project or enterprise as measured by discounted cash flow technique. It is also known as the marginal efficiency of capital.

### International Bank for Reconstruction and Development (IBRD)
It is a specialised agency which helps raise standards of living of people of developing countries, by making loans to governments or guaranteeing outside loans. It lends on broadly commercial terms, either for specific projects or for more general social purposes. Funds are raised on the international capital markets. IBRD and its affiliates, the International Development Association (IDA) and the International Finance Corporation (IFC), are often known as the World Bank. It is owned by the governments of 192 countries.

### International Finance Corporation (IFC)
It is an affiliate of the International Bank for

Reconstruction and Development (IBRD) established in 1956 to provide assistance to the developing countries. Although the IFC and IBRD are separate entities, both legally and financially, the IFC is able to borrow from the IBRD and reloan to private investors.

## International Monetary Fund (IMF)

It is an independent organisation having a special relationship with the United Nations to promote international trade, employment and real income in its member countries, and stability of exchange rates, the latter being fixed in relation to the value of gold and the US dollar. Member states pay into the Fund a specified quota, of which 25 per cent must be in gold. The IMF has a Managing Director, a Board of Executive Directors, and a Board of Governors representing each of its member states.

## international systems

It refers to systems of metric units of measurement that has gained widespread acceptance as a means of handling all forms of measurement. The International Organisation for Standards (IOS) has developed a wide range of recommendations based on SI units. Basic units of the SI system include the metre (length), the kilogram (mass or weight), the second (time), and the ampere (electric current).

## Internet

It is an international network of computers connected by modems, dedicated lines, telephone cables, and satellite links, with associated software controlling the movement of data. It offers facilities for accessing remote databases, transfer of data between computers, e-mail

Internet

and a host of other facilities and functions.

## interpolation
The term is used for estimation of the value of an unknown quantity that lies between two of a series of known values. For example, one can estimate by interpolation the population of a country at any time between known 10-year census figures.

## intestate
It is a person who dies without having made a will. The estate, in these circumstances, is divided according to the rules of intestacy. The division depends on the personal circumstances of the decreased.

## intrapreneurship
It implies a method of obtaining flexibility among managers by identifying people who are likely to set up their own business, then enabling them to act as entrepreneurs within the company.

## intrinsic value
It is the inherent value of material before the added value of manufacture, etc.

## inventory
It is an accounting term for the cost of materials being processed in a firm at a given point in time, including raw materials, work-in-progress and finished goods.

Inventory

## inventory turn
It describes the number of times inventory turns during a year. It is normally calculated by dividing the average inventory level into the annual inventory usage.

## inventory turnover
It can be defined as the cost of goods sold, decided by the average inventory investment. The inverse of the inventory turnover ratio is an estimate of the cycle time. It can be mathematically established that inventory turnover should increase with an increase in demand. A

**Dictionary of Business**

caution should be exercised in benchmarking inventory turnover ratios between firms that have differing demand rates, or whose demand rate is changing drastically over time. Technically, sales decided by the average inventory investment is coverage.

### investment appraisal
It refers to analysis and evaluation of the return on investment of money, etc. Such appraisal is also applicable to all management activities, etc. even where it may not be possible to quantify the return precisely.

### investment bank
A bank that specialises in new issues and then selling them in smaller batches to investors.

### investment review board (IRB)
It is a decision-making body, consisting of senior programme managers, financial managers and information managers. The body is responsible for making decisions about IT projects and systems, based on comparisons and trade-offs between competing projects and an emphasis on meeting mission needs and improving organisational performance.

### investment strategy funds
These are investment trusts, which act upon the investment strategies of the respective offers for the different risk classes. Such funds invest worldwide in different instruments, depending upon risk class shares and/or obligations. Investment strategy funds also make allocation of fund, strategy of fund, portfolio funds, and investments objective fund, administration of an estate fund or mixed funds.

### investment trust
It refers to any company that exists to invest its capital in other companies, usually in quoted securities but at times more speculatively. An investment trust has the advantage of giving small investors an opportunity to spread their investment widely and therefore safely.

### invisible earnings
The earnings from abroad that contribute to the balance

Dictionary of Business

of payments (BOPs) as a result of transactions involving services such as insurance, banking, shipping, tourism, among others, rather than the sale and purchase of goods.

## irritation strike
It is a type of industrial action in which workers work badly and wastefully rather than directly going on strike.

## issuing house
A financial institution usually a merchant bank, which handles for client companies, the raising of capital by new issues of shares, bonds, debentures, securities, etc.

## item profile
It refers to data that describes the characteristics of an item. It includes physical characteristics like size and weight, transactional characteristics such as time consumed, and units sold or group characteristics like sales channel, commodity and hazardous classification. Item profiles are used in warehouse design and slotting.

# J

### JICNARS
It stands for joint industry committee for national readership surveys.

### job-and-finish
A system under which workers are free to leave work when they have completed an agreed amount of work rather than waiting until the normal knocking-off time.

### jobbing
It is a type of process in which small numbers of products are made to order. It involves high levels of skill and the movement of resources to the product.

### job classification method
It is a non-analytical job evaluation technique which involves the allocation of jobs into predetermined job levels. The features of each grade will normally be defined in terms of level of responsibility or skill involved in it.

### job cover plan
It is a plan, usually presented in the form of a chart, and which carries a note of all the jobs and tasks in the firm or unit, both at present and in the predictable future, and of the extent to which each employee is capable of carrying out each of them. Special note is made of problems like understaffing or overstaffing of individuals; overworking in a manner that is damaging to their performance; employees able to take on other jobs if necessary; any impending technological change that will affect the demand for skill, among other things.

### job knowledge test
It is an achievement test in a particular job or skill or range of skills. It is not concerned with testing an individual's potential after further training and/or experience, but only his/her skill for a specific job.

### job production
It refers to manufacture of single product to individual specifications. It differs from the quantity production of batch production; the standardised production of

mass production; and the continuous productions of process production or assembly line or flow line production.

### job ranking
The term is used for job evaluation technique for determining the relative position of each job by comparison with all other jobs, albeit without indicating the extent of different levels.

### joint and several liability
It can be defined as a liability that is entered into as a group, on the understanding that if anyone of the group fails in his undertaking, the liability must be shared by the remainder.

### joint product
Two or more products requiring the same raw materials and processing.

### joint venture
It is a commercial undertaking entered into jointly by two or more entities. Such ventures are usually governed by the State's Partnership Act, but they differ from partnerships in that they are limited by time or by activity. Generally, separate books are not kept and the joint ventures will have a profit or loss sharing ratio for the purpose of the joint venture only. Joint ventures have become increasingly common as companies cooperate with each other in globalised markets to share costs and exploit new technologies.

### junk bonds
They are high yielding but low grade bonds where security is below average or which may be conditional upon the acquisition of assets through a takeover.

### just in time (JIT)
It is an approach to manufacturing that aims to reduce stocks or raw materials and finished goods, excess transport, and levels of scrap and defective units. The traditional systems isolate operations from the environment, for example, by uncoupling inventory. JIT strategy recognises that without protection processes can go wrong but, if they do, the right reasons should be found instead of trying to put the process right.

**Dictionary of Business**

# K

### Kaldor-Hicks efficiency
In economic theory, an alteration in the allocation of resources is said to be Kaldor-Hicks efficient when it produces more benefits than costs.

### Kanban inventory system
It is a card system of inventory control used in the just-in-time (JIT) production system which involves production lines calling off exactly the number of parts needed.

### kangaroo court
The term is used for an informal court with no legal standing such as one conducted by workers to try a colleague.

### keepwell
It refers to a guarantee by a holding company that it will maintain financial backing for a subsidiary for a stated period. The usual purpose is to enhance the creditworthiness of the subsidiary.

### keyed advertisement
An advertisement that is coded so that there can be an indication of the response to it. Thus, the same advertisement appearing in several publications may be coded to depict different publications.

### key task
The task which conditions the time and/or quality of related tasks and the total job or operation which all these form together.

### key task analysis
It is an analysis of key tasks to be performed, levels of performance required and methods of checking actual against desired performance.

### key worker approach
It is a system of work where one highly trained person takes a lead in group working and is trained to teach and disseminate knowledge and techniques.

### kicked upstairs
The term is used for someone

who is promoted in order to remove him or her from a position in which his/her inefficiency is creating problems.

## kiting

It is an informal term for the dishonest practice of improving the apparent cash position in a company's accounts by paying a large cheque on the last day of the accounting period from one of its current accounts into a second current account. Since the first account will not have been debited, but the second account will have been credited, the overall cash position is temporarily overstated. It is also known as window dressing.

## kits, kitting

In HR management, it denotes grouping individual items together for future use. In a manufacturing context, 'kits' of parts are often put together in boxes and given to workers to assemble. In a distribution context, kits of parts are prepared to be packed and shipped.

## know-how

It is the ability to achieve a desired result. It may be the most valuable knowledge element of all. It is predictive and reflects the person's, or organisation's ability to act and achieve its goals.

Know-how is built on another key knowledge element and understanding, i.e. 'what is', 'what was' and 'why', that deals with knowing historic cause and effect, and thus, determine the current state of things.

## knowledge assets

These are parts of an organisation's intangible assets that relate specifically to knowledge, like know-how, best practices, intellectual property, etc. Knowledge assets are often divided into (a) human, viz. people, teams, networks and communities; (b) structural, i.e. codified knowledge that can be found in processes and procedures; and (c) technological like the technologies that support knowledge sharing such as databases and intranets.

# L

## labour
It is a generic term for workforce or the human physical and mental effort and skills involved in industry, enterprise and commerce.

Labour

## labour code
A code used in some countries to regulate the relationship between employer and employee.

## labour force
It refers to population working or available for work.

## labour hoarding
It denotes a situation where a firm employs more labour than immediately necessary to guard against the possibility of being caught with insufficient labour later. The situation occurs in conditions of full employment, inflation, and/or boom.

## labour-intensive
It is an industry where there is high use of labour with complementary low capital investment and mechanisation. It is opposite of capital-intensive.

## labour law
It simply means employment legislation dealing with relations between employer and employee and industrial relations in general.

## labour market
The term defines the availability and demand for particular kinds of labour and skill, considering factors like wage levels, terms and conditions of employment,

activities and needs of competing employers, outflows from educational institutions, travel to work areas, local economic conditions, etc. Labour markets exist internationally, nationally, locally and as internal labour market, within a particular location, e.g. a city.

## labour mobility

It is the extent to which workers are prepared to change jobs geographically and/or in occupational terms, and the factors influencing their attitudes.

## labour-only subcontracting

It is a situation where a contractor, particularly in the construction industry, obtains from a subcontractor, labour, but not materials or components. It is also known as gang system.

## labour relations

The term is synonymous with industrial relations though a distinction between them is that industrial relations are concerned with union-management relations.

## labour stability index

It is the ratio of number of employees who have been employed by a particular employer for at least a year to the number of those who were employed by the firm a year ago.

## laissez-faire economy

An economy where forces operate freely without intervention from government policy. It is believed that such an economy is non-existent these days.

## last-in, first-out (LIFO)

It denotes the following:
1. In terms of stock valuation, it is the method of valuing stocks that assumes that all issues or sales are charged at the most current cost, but stocks are valued at the oldest cost available.
2. In stock rotation, it refers to the method whereby the goods which are the newest goods in stock are sold or consumed first.
3. In redundancy situations, it means the first employees to be made redundant are those most recently recruited.

## late finish date (LFD)

In the critical path method, it is the latest possible point in time that an activity may be completed without delaying a specified milestone.

## late start date (LSD)
In the critical path analysis method, it implies the latest possible point in time that an activity may begin without delaying a specified milestone.

## laying off
It refer to the following:
1. It means suspending or terminating the employment of workers because there is no work for them to do. If the laying off involves a permanent termination of employment, redundancy payments will have to be paid.
2. Lay-off is also described as a situation where an employer is unable to continue employing workers, usually for lack of work, and suspends their employment. This may happen, where there is recession and consequent lack of demand for goods and services.

## leading and lagging
It refers to the following:
1. Techniques used at the end of a financial year to enhance a cash position and reduce borrowing.
2. The use of similar techniques to benefit from the expected change in a currency value.

## leading method
It is a marketing technique used in preparing forecasts in a particular area, wherein an analysis is made of trends or economic indicators that are known to be related to the data being forecast.

## lead manager
A bank or other financial institution chosen to underwrite a new issue of bonds or to head a syndicated bank facility.

## lead rate
It refers to extra payment made to an employee called upon to use exceptional skills or to take extra responsibility.

## lead time
It denotes the time which must be allowed for the completion of a job or operation. It may be manufacturing time or the time to be allowed for orders bought out goods to be met.

## lead users
These are the first users of a new product or service, who are asked to assess its advantages and disadvantages in relation to those of its competitors' products.

Dictionary of Business

## leapfrogging
It refers to the process by which a successful pay claim by one group of employees tends to encourage pay claims by further groups, often on the grounds that pay differentials should be maintained.

## learning curve
It refers to the following:
1. Representation in graph form of rate of progress of trainees. It is also known as skill acquisition curve. The rate of improvement is shown by plotting production against time.
2. A mathematical model that relates the cost per unit to the cumulative number of units produced. The curve usually has a slow beginning and then a steep acceleration before it settles down to reach the plateau, i.e. a period of stability or consolidation.

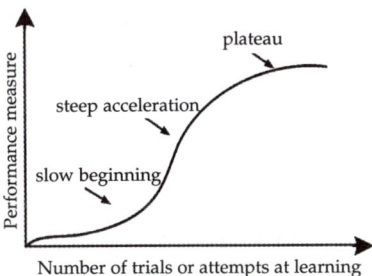

**Learning curve**

## learning organisation
It describes an organisation which encourages and supports learning by everyone at all levels in the organisation and also recognises a corporate learning process for itself.

## learning plateau
It refers to the temporary flattening out in trainee or student's learning curve. Sometimes, it represents period of consolidation in acquisition of skills.

## lease
It is a document which the owner of buildings, land, factory equipment, office equipment, or transport, etc. signs, over its use to another individual or company, for a particular period of time at a particular rent.

## least-squares
It is a method devised by the French mathematician Legendre for calculating the regression line which gives the best representation for a set of observed values so that the line may be used to predict the approximate value of one variable, given a known value of the other.

## letter of credit (L/C)
The documentary credit issued by a bank or similar institution allowing a borrower to draw bills of exchange on it for specified purposes. In the case of international trade, an overseas buyer may arrange for a bank in the country of the vendor with a letter of credit accepting a bill of exchange drawn on it against delivery of the relevant export shipping documents. It may be revocable or irrevocable, confirmed or unconfirmed.

An irrevocable L/C cannot be cancelled by the person who opens it or by the issuing bank without the beneficiary's consent, while a revocable L/C may be revoked. In an irrevocable L/C, the negotiating bank guarantees to pay the beneficiary, even if the issuing bank fails to honour its commitments. In an unconfirmed letter of credit, this guarantee is not given. A confirmed irrevocable letter of credit therefore provides the most reliable means of being paid for exported goods.

## leverage
It refers to the following:

1. A US term for gearing.
2. The use by a company, of its limited assets to guarantee substantial loans to finance its business.

## leveraged buy out
Abbreviated as LBO, it is a condition or situation where, in a bid for a company, the management provides only a small part of the capital received and the banks supply the balance of the equity or loan capital.

## liability
It can be defined as any form of debt owed to others. Current liabilities are short-term debts which must be settled within 12 months of the financial year. Secured liabilities are claims that have some or securities pledged to ensure satisfaction in the event of default. Contingent liabilities are those which may materialise in the event of some happening, e.g. a default under bank guarantee.

## licensing
In international marketing, it is an agreement by which a company permits a foreign company to set up a business in the foreign market using

**Dictionary of Business**

## lien

It is the right to retain goods until the seller has been fully paid. When goods are sold on credit, no lien exists until the credit period has expired.

## lieu days

It refers to holidays taken in lieu of unpaid overtime.

## lieu payment

In some countries, it is amount paid to an employee as compensation for not being able to join a payment-by-results scheme, etc.

## life-cycle cost

In business, it is the overall estimated cost for a particular object over a period of time corresponding to the life of the object, including direct and indirect initial costs in addition to any periodic or continuing costs for operations and maintenance.

## lifestyle

It consists of the activities, interests, opinions, and values of individuals, which provide a profile of a person's whole pattern of behaviour and interaction with the world. Lifestyles are important in marketing because they influence the way in which people make purchases. The technique for measuring lifestyle is part of psychographic segmentation.

## limited company

It can be defined as a company in which the liability of the members in respect of the company's debts is limited either by shares, in which case the liability of the members on a winding-up is limited to the amount unpaid on their shares, or by guarantee. In the latter case, the liability of members is limited by the memorandum to a certain amount, which the members undertake to contribute on winding up.

## limited liability partnership

It is a legally recognised entity under the Indian Partnership Act, 1932. This type of business organisation is intended to combine the flexibility of a traditional partnership with the corporate notion of limited liability. Persons intending to set up a limited liability partnership must register it with the Registrar of Companies.

## line and staff management

It is a system of management used in large organisations in which there are two separate hierarchies:

1. The line management side, which is comprised of line managers with responsibility for deciding the policy of and running the organisation's main activities.

2. Staff management and its separate staff managers who are responsible for providing such supporting services as warehousing, transport, personnel management, and plant maintenance.

## line filling

It means adding products to an existing line of products in order to leave very little opportunities for competitors. It can be horizontal or vertical. In horizontal line filling, a mobile manufacturer may produce machines with a variety of features, and functions, multi-recording memory, etc. at the top end of the price range, and relatively cheap cost-effective machines at the lower end. In vertical line filling, a manufacturer may produce a wide variety of brand names within a single product line.

## linked subcontracting

It means making employees redundant, and then hiring their services back as independent subcontractors.

## liquid assets

These are assets that can be quickly converted into cash. These include cash at bank, cash in hand, easily marketable securities, book debts, bills receivable, etc.

## liquidation

It refers to legal procedures which cause a company to be formally closed down and cease its existence.

## liquidator

The term is used for a person appointed by a court, or by the members of a company or its creditors, to regularise the company's affairs on winding up. In the case of a member's voluntary liquidation, it is the members of the company who appoint the liquidator. In a creditors' voluntary liquidation, the liquidator may be appointed by company members before the meeting of creditors, or by the creditors themselves at the meeting.

The liquidator has a relationship of trust with the company and the creditors as a body. A liquidator appointed in a compulsory liquidation is an officer of the court, and is under statutory obligations not to profit from the position.

## liquidity

It refers to the extent to which a company has access to cash or can convert some of its assets into cash without substantial loss in value. It shows the ability to meet financial obligations in cash or its equivalent.

## liquidity trap

It can be described as situation in which investors hold on to cash because they are worried about the likelihood of a fall in the price of financial assets. According to a noted economist J.M. Keynes, in such a situation, monetary policy becomes ineffective because monetary expansion will not lower interest rates.

## liquid ratio

It can be defined as the ratio of assets minus stocks to current liabilities. This may be a safer yardstick for a company than current ratio because it does not involve reliance on stocks which, at least at the critical time, may not be readily saleable.

## load

It refers to the following:
1. In manufacturing, load implies the amount of production scheduled against a plant or machine.
2. In warehousing, it is described as the materials being handled by a piece of equipment.
3. In transportation, load is described as the materials being transported.

Load

**Dictionary of Business**

## load balancing
The term is used for a specialised function provided by third-party application providers. Load balancing software designed to distribute web content requests from a single URL, accessed by an end-user, to any number of production servers. In this way, multiple production servers can be used to serve web content to a larger audience base.

## loading
It denotes the following:
1. In cost accounting, it refers to adding overhead to prime costs.
2. In mutual funds, it is the additional amount to the market price of shares and stocks to cover administrative costs, brokerage, etc.
3. In general sense, it means the extra amount added to cover some contingency.

## load levelling
In project planning and manufacturing contexts, it is desirable to have a level workload for resources like machines, tools, people, etc. over a period of time. Some finite planning systems attempt to create schedules that require about the same amount of a resource in every period. This is known as level loading.

## local option
It is a situation where local government or management has the right to decide an issue without reference to higher authority.

## localisation
It means altering the content of a product such as a web site or computer program, to make it suitable to users in a particular country or language group.

## locater systems (LS)
These are inventory tracking systems that enable to assign locations to inventory to facilitate greater tracking and the ability to store product randomly. Before the advent of locater systems, warehouses needed to store product in some logical manner in order to be able to find it. By using the locater systems, space utilisation can be increased by slotting the product by matching the physical characteristics of the product to allocation whose physical characteristics match that of the product.

## lock-out
Also called shut out, it is the situation in which the employer brings pressure to bear on employees by refusing them access to the workplace.

## logo
It is a company's or organisation's symbol, badge or name style.

**GlobalELT**
ENGLISH LANGUAGE TEACHING BOOKS

Logo

## Lombard street
The term is used to mean the UK banking and financial world. Lombard street is actually a street in the city of London named after the money changers and bankers who originally came from Lombardy to London in the 18th century.

## London interbank offered rate
Abbreviated as LIBOR, it is the rate of interest at which banks lend to each other on the London interbank market. The loans are for a minimum of £ 250,000 and for periods up to five years. It is the most significant interest rate for international banks. It is also used as a benchmark for lending to bank customers and as a reference rate for many derivatives.

## longitudinal design
It is a marketing research design in which the views of a fixed population sample are depicted over a period to trends and changes in audiences. Many consumer panels, TV audience panels, and readership panels belong to this type.

## longitudinal flue space
It can be defined as the space between the rows of back-to-back racking. Flue spaces allow the water from an overhead sprinkler system to reach lower levels of the rack. Usually, a longitudinal flue space of at least 6 inches is required. Such space is measured as the distance between the loads, not the distance between the racks.

## long-term liabilities
These are liabilities which will not have to be met within the next three years.

**Dictionary of Business**

## loose rate
The term describes the situation where the piece work rate for completing a job, as established by a rate fixer, is such that it enables a worker to earn bonus relatively easily. In it, a work group may informally hold back production under a fiddle or quota restriction for fear of rate cutting.

## loss ratio
The term refers to the ratio between the total of the premium paid to an insurance company and the total value of the claims settled by the company.

## lot
It refers to one or more components or finished devices that consist of a single type, class, model, size, composition or software versions that are manufactured under essentially the same conditions and that are intended to have uniform characteristics.

## lot size
It denotes the quantity that is ordered. When one deals with suppliers, one typically calls this the order size, when dealing with manufacturing orders placed on owner's own factory, then it is called the lot size or batch size.

## lowest replaceable item
It is the lowest level component at which maintenance will be performed or discrete configuration enforced. However, sometimes the lowest is known as the smallest.

## LTL
It is abbreviation for less than truckload, viz. a small shipment that does not fill the truck or a shipment of insufficient weight to qualify for a truckload quantity discount.

## luddites
Luddites were groups of workers who violently opposed the introduction of machinery in factories in the early 19th century in the UK. The term is used to describe workers opposed to changes in technology and introduction of new working methods.

## lump labour
It is a type of labour seen particularly in the construction industry and is

sometimes called labour-only sub-contracting. Lump labour workers are self-employed and are paid a lump sum per day's work or per quantities of completed work, either by the contractor who in turn is paid by the company lump sum for the work done or by the company directly.

## lump sum

It refers to the following:
1. A sum of money paid all at once, instead of in instalments.
2. A sum of money paid for freight, irrespective of the size of the cargo.
3. An insurance benefit such as a sum of money paid on retirement or redundancy.

# M

### machine ancillary time
A situation when plant is not being used for production so that setting up, cleaning, etc. can take place. Machine ancillary time is thus production time lost for genuine reasons considered necessary for continued efficient production.

### machine hour rate
It is the rate at which the use of equipment is charged for estimating and costing purposes.

### machine idle time
It is a situation when a machine is available for production work but is kept out of action by lack of materials, labour, orders, etc.

### mail order selling
It refers to selling against orders received through the post directly from consumers, purchasers or agents. Such orders may be in response to advertisement of the direct response promotion or coupon advertising kind.

### maintainability
It refers to the following:
1. The probability that a failed system can be made operable in a specified interval.
2. Ability of an item under stated conditions of use to be retained in or restored to, within a given period of time, a specified state in which it can perform the requisite functions.

### maintenance, repair operations
These are items purchased for a firm that are not used directly in the product. Lubricants, cutting for machines, etc. are examples. These items are generally not handled by the firm's ERP system, but are often significant expenditure items for many manufacturing firms.

### make-up pay
It denotes payment made on payment-by-results basis to a worker who has not reached an agreed minimum level of payment, irrespective of the amount of work achieved.

## make versus buy decision

The manufacturing firms often have to decide between making a part or product and buying it from supplier. These decisions have strategic implications. One of the most difficult aspects of this decision is how to handle overheads. If the firms completely ignore overheads, the decisions will generally be in the direction of in-sourcing; if they fully allocate overheads, decisions will generally go in the direction of outsourcing and can lead the firm into the death-spiral where the more they outsource, the more overhead they have, leading to more outsourcing.

## make-work

It refers to work done to keep employees occupied rather than to produce goods or services of marketable value.

## managed costs

These are costs over which there is some degree of management discretion during the progress of a project so that there is some scope for varying expenditure once the project is underway. It is opposite to costs to which management is virtually irrevocably committed once the project is launched.

## mandate

It refers to instructions given by an organisation to its representative on how he or she should vote on particular issues at a meeting or conference.

## manifest

It is a list of all the cargo carried by a ship or aircraft. It is signed by the captain before being handed to the customs on leaving and arriving at a port or airport.

## manpower analysis

It is the first stage in manpower planning in the individual firm. In it, all the employees in the firm or unit are analysed by age, length of service, job title and wider occupational category. Manpower analysis may also involve an assessment of the effects of labour turnover, on the basis of the number of leaves in the previous year.

## manpower deficit

It can be described as excess of jobs available over manpower available.

**Dictionary of Business**

## manufacturing account

An accounting statement forming part of the internal final accounts of a manufacturing organisation for a particular period. It shows direct cost of sales, manufacturing overheads, total production cost, and cost of goods manufactured.

## manufacturing cell

It can be defined as a mini-production line engaged in processing similar parts or products that require similar or identical operations. While a cell does not always make the same parts, it does make the same family of parts or products. The machines and fixtures within the cell are usually arranged close to each other so that there is no need to allow for storage between the operations or handling with hand trucks or pallet jacks.

## manufacturing execution system

Abbreviated as MES, it is a system that provides real-time information on manufacturing operations from the time. In it, an order is started until it is completed in a factory. MES does not plan order launch dates or order sizes. It rather focuses on collecting data and planning the detailed operations after an order has been started. Function of this system includes resource allocation and status, dispatching production orders, data collection and quality management, etc.

## manufacturing resource planning (MRP)

It is the process for determining material, labour and machine requirements in a manufacturing environment. MRPII is the consolidation of material requirements planning, capacity requirements planning, and master production scheduling. MRP was originally designed for materials planning only. When labour and machine planning were incorporated, it became known as MRPII.

## man-up

The term denotes lift trucks designed to raise the operator with the load. The most common types of man-up vehicles are turret trucks.

## MAPI method

It refers to the method for

evaluating machinery replacement decisions. There are two basic methods. One focuses attention on comparisons for one year immediately ahead by means of using a relatively simple two-page computing form. The other is relatively basic MAPI method which lays emphasis on the return to be expected over the asset's full life.

## marginal accounts

The term is used for accounts relating to firms whose credit rating is poor and the prospectus is questionable.

## marginal costing

It is the technique of costing in which costs are segregated into fixed costs and marginal costs which are the variable costs, i.e. those which tend to vary in relation to output. The marginal costing procedure is first to segregate fixed costs and then to apportion only the marginal costs to products or processes. The fixed costs are not charged to production and are written off to the profit and loss account in the year in which they are incurred.

## margin call

It is a call to a client from his commodity broker or share broker to increase his margin, i.e. the amount of money or securities deposited with the broker as a safeguard. This usually happens if the client has an open position in futures or cash in a market that is moving adversely for the position held by him.

## margin of safety

It is the extent to which sales volume or revenue exceeds the break-even point. The sales performance or target being checked is pinpointed on the sales revenue line above the break-even point in the chart. The margin of safety in financial terms is read off on the dotted vertical axis called 'margin of safety' (cash)' axis. Alternatively, the margin of safety in terms of volume of product is read off on the dotted horizontal 'margin of safety' (units). All managements aim to achieve a reasonable margin of safety in order to be able to withstand any significant decline in sales and/or production.

## market

It is a generic term for the number of customers or

potential customer units which have in common one or more easily identifiable and recognisable characteristics, including geographical location, income level, demand patterns, buying needs, habits, taste, etc.

Market

## market and sales forecasting

The term encompasses policies and techniques concerned with the potential and prospective sales volume or market trend for the individual product and with setting a sales target for such a product.

## market assessment

It implies identifying and evaluating all the relevant factors which affect a company's current or potential market. The process of market assessment involves the following:
1. Identifying the market and the characteristics of buyers.
2. Establishing the overall market structures and size.
3. Identifying the external factors which could affect market size and the competitive situation, including competitors' activities, national and international economic situations, etc.

## market diversification

It denotes to sell to different purchasers or in different markets through product diversification, establishing new markets, etc.

## market economy

It is defined as an economy based on the production of goods and services for sale rather than for the personal consumption of the producer and his/her dependents.

## market failure

It is a situation in which a market does not operate efficiently. The factors that may cause such failure include the possession of market power by transactors, externalities, or information problems.

## market forces

These are the forces of supply and demand that in a free market determine the quantity available of a particular product or service and the price at which it is offered. Generally, a rise in demand causes both supply and price to increase, while a rise in supply causes a fall in price as also a drop in demand, although many markets have individual features that modify this simple analysis.

## marketing

It is defined as the process of planning and executing the pricing, promotion, and distribution of products and services to create exchanges that will satisfy the needs of individual, groups and organisations. Marketing a product involves tasks like anticipating changes in demand, promotion of the product, ensuring that its quality, availability, and price meet the needs of the market, and providing after-sales service.
Marketing is a creative management function which promotes business and employment by assessing needs of the end user of products or services, initiates research and development, and produces various types of products and services which can be profitably provided to satisfy market requirements.

## marketing control

It is the process of monitoring sales results and costs vis-a-vis targets and budgets and taking action when required to exploit opportunities. It is also done through keeping a track of competitors' activities and changes in the marketing environment as well as revising overall marketing plans.

## marketing department

It is a subgroup of employees in a form which invents strategies for selling the company's products.

## marketing mix

It refers to the factors controlled by a company that can influence consumer's buying of its products. The four components of a marketing mix are:
1. The product—its quality, branding, packaging, and other features.
2. Pricing—the recommended retail price, and credit terms, etc.
3. Promotion—sale promotion.
4. Place—where to sell the

**Dictionary of Business**

product, etc.
The potential profitability of a particular marketing mix relates its acceptability to its market.

### marketing myopia
It implies a failure to define an organisation's purpose in terms of its function from the consumer's point of view. It ignores the needs of the consumer in more general terms rather than product-specific terms.

### marketing-oriented company
It is a company that tends to manufacture what are the consumer or customer needs, rather than what best suits its production and technical facilities.

### marketing strategy
It implies a plan identifying what marketing goals and objectives will be pursued to sell a particular product or product line.

### market leader
It is a company which has the largest share in a market for particular goods or services. For example, Infosys is market leader in IT solutions.

### market overhang
The term is used for the situation in which sellers, apprehensive about falling prices, prefer to postpone their sales until there is greater market demand. By reducing transactions, this behaviour can itself delay the expected recovery.

### market penetration
It can be described as proportion expressed as a percentage of the actual market volume that is generally met by a particular company or its products. A further and related important indicator is market saturation, which is the proportion, that the actual market volume is of market potential.

### market research
It refers to the following:
1. Getting an idea of which way trends are going and to find out who else is doing the same thing.
2. An investigation of the participants in a market.

### market risk
It refers to the risk, which depends on factors, which affect the entire market and not an individual portfolio.

## market saturation
It denotes the proportion, usually expressed as a percentage, showing the relationship of actual market volume to market potential.

## market segmentation
It is an analysis of the purchasers in a market by reference to characteristics like buying behaviour, demand patterns, socio-economic status or age in order to divide the market into sectors or segments in each of which the customers are of similar nature and are influenced by similar nature. After effecting market segmentation, marketing effort can be directed more specifically to defined segments.

## market share
It implies sales of a product in a particular market segment as a proportion of the total sales or actual market volume in that segment.

## market-to-book ratio
It refers to the common method of valuing knowledge-intensive companies. It is equal to price per share × total number of shares outstanding divided by book equity, which is the equity portion of a company's balance sheet.

## mark-up
It refers to the following:
1. Difference between wholesale price and retail price.
2. The difference between prices at various stages between the prime producer and the final supplier to the consumer.
3. Also an increase in price of a product or service.

## master production schedule (MPS)
It is a time-phased plan specifying when the firm plans to build each end item. The aggregate plan, for example, for a furniture company may specify the total number of sofa sets it plans to produce in the next month or next quarter. MPS identifies the exact size and qualities and also states period by period, how many and when each of these sofa types is needed.

## matched bargain
A situation where there is a narrow or small market for shares, and a scale can only be effected if a purchaser is immediately willing to buy.

## material
It is a generic term covering systems, equipment, stores, supplies, etc. including related documentation, manuals, computer hardware and software, among other things.

## materiality
It is the extent to which an item of accounting information is material. A piece of information is considered material if its omission from a financial statement could influence the decision-making of its users. Materiality is thus not an absolute concept but is dependent on the size and nature of an item and the specific circumstances in which it may arise.

## material requirements
It refers to a system to support manufacturing and fabrication organisations by the timely release of production and purchase orders, using the production plan for finished goods to determine the materials required to make the product. Orders for dependent demand items are phased over a period of time to ensure that the flow of raw materials and inventories in process match the production schedules for finished products. The three main inputs are the master production schedule, inventory status records and producer structure records.

## material review board (MRB)
It is a standing committee that determines the disposition of items that have questionable quality.

## materials building
It is a term for application of analytical methods and equipment design considerations to the problems of storing, packaging and moving products and materials in any form in the prescribed sequence and sending them to the locations required. The aim is to use safest and most economical methods, equipments, containers and handling devices.

## maturity date
It is the date on which a document such as a bond, bill of exchange, a fixed deposit, recurring deposit, national saving certificate, or

## mean absolute per cent deviation

insurance policy becomes due for payment. In case of redeemable government stocks, the maturity date is known as the redemption date.

## mean absolute per cent deviation

It is the average forecast error, either positive or negative, which is calculated as the sum of absolute value of forecast error for all periods, divided by the total member of evaluated periods.

## mean time between failure

It refers to the average time that a component is expected to work without failing. It is a good measure of the reliability of a product and is often described as a 'bath-tub curve', which suggests that most components fail either at the beginning of the product life, or towards the end of the expected product life.

## mean time to repair

It is a measure of the average time required to fix something such as a machine. It is in effect a measure of the complexity of a repair job.

## measured daywork

It is a method of assessing wages in which a daily production target is set and a daily wage agreed upon this basis. If the target is reached, the worker receives the agreed daily wage, but if it is not reached, the worker is paid pro rata.

## mechanical aptitude test

It is a test used in personnel selection to assess the ability to understand how movement can be transmitted mechanically.

## mediation

It refers to the intervention of a neutral third party in an industrial dispute. The aim is to enable the two sides to reach a compromise to resolve their differences. The mediator usually proceeds by seeing representatives of each side separately and then together. In case the mediator has power to make binding awards, the process is called arbitration but if the mediator can only suggest means of settling the dispute, it is known as conciliation.

## medium-term

Also called intermediate term, it denotes a time period of medium duration, the extent of which may differ according to context. In accounting, medium-term liabilities are those falling due between one and five years; in money markets, it means maturities of greater than a year; in bond markets, a period of five to ten years.

### meltdown
The term is used for disastrous and uncontrolled fall in share prices. It is now increasingly used for economic slowdown, affecting large number of companies, institutes, and resulting in general layoff.

### mercantile agent
It refers to a person who has authority, in the ordinary course of business, to buy, sell or consign any goods entrusted to him/her by the principal. Mercantile agents are also called commercial agents.

### mercantile credit
Also known as commercial credit, it refers to the allowable limits of a transaction. It covers business between manufacturer and wholesaler and other levels of the trade before it reaches the end user. It is also a term for transactions prior to manufacturing, e.g. when materials and components are supplied to the manufacturer.

### merchandising
It refers to the following:
1. In marketing, a term for manufacturing or wholesaling by a company directly to encourage sales promotion by the retail outlets it serves.
2. Using psychological persuasion on consumers at the point of purchase without the use of personal salesmanship.
3. Planning the range of products to be sold and promoted.

### metric system
It is a system of measurement based on the decimal system. It was first formalised in France at the end of the 18th century and by the 1830s, it was being widely adopted in Europe. With the advent of metric system, certain traditional units such as the hundred weight, ton, pound, ounce, yard, foot, inch, gallon, bushel, square mile, cubic yard, and cubic foot are being less used for the purpose of trade.

**Dictionary of Business**

## micromarketing
It is a form of target marketing in which companies make their marketing programmes to cater the needs of a narrowly defined geographic, demo-graphic, or behavioural market segment.

## middleman
The term is used for wholesaler, agent or other businessman coming between the producer or the manufacturer and retailer in the sales chain. His basic role in the distribution of goods is to buy from the producer and sell to the retailer.

## migrant worker
A worker who has come from another country to work. Attracted by greener pastures in the country or region to which they have migrated, such workers may or may not bring their family with them. In many cases, they will be sending a substantial proportion of their earnings back to their native country. This can have an adverse effect on the balance of payments of countries that attract substantial numbers of migrant workers.

## min/max inventory system
It is a simplistic inventory system in which a minimum quantity and maximum quantity are set for an item. When the quantity drops below min, the management orders up to the max.

## mismatch
It refers to the following:
1. Any financial position that is not perfectly offset by anything.
2. The situation in which the assets and liabilities are not matched, typically because the bank borrows short-term and lends long-term.
3. A situation when supply fails to match the demand for goods, leading to inflation.

## misrepresentation
It refers to an untrue statement of fact, made by one party to the other in the course of negotiating a contract, that makes the other party to enter into the contract. A false statement of law, opinion, or intention does not constitute a misrepresentation. Unless the representee relies on the statement so that it becomes an inducement to enter into the contract, it is not a misrepresentation.

**Dictionary of Business**

## mistake

In law, it is a misunderstanding or erroneous belief about a matter of fact or a matter of law. Mistake is particularly important in the law of contract. Mistakes of law have no effect on the validity of agreements. When a mistake of fact does so, it may render the agreement void under common law rules, in which case it is referred to as an operative mistake, or it may make it voidable, i.e. liable, subject to certain limitations, to be set aside under the rules of equity.

## mixed model assembly

It implies the practice of assembling more than one product during any period of time. For example, an assembly worker might see three units of product X, then two units of product Y, then four units of product X, etc. The alternative to this policy is to make large batches of each product and then switch over to the other product.

## mobility of labour

It describes the extent to which workers are willing to move from one region of country to another or to change from one occupation to another. In horizontal mobility, there is no change of status, whereas in vertical mobility, it does bring a change in status. An upward change in status will increase a worker's mobility, whereas a downward change will reduce it.

## model

In business, it is a representation of a set of components of a process, or system. A model is generally developed for understanding, analysis, improvement, and replacement of the process if required.

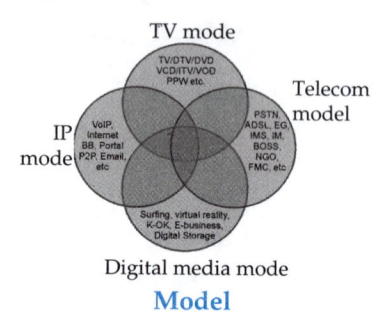

Model

## model-driven DSS

It is a type of DSS that emphasises access to and manipulation of a model, for instance, statistical, financial, optimisation and simulation. Simple statistical and analytical tools provide the elementary level of functionality. Model-driven

DSS generally uses complex financial, simulation, optimisation, and expert models to provide decision support. Model-driven DSS uses data and parameters provided by decision makers to aid them in analysing a situation.

## modular design

It is a design based on organising a complex system like a large programme, an electronic circuit or a mechanical device as a set of distinct components that can be developed independently and then plugged together. It may appear a simple idea, but experience shows that it is quite complex. The effectiveness of a technique depends critically on the manner in which systems are divided into components and the mechanisms used to plug components together.

Modular design

## modularity

It is a general systems concept, a continuum describing the degree to which a system's components can be separated and recombined and it refers both to the tightness of coupling between components and the degree to which the rules of the system architecture enable the mixing and matching of components.

## monadic testing

It denotes a technique used in marketing research in which consumers are presented with a product to test on their own, instead of being asked to compare it with a competing product.

## monetary measures

These are measures taken by the government to counteract deflation or inflation by controlling the amount of spending power available to banks, by changes in bank rate, minimum lending rate, etc.

## money at call and short notice

It is an asset that appears in the balance sheet of a bank. It includes funds lent to discount houses, money brokers, the stock exchange, corporate customers and often to other banks. At call, money is repayable on demand, whereas short notice money implies that notice of repayment of up to 14 days will be given.

### money broker
The term is used for financial institution that specialises in dealing in the money market in short-term securities and loans and in precious metals like gold, and foreign currencies. Other types of institution dealing in the money market are acceptance houses, commercial banks, and discount houses.

### moneylender
A person whose business is to lend money, other than pawn-brokers, corporate bodies with special powers to lend money, banks, or insurance companies.

### monitor
It is the management role classification identified by Mintzberg, which requires the manager to solicit and assemble contextual information, enabling him or her to understand events and situations within the organisation.

### monopolistic competition
It can be defined as a market for a particular product or service in which there are many competing sellers offering similar but non-identical goods. Such a market resembles perfect competition in that there are a multiplicity of buyers and sellers and few barriers to entry. But, since each specific good can only be obtained from one seller, the producer acquires a power to influence market prices—a condition that would not exist under perfect competition.

### monopoly
It can be defined as the situation where at least one-third of a local or national market is controlled by one company, corporation or group of people. In India, monopolies have been curbed since Independence.

### monopsony
It is the situation where one purchaser has sole control of a market for products, services or labour even though there may be several sellers.

### moonlighting
It means doing a second job,

**Dictionary of Business**

usually in the evenings, in addition to one's normal daytime job.

## moral hazard

It can be described as the situation in which a person or organisation has no incentive to act honestly or with due prudence. The term is used in the insurance world, where a typical example of a person exposed to moral hazard would be the owner of an insured car or bike, which has little or no incentive to guard against theft.

## moral suasion

It is use of argument and persuasion, rather than coercion or legislation, to influence the activities of those within its purview.

## moratorium

It refers to the following:
1. An agreement between a creditor and a debtor to allow additional time for the settlement of dues.
2. A period during which one government permits a government of a foreign country to suspend repayments of a debt.
3. A period during which all the trading debts in a particular market are suspended owing to some exceptional crisis in the market.

## mortgage

It refers to the following:
1. A condition when a financial organisation, e.g. a building society or an insurance company makes a loan to a mortgagee, either an individual or a company, the mortgagee retaining qualified ownership of the property as security for the loan.
2. Temporary and conditional pledge of property to a creditor bank of finance company as security against a debt.

## moving average

It is simple arithmetic technique for updating the accuracy of short-term forecasting which is based on extrapolating from past performance. For example, the forecast of demand for a particular product may be based on the average sales in, say, the previous three months. Thus, for the 4th month, the forecast would be the average of sales in months 1 to 3 but for 5, using a moving average, the average would move forward one month and be based on sales in months 2 to 4.

**Dictionary of Business**

## moving-parity
It is a method that gives a compromise between fixed parity and floating exchange rates by automatically adjusting the par rate for a currency according to a moving average of the rates of previous months.

## MRP generation
It refers to the running of the programs that convert demand into planned orders. Depending on the operation, MRP generation may be run daily, weekly, or even monthly. This processing requires a lot of system resources hence it is generally confined to off hours or week-end processing.

## multi-employer bargaining
Also called association bargaining, it is a form of collective bargaining in which a number of employers participate, as in industry-wide bargaining, sometimes through an employers' association.

## multi-national company
The term is used for commercial organisations with whole of majority ownership of interests or subsidiaries in several of countries, the commercial strategy of the organisation tending to be international in its approach.

## multi-national enterprise
It refers to a corporation that has production operations in more than one country for various reasons, including securing supplies of raw materials, utilising cheap labour sources, servicing local markets, taking advantage of tax and interest differences, and bypassing protectionist barriers.

Multi-national enterprise

# N

### named vote
Vote taken at a board meeting by recording by name the way in which each voter votes. This procedure is reserved only for very important issues.

### name screening
It is a market research technique for checking that the prospective name of a product or service conveys the intended image, and avoids confusion with other brand names.

### narrow money
It is an informal name for M0, or sometimes M1, i.e. the part of the money supply that can directly perform the function of a medium of exchange.

### national agreement
It is an industry-wide agreement on wages and conditions of employment, made between the appropriate employers' association and trade unions.

### national bank
It refers to the following:
1. The central bank of a country.
2. In the US, one of the privately-owned banks which by law must be an investing member of its respective district Federal Reserve Bank.

### national debt
It implies debt owed by a national government, generally in the form of a combination of short-term and long-term loans.

### national procedure agreement
It refers to an agreement made between the employers' associations and the trade unions in a particular industry to lay down the procedure to be followed in the event of industrial disputes, etc.

### natural wastage
It is the process of reducing number of people employed in a firm or organisation by not taking new employees to replace those leaving by themselves or retiring. It is preferred to making employees redundant after a

decision has been taken to lay off, especially if this decision is the result of the introduction of a new management systems. It is treated with suspicion by employees.

## near money (quasi money)

It refers to an asset that is immediately transferable and may be used to settle some debts, although it is not as liquid as currency. Bills of exchange are examples of near money. Other examples are deposits, treasury bills, surrender value of life insurance policies, etc.

## need recognition

It is the first stage of consumer buying behaviour, in which the consumer recognises a problem or need.

## negative demand

A market is said to be in a state of negative demand if a major part of the market dislikes the product.

## negative inventory

It is an inventory system whereby the in-hand inventory balance is listed as a quantity less than zero.

## negative motion

It refers to a motion moved at a board meeting with entirely negative intent. It should not be accepted by the chairperson because it makes no more contribution to the work of the meeting than if it had been left unsaid.

## negative strike

It denotes industrial action to fight against a worsening of wages and/or working conditions.

## negotiable instruments

These are documents representing freely assignable rights in a contract. Examples of negotiable instruments are cheques, bearer bonds, bills of exchange, promissory notes, etc.

---

**Promissory Note**

I, Jane Monroe, do promise to pay City Finance the sum of $50,000. Repayment is to be made in the form of 300 equal payments at 6% interest, or $322.15 payable on the 1st of each month, beginning 8/1/2005 until the total debt is satisfied.

Signed.

*Jane Monroe*
7/1/2005

---

Negotiable instrument

## negotiating rights

A condition where a trade union has the established right to enter into full negotiations and collective bargaining with employer. These rights often have more impact on management prerogative.

### net
The term indicates that the full amount of any discount thereon would be contrary to the terms of the contract.

### net asset value (NAV)
For investment trusts, it is the market value of all shares and stock owned, divided by the number of trust shares.

### net effective distribution
It refers to the proportion of shops in a survey that actually have the product being surveyed in stock at the time of an audit.

### net investment
It is the level of investment after depreciation of equipment and stocks has been deducted from gross investment. It is a better indication than gross investment of the provision made for future economic growth.

### net present value (NPV)
It denotes a method of capital budgeting in which the value of an investment is calculated as the total present value of all cash inflows and cash outflows less the cost of the initial investment. If the net present value is positive, the return will be greater than that required by the capital markets and the investment should be considered.

A zero NPV indicates that the project repays the capital invested, plus some minimum acceptable return, while a negative NPV is virtually a losing proposition.

### net profit
It is gross profit minus the cost of marketing, finance and administrative functions. In a marginal costing system, net profit is sales revenue minus marginal costs minus fixed costs.

### net receipts
It is the total amount of money received by a business in a specified period after deducting costs, raw materials, taxation, etc.

### net worth
It can be defined as the value of an organisation when its liabilities have been deducted from the value of its assets. However, net worth so defined can be misleading

because balance sheets rarely show the real value of assets.

## new product development (NPD)

It is a marketing procedure in which new ideas are developed into viable new products or extensions to existing products or product ranges. However, new ideas, which are generated either internally or by feedback from consumers, have to pass through many stages. They are first screened for prima facie viability. Those that pass this test are further put to concept tests and a detailed analysis of their potential profitability is made. Any ideas that survive these obstacles are subjected to extensive product development.

## next business

It refers to the motion moved from the floor of a meeting or conference with the object of ending discussion on the item of business in hand. If the motion is seconded and then carried, the meeting abandons the item in hand and moves to the next item on the agenda.

## niche players

These are specialists in particular areas or activities, in financial services.

## niitmash system

It is a Russian classification and coding system for components.

## no-claims bonus

It refers to a reward in the form of premium discount given to policyholders if they complete certain period without making a claim. The system is mostly used in motor insurance. Such bonus is allowed for remaining claim-free and is not dependent on claim for a particular accident.

## nominal account

It is a ledger account that is not a personal account in that it bears the name of a concept such as bills receivable, bills payable, bad debts, investments, etc. rather than the name of a person.

## nominal price

It refers to the following:
1. A minimal price fixed for the sake of having some consideration for a transaction.
2. The price given to a security

when the same is issued. This is the maximum amount the holder can be required to contribute to the company.

### nominal value
Also called par value, it is the value of a share when it was issued, as stated on its share certificate and in the company's Memorandum of Association, and not its market value which may be above, at, or below par.

### nominee
A person named by another to act on his/her behalf, often to conceal the identity of the nominator.

### nominee holdings
It refers to shares held in a company through a nominee, not disclosing the owner's identity. Where such anonymous holdings are built up in preparation for a takeover bid, this process is known as warehousing.

### non-executive director
He is the member of company board of directors who does not have executive responsibility within the company but is valued for his/her external experience and objective judgement.

### non-marketable securities
Securities that are not sold on financial markets such as national savings certificates.

### non-recourse finance
It implies finance raised in a manner that it does not hold the applicant responsible for any failure to repay an export finance house, which may lend directly to the overseas buyer without recourse to the exporter.

### non-resident
It is the status of an individual who has moved to another country, either for employment or permanently. NRI's liability to tax in India is restricted to income from sources within this country.

### non-stock corporation
A corporation which has no issued share capital. Mutual savings banks, credit unions, charitable bodies, etc. fall in this category.

### no-poaching agreement
An agreement made by trade unions not to try to recruit each other's members.

### nostro account
A bank account conducted by an Indian bank with a bank in

another country, usually in the currency of that country.

### not negotiable
These are words marked on a bill of exchange, including cheque, indicating that although it can still be negotiated, the holder cannot obtain a better title to it than the person from whom it was obtained, thus providing a safeguard if it is stolen.

### notary public
A legal practitioner, usually a solicitor, who is empowered to attest documents, notes and dishonoured bills of exchange.

### numeric control
It is the operation of machine tools and other processing machines by a series of coded instructions. The numerical data for these instructions is stored in a computer system. A system which has a computer controlling more than one machine tools is called direct numerical control (DNC).

### nursed account
The account of a supplier with a particular customer who has always been paid on time so that he/she can be relied upon for a good trade reference.

Notary public

# O

## obligation
It generally refers to the duty of a borrower to repay a loan and that of the lender to ensure that the securities held by him/her are kept safely to return the borrower after the loan has been fully paid.

## odd pricing
Pricing goods at odd amounts, e.g. £599 instead of £600. It is done in the belief that these seemingly lower prices will attract more customers and give larger sales volume.

## offer
It is the price at which a seller makes it known that he is willing to sell something. If there is an acceptance of the offer, there is a legally binding contract. In law, an offer is distinguished from an invitation to treat, which is an invitation by one person or firm to others to make an offer.

## official receiver
The term denotes a person appointed by the court to act as a receiver in bankruptcy and winding-up cases. The High Court and each county court in UK, that has jurisdiction over insolvency matters has an official receiver, who is an officer of the court.

## offset
It refers to the following:
1. The right enabling a bank to seize any bank account balances of a guarantor or debtor if a loan is in default.
2. A code on the magnetic strip of a plastic card that, together with the personal identification number (PIN), verifies that the user of the card is entitled to use it.
3. A printing technique where the inked image is transferred from a place to rubber cover and then to printing surface.

*Offset printing*

### offshore fund
It refers to any fund held outside the country of residence of the holder.

### off-the-shelf company
It is defined as a company that is registered with the Registrar of Companies. Although it does not trade and has no directors, yet it can be sold and reformed into a new company with the minimum of formality and expense.

### omnibus research
It is marketing research based on multiple questionnaires sent out regularly to a panel of respondents.

### on stream
It denotes the following:
1. An integral and/or continuous part of a process or activity.
2. A specified investment or asset which is providing the expected revenues.

### online service provider
Abbreviated as OSP, it refers to an Internet service provider, having a large amount of specially developed content available to subscribers. The distinction between an ISP and an OSP depends on the amount of premium content offered as part of the service.

### ONS
It is abbreviation for Office for National Statistics. The information statistics available at ONS is very useful for various types of business.

### open account scheme
It is a scheme operated in the UK under which the Export Credit Guarantee Department guarantees to an exporting firm's UK bank, the financing of short-term transactions made on open account terms.

### open account terms
These are agreed terms in export trading, where an overseas buyer is instructed to make payment to the exporters bank's overseas correspondent.

## open-door policy
It is an import policy in which all goods from all sources are imported in the country on the same terms, usually free of import duties.

## open general licence (OGL)
It is an import licence for goods on which there are no import restrictions, and hence no import license is required.

## open indent
It is an order to an overseas purchasing agent to buy certain goods, without specifying the manufacturer. It is opposite to closed indent in which manufacturer is specified.

## opening stock
It is the inventory held by an organisation at the beginning of an accounting period, usually the start of financial year, as raw materials, work-in-progress, or finished goods. The closing stocks of one period become the opening stocks of the succeeding period.

## open-loop control
It is a system in quality control where the control of a process has a predictable relationship with the quality of the output. Output need not be measured and the emphasis is on setting the controls.

## open market operations
It means buying and selling of securities in the open market by a central bank such as the Bank of England and the Reserve Bank of India. Central banks use such operations, as well as issue directives to banks, to regulate the money supply.

## open position
Also called naked position, it is a trading position in which a dealer has commodities, securities, or currencies bought but unsold or unhedged, or sales that are neither covered nor hedged.

## operating leverage
It is the ratio of fixed costs to total costs. The higher the ratio is, the more sensitive is overhead recovery to volume forecasting errors.

## operating profit or loss
It is the profit or loss made by a company as a result of its principal trading activity. This is arrived at by deducting its operating expenses from its trading

**Dictionary of Business**

profit, or adding its operating expenses to its trading loss.

## operation
It is a generic term for the overall work environment that includes the facilities and all activities that occur within it. While discussing MRP and related topics, an operation is a specific step that exists in the routing of a manufacturing process.
It encompasses a set of activities concerned with transforming resource inputs into desired outputs, in which all purposeful organisations are involved.

## operational risk
It is defined as the risk of direct or indirect loss resulting from inadequate or failed internal processes and systems, or from some external events. The control of operational risk has been the object of much attention since the 2004 Basel II accord concerning the capital adequacy of banks.

## operations strategy
It refers to policies for using the firm's resources to support the business unit's strategy for gaining a competitive advantage. Such policies are normally defined in terms of the operations objectives of cost, quality, flexibility, and service. Firms gain a competitive strategic advantage by avoiding trade-offs between these objectives.

## opitz classification
It is a German classification and coding system for tools and components, based on shape, characteristics and significant features, using a five-digit primary code. A four-digit supplementary code provides information on dimensions, material, form and accuracy.

## opportunity costs
It can be defined as the cost in terms of lost income or profit of the foregone alternative investment or course of action. If the management is unable to make a decision or take an opportunity that would have produced a better net return than the decision it does in fact make, the lost revenue is an opportunity cost. Opportunity costs may be deliberately calculated when evaluating alternative investment or other marginal decisions.

Dictionary of Business

## optimised production technology (OPT)

It is a computer-based system for planning, production and the allocation of resources. It can be distinguished from other methods that aim to use machines to their full capacity. Maximisation of throughput in areas that have no bottlenecks increases the build-up of work in these areas, and thus locks up capital in work-in-progress. Although an appropriate quantity of work is necessary, too much of it proves harmful.

## optional replenishment

The term is used to describe the action of ordering or producing up to the max in a min-max system, even though inventory has not reached the min.

## order cost

It can be defined as the sum of the fixed costs that are incurred each time an item is ordered. Such costs are not associated with the quantity ordered but primarily with physical activities required to process the order. For purchased items, these costs usually include the cost to enter the purchase order and requisition, any approval steps, the cost to process the receipt, invoice processing and vendor payment. In some cases, a part of the inbound freight may also be included in order cost.

In manufacturing, the order cost includes the time to initiate the work order, and time associated with picking and issuing components excluding time used in handling specific quantities.

## order of magnitude

It is an estimate made without detailed data, usually produced from cost data, during the formative stages of an expenditure programmes for initial evaluation of the project.

## order profile

It refers to data describing the characteristics of inbound, outbound or internal orders. Examples of characteristics of an order profile include line items per order, units per order, weight per order, destination, shipment method order type, among other things. Such characteristics are usually broken into logical groups like breaking line items per order into groups of

1 line item, 2-5 line items, 6-10 line items, 11-25, and so on.

## order qualifier, order winner

It implies a screening criterion that permits a firm's products to be considered as possible prospects or items for purchase. An order winner is a screening criterion that differentiates the products or services of one firm from those of another and then makes a crucial difference in the buyer decision process.

## order-call ratio

It is the relationship between the number or value of orders placed and number of calls made by salespeople or representatives, necessary to obtain them over a specified period of time.

## ordinary activities

The term is used for any activities undertaken by an organisation as part of its business and any related activities in which it engages in furtherance of these activities.

## ordinary shares

These are shares which constitute the equity capital of a company and take precedence after debentures and preference shares in entitlement to the company's distributed profits.

## outward trade mission

It is a term in the UK for a group of British business people going overseas to sell UK goods and services with financial support from the Department of Trade and Industry and with the sponsorship of a trade association chamber of commerce.

## outwork

It refers to work carried out for a company outside its own premises, especially by people working in their own home. It is also known as the putting out system.

## overall equipment effectiveness

Abbreviated as OEE, it is a key metric for lean operations and is used extensively in TPM applications. It is calculated as follows:
OEE = (Availability rate) x (Performance rate) x (Yield rate).
Availability rate is (Operating time less downtime)/(Total operating time) and reflects downtime losses due to

changeovers, equipments failures and start-up losses. Performance rate is total output or potential input at rated speed and reflects speed losses due to idling and minor stoppages or reduced speed operation. Quality rate is good output or total output and is a function of defects and rework. There are six big losses, viz.
1. Losses of quantity due to defective products and losses of time owing to decreased productivity from equipment breakdown.
2. The adjustment losses which stem from defective units and downtime that may be incurred when equipment is adjusted to shift from producing one kind of product to another.
3. Idling and minor stoppage losses relatively frequent and resulting from brief periods of idleness when between units in a job.
4. Reduced speed losses occur when equipment is run at less than the design speed.
5. Quality defects and rework are product-related defects.
6. Start-up losses are yield losses incurred during early production, i.e. from machine start-up to steady state.

## overall market capacity

It refers to the amount of a product or service that could be absorbed in an overall market without taking into account price or market segmentation considerations. Thus, the future overall market capacity for dwelling units would include consumers who would like to own a car but are either unable or unwilling to pay the existing price.

## overbought

It denotes the following:
1. The situation of having purchased more of a good than one needs or has orders for.
2. Having purchased more securities or commodities than are covered by margins deposited with a broker.
3. The market that has risen too rapidly as a result of excessive buying.

## overdraft

It is a type of loan made to a customer with a cheque account at a bank or building society, in which the account is allowed to go into debit, up to a specified limit. Interest is charged on the daily debit balance.

## overheating
It is the state of an economy during a boom, with increasing aggregate demand, leading to rising prices instead of higher output. Overheating reflects the inability of some firms to increase output as fast as demand, which therefore profit from the excess demand by raising prices.

## overseas company
The term is used for a company incorporated outside India that has a branch or a subsidiary company in India. Overseas companies with a place of business in India have to make a return to the Registrar of Companies, giving particulars of their Memorandum and Articles of Association, directors, etc. along with the latest balance sheet and profit and loss account.

## oversold
It denotes the following:
1. The condition of having sold more of a product or service than one can produce, purchase or supply.
2. A market that has fallen sharply as a result of excessive selling.

## overtrading
It refers to the following:
1. A situation where a company expands in such a way that, even if it is highly profitable, it cannot pay its own way for lack of working capital and thus, has liquidity problems.
2. Trading by an organisation beyond the resources provided by its existing capital. It tends to lead to liquidity problems as too much a stock is bought on credit and too much credit is extended to customers. Ultimately, there is no sufficient cash available to pay the debts as they arise.

## ownership
It refers to rights over property, including rights of possession, exclusive enjoyment, destruction, etc. In Indian common law, land cannot be owned outright, as all land belongs to the state and is held in tenure by the owner.

# P

## pacing
It describes the rigidity of time allowed in assembly or flow line work for completing certain operations or jobs.

## package deal
It implies an agreement which covers a number of issues and points, providing a package in which different parties make concessions on particular aspects for achieving a total agreement considered to be of overall advantage to all concerned.

## pack to order
Also called pack demand, it is similar to 'assemble to order' except that assembly of products is not required. A country and language specific label is put on the box which is shipped to the distributor in the country.

## paid-in surplus
It can be described as share premium, i.e. money received by a company or corporation for the issue of its shares over and above their nominal value.

## paired comparisons
It is a technique used in marketing research in which consumers are presented with pairs of competing products and asked to choose the one they prefer. Such technique can be used to compare a number of brands such as of toothpaste, giving respondents two at a time to compare. The number of times each brand is selected as a preference in a large number of such tests reveals an order of brand preference.

## pallet inverter
It is a type of stationary equipment used to transfer product between different types of pallets such as transferring from wood to

Pallet inverter

plastic pallets or from pallets to slip sheets. A load on a pallet is placed in the pallet inverter and the entire load is rotated 180 degrees allowing for removal of the original pallet and replacement thereof with another.

## paperless
The term is used for referring to processing in the warehouse or on the shop floor. Paperless generally suggests that the direction of tasks and execution of transactions are conducted electronically without the use of paper documents. This is usually accomplished with fixed or portable computers, barcode scanners, RFID readers, light-signalling technology, or voice technology.

## paper profit
The profit shown by the books or accounts of an organisation but which is not a realised profit. This is generally for one of three reasons:
1. Because the value of an asset has fallen below its book value.
2. Because the asset, although nominally showing a profit, has not actually been sold.
3. Due to the fact that technically bookkeeping shows some activity to be profitable when it is not.

## parametric estimating
It is an estimating technique that uses a statistical relationship between historical data and other variables to calculate an estimate.

## parenting
In business, it is the way in which the directors of main holding company of a large group manage their relationships with the subsidiary companies or business units.

## participating interest
It refers to an interest held by one organisation in the shares of another organisation, provided such shares are held on a long-term basis for the purpose of exercising some measure of control or influence over the organisation's activities.

## participation
The term encompasses a variety of ways of increasing the involvement and commitment of employees to their own jobs and to

corporate goals. Originally, participation meant that the system of ownership needed changing as in guild socialism. Nowadays, participation implies some form of profit-sharing and involvement in decision-making through joint consultation, project groups, etc.

## passing off
It denotes conducting a business in a manner that misleads the public into thinking that one's goods or services are those of another business. The common form of passing off is marketing goods with a design, packaging, or trade name that is quite similar to that of someone else's goods.

## pathfinder
It is a summary of a business plan prepared to attract initial interest among potential financial bankers.

## pathfinder prospectus
It is an outline prospectus concerning the floatation of a new company in the UK. It includes sufficient details to test the market reaction to the new company but not its main financial details.

## pawnbroker
The term is used for a person who lends money against the security of valuable goods used as collateral. Borrowers can reclaim their goods on repayment of the loan and interest within a stated period. But, if the borrower defaults, the pawnbroker is free to sell the goods.

## payback
It is a technique for forecasting when a project-enterprise will reach its break-even point. Ordinary payback is simple while discounted payback is more sophisticated and allows for the need to recover the investment, but get some return on it.

## payee
It is a person or company to be paid. In the case of a cheque payment, the payee is the person or company to whom the cheque is made payable.

## payment in due course
It is the payment of a bill of exchange when it becomes due. Legally, the payment should be as per apparent tenor of the instrument.

**Dictionary of Business**

### payment on account
It denotes the following:
1. A payment made for goods or services before such goods or services are finally billed.
2. A payment towards meeting a liability that is not the full amount of the liability.

### payment system
It refers to a procedure relating employees' pay to their effort or work and, establishing administrative, negotiating and disputes handling machinery. The two basic methods of payment are:
1. Time-related payment, i.e. so much per hour.
2. Payment-by-results, i.e. performance-linked pay.
These two methods are often combined in a payment system.

### payoff
It is the value of a portfolio or a single financial obligation at a specified date or at the expiry of an instrument. The value is usually calculated in absolute terms and also sometimes in terms of the gain made over a given time period.

### p-chart
It is a quality control chart that shows per cent defective parts made in the process. A sample of parts is collected from the process every so many parts or time periods. The per cent defective parts in the sample is plotted on the control chart and a determination made whether the process is under control or not.

### peaceful picketing
It is peaceful, non-violent persuasion by strikers seeking to dissuade black-leg labour from replacing them or their employer's customers from dealing with him or her.

### peak absences
These are points in a demand cycle where the workload or demand is relatively light.

### peak loads
These are points in a working cycle where the work or demand is at its heaviest.

### peering arrangement
An agreement made between independent networking companies governing the way in which Internet traffic moves between their networks.

### peg
It is the exchange rate normally acceptable to the

central bank of the country concerned.

### penetration pricing
It implies launching a new product at a low price in order to quickly capture as large a share of the market as possible. It is opposite to skimming, i.e. putting the product on sale at a high price and then reducing the price by stages.

### pensionable salary
It is that part of a person's salary or earnings which is taken into account in calculating entitlement to pension. This may be total earnings or it may exclude items like as bonus, commission, overtime, and premium payments.

### pensionable service
It refers to years of employment taken into account for the purposes of calculating the level of pension due.

### PERA system
It is a classification code for components covering material, initial form like length, diameter and batch size. It was developed by the Production Engineering Research Association in the UK.

### perceptual distortion
It is a term used in marketing research for the extent to which an interviewee's assessment of a product is distorted by his or her own interests and values.

### perceptual mapping
It refers to the use of mathematical psychology to understand the structure of a market. In it, the consumer images of different brands of a product are plotted on a graph or map. The closer two brands are on the map, the closer they are as competitors.

### perfect competition
It can be defined as a market in which no buyer or seller has the power to influence prices, and there is an equilibrium of supply and demand. For such a market to exist there has to be a multiplicity of small buyers and sellers, no barriers to entry, and perfect information about prices. The goods should be offered by the various sellers and undifferentiated to prevent the development of monopolistic competition.

**Dictionary of Business**

## performance measurement

It is a set of measures used in ratio analysis or management ratios, normally as an integrated set or hierarchy of ratios. Such measures might include return on capital, capital turnover, unit profit, output per worker, labour intensity and value added.

## performance quality

It denotes the product design standard set for the product and service attributes.

## period of grace

It is the period of time normally allowed to a party to a contract to meet the obligations laid upon him or her under the contract. Such a contract may be voluntary such as an undertaking to repay a loan, or one imposed statutorily or by custom, e.g. a permit or licence required or payment for services such as power supply.

## period order quantity (POQ)

It can be defined as a simple lot sizing rule that defines the order quantity in terms of supply for the period. It is implemented in manufacturing resource planning (MRP) system simply by adding up the next POQ periods of net requirements.

## peripherals groups

It refers to employees who are on temporary contract used only when demanded by production, etc. levels, thus giving management numerical flexibility. They are complemented employment but have an obligation to contribute to functional flexibility.

## perishable dispute

It denotes strike over issues which the management would resort to by default if the workers did not act immediately.

## perks

It is an informal word for perquisites, the benefits arising as a result of employment, in addition to regular remuneration. Perks are privileges that are expected mainly by senior employees. Company car, rent free accommodation, insurance, gym facilities are examples of perks.

## permanent diminution in value

It refers to a fall in the value

of an asset that is unlikely to be reversed. The fixed asset must be shown in the balance sheet at the reduced amount, which will be the estimated recoverable amount. A provision has to be made through the profit and loss account.

## permanent establishment
It implies fixed place of business that a taxpayer of one country has in another country, thus rendering the taxpayer liable to that second country's taxation too.

## per pro
It is an abbreviations for per procuration which denotes an act by an agent, not acting on his own authority but on that of his principal. It is used when signing letters on behalf of a firm or someone else, if formally authorised to do so.

## personal account
It is an account in a ledger that bears the name of an individual or of an organisation. It shows the state of indebtedness of the named person to the organisation keeping the account or vice versa.

## personality promotion
It is in fact a sales promotion technique where publicity is given to the fact that a known personality will give prizes in a neighbourhood to users of the product they are promoting.

## petty cash
It is the amount of cash that an organisation keeps in notes or coins on its premises to pay small items of expenses. It is distinct from cash, which normally refers to amounts held at banks.

## phantom bill of material
It is a bill of material coding and structuring technique used primarily for transient sub-assemblies. It represents an item that is physically built but rarely stocked before being used in the next level in the bill of material.

## phantom stocks
It is a form of bonus plan in which participants receive partial or complete financial benefit of stock of share ownership without actually owning any stock.

## phantom withdrawals
It is the removal of funds from bank accounts through automated teller machine (ATM) by unauthorised

means and without the knowledge or consent of the account holder.

## Phillips curve

A curve devised by A.W. Phillips in the UK to relate changes in money wage rates to the percentage of the labour force which is unemployed.

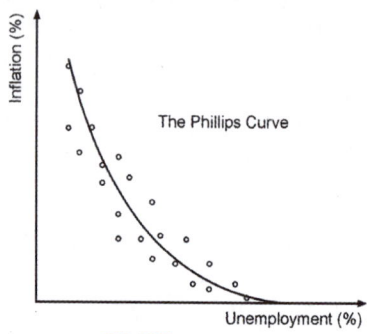

Phillips curve

## physical distribution management

It can be defined as the study, control, and management of all the factors involved in the distribution of materials and finished goods. It involves an integrated approach to materials handling, protective packaging, transport, warehousing, inventory control, etc.

## physical inventory

The term is used for the process of counting all inventories in a warehouse or plant. Operations are usually shut down during a physical inventory.

## pick-to-light

It is a system consisting of light displays for each pick location. The system uses software to light the next pick and display the quantity to pick. Such systems have the advantage of not only increasing accuracy, but also increasing productivity. Since hardware is required for each pick location, pick-to-light systems are easier to justify cost where very high picks are involved. Carton flow rack and horizontal carousels are good applications for pick-to-light.

## piece rate

It is a payment system in which an employee is paid a specific price for each unit made. The rate is therefore directly related to output and not to time.

## pie chart

Also called circle chart, it is a diagram consisting of a circle with radii dividing it into sectors proportional in area to the relative sizes of the quantities represented.

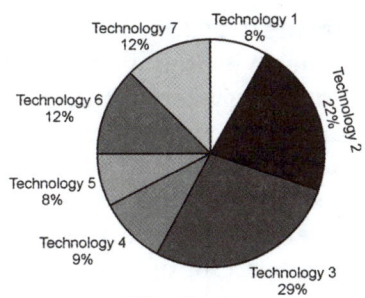

Pie chart

## pioneer product
It is a product of entirely new design and/or function. It is distinct from a market follower, which is a product introduced to compete with existing products, and from a brand leader that is already well established in its field.

## pilot production
It implies initial production of a product in shop floor conditions, to establish the best production methods and system. It is normally introduced in conjunction with the test marketing of a new product.

## pinwheel or pinwheeling
It is a method for loading trailers where you alter the direction of every other pallet. Pinwheeling is used to load more pallets on trailer when the depth of the pallet is longer than half the trailer width, but the depth plus the width is less than the trailer width. It can be used as a productivity/space utilisation compromise or to reduce load shifting when loading pallets where the depth of the pallet is less than half the trailer width.

## piracy
It refers to the following:
1. An illegal act of detention, robbery, pilferage, etc. committed on a ship or aircraft. It excludes acts committed for political purposes and during a war. In marine insurance, it includes any form of plundering at sea.
2. An infringement of copyright. The usual remedy is for the copyright holder to obtain an injunction to end the infringement.

## pitch
It refers to any sales presentation by a salesperson to a buyer. The term is also used in advertising to describe an agency presentation to a prospective client.

## Pittler classification
It is a method of classifying and coding components, using a nine-digit code to

summarise a wide range of information about components.

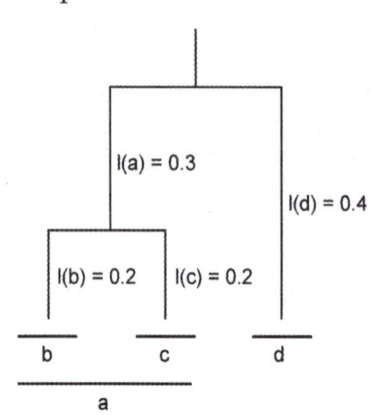

```
         |
       ──┴──────────┐
       │            │
   I(a) = 0.3   I(d) = 0.4
   ┌───┴───┐
I(b) = 0.2  I(c) = 0.2
   │       │        │
   b       c        d
   ─────────────────
            a
```

**Pittler classification**

## plain time rate

It implies time rate or time related payment to emphasise that it does not include bonus or premium payment.

## planned learning experience

It refers to the system where an employee or trainee is directed to undertake work that is selected for the particular employee or trainee as being particularly relevant to complementary training he/she is receiving or to his/her career development. Such experience often involves job rotation between different types of work.

## planned order

The term is used within MRP and DRP system for system-generated planned order quantities. Such orders only exist within the computer system and serve multiple functions. One of its functions is to notify the materials' planner or buyer to produce or order materials. This is done by converting a planned order into a purchase order, shop order or transfer order. Another function is used by the MRP or demand resource planning (DRP) system to show demand, which is used by subsequent MRP and DRP programs to generate additional planned orders.

## planned unit development (PUD) areas

These are areas planned and developed as one entity, by a single group. Planned unit development usually includes a variety of uses, including different housing types of varying densities, open space, and commercial uses.

## planning programming budgeting system

It is a business management technique in USA based on the industrial management of program budgeting. It has

**Dictionary of Business**

also been introduced into other countries, including the UK where it is often called output budgeting. It is an integration of a number of techniques in a planning and budgeting process for identifying, costing and assigning a complexity of resources, for establishing priorities and strategies in a major program, and for forecasting costs, expenditure and achievements for the current financial year or over a longer period.

## planogram

It can be defined as a plan for retail space allocation, designed to maximise the return on investment (ROI) for the retail space. A good planogram allows inexperienced employees to properly maintain shelf stock, etc. The advantages of planogram system include better control of inventory investments, improved inventory investments, improved inventory turnover, reduction in labour cost, increased sales and increased profit, and more satisfied customers.

## plant and machinery

It is a generic term for equipment required to operate a business. Capital allowances are available for plant and machinery. The Yarmouth case in France, defined plant and machinery as "whatever apparatus is used by a businessman for carrying on his business; not his stock in trade which he buys or makes for resale, but all goods and chattels, fixed or moveable, live or dead, which he keeps for permanent employment in the business".

## plant principles

These are principles that characterise and specify the fund. The investor receives information about the securities, the currency, securities held in the portfolio, and the geographical range of the plants.

## plastic money

It is a colloquial name for a credit card, cash card, debit card, or a multifunctional card.

Plastic money

### platform strategy
It refers to a new product development strategy that plans new products around a small number of basic product designs that allow many different final products with differing features and functions. This strategy is well established in the automotive industry.

### poaching
It is the practice by less scrupulous firms of luring trained workers from other firms rather than investing in training themselves.

### point of sale (POS)
It is a data collection device where the products are sold, generally scanning and cash register device in a retail store. POS data is a rich source of data that can be used to inform the entire supply chain.

### points rating method
It is a method of evaluating jobs numerically by analysing component job factors in detail and giving them points or values from within a defined range.

### political strike
It denotes an industrial action in which the cause of the action is not directly related to the strikers' conditions of work or wages, but to a wider situation or principle.

### pop up sorter
It is a sorting equipment integrated into conveyor to move materials off the conveyor at fixed points. Such sorters are installed in fixed positions and may consist of a series of wheels, and small belts that are normally located slightly below the conveyor rollers. The wheels and belts are momentarily raised to enable diverting materials off the conveyor.

### portal
It is a website that seeks to act as an attractive user-friendly access point to the Internet. Portals provide services like e-mail, instant messaging, etc., content such as news, listings of events, etc. and search engine to search the rest of the web.

### porter's five forces
It is a framework for analysing the balance of power within a particular industry. It identifies five forces in the microenvironment that drive competition and threaten

a firm's ability to make profits:
1. Rivalry between existing competitors depending on their number, size and relative market shares.
2. The threat of new entrants.
3. The threat of substitutes, viz. products in another industry that the consumer may see as alternatives.
4. The strength of buyer power.
5. The strength of supplier power.

## portfolio investment
It refers to investment by an investor or a mutual fund in a range or portfolio of shares or securities, normally to spread the risk.

## position
It is the extent to which an investor, dealer, or speculator has made a commitment in the market by buying or selling securities, currencies, commodities, or taken any financial obligation.

## position a product
It denotes the following:
1. To differentiate a product from competitors' products.
2. An attempt to convince customers that this product will satisfy their desires.

## position guide
A US term for a document outlining the responsibilities, duties and authorities of specific jobs. It is synonymous to job description.

## positioning
It implies a marketing strategy that will position a company's products and services against those of its competitors in the minds of consumers.

## post-entry closed shop
The factory or workshop where the employees are required to join a particular trade union after taking up employment if they are not already members.

## post hoc segmentation
It refers to the process of segmenting a market or markets empirically.

## post implementation review (PIR)
In business management, it is an evaluation tool that compares the conditions before the implementation of a project with the actual results achieved by the project.

## postponement
It denotes a manufacturing or distribution strategy whereby

specific operations associated with a product are delayed until just prior to shipping. Storing product in a generic state and then applying custom labels or packaging before shipping is an example.

## post-test
It refers to the following:
1. A sales promotion test to check how effective a sales or advertising campaign has been.
2. Test at the end of a training program to check the performance of trainees.

## postural discrimination
It is a form of psychomotor skill, i.e. individual's ability to respond to postural or physical cues, as distinct from visual cues, in adjusting working position.

## potential acquisition valuation method
It is a systematic approach, involving ten stages to evaluate investment proposals. It analyses costs involved and the expected return on investment.

## potential demand
It refers to the future demand likely for a product or service. The magnitude of the potential demand for a product is determined by the number of people who have needs which will be satisfied by the product, as also the quantity of the product that will satisfy those needs.

## potential entrant
The term is used for an organisation that is poised to enter a market and would do so if there was a small price rise or a reduction in barriers to entry.

## potential market
It is composed of consumers who profess some level of interest in a particular product or service.

## poverty trap
A country has a system of social security benefits payable to the lowest paid. Poverty trap is the level of wage payment at which an increase in wage does not practically benefit the recipient because it is cancelled out by a loss of social security benefits.

## predictive maintenance
It refers to the practice of monitoring a machine with a measuring device that can predict when it is likely to fail.

## pre-emption
It is the right of a person to be the first to be asked if he or she wishes to enter into an agreement at a specified price, e.g. the right to be offered an apartment at a price acceptable to the vendor before it is put on the open market.

## pre-emption rights
These comprise the principle, established in company law, that existing shareholders should be offered a proportion of certain classes of newly issued securities before they are offered to anyone else and upon terms that are at least as favourable.

## preference shares
These are shares which take precedence over ordinary shares of a company but take their turn after debentures both in the payment of dividends and in the settlement of claims in the eventuality of a company going into liquidation.

## preferential creditor
It is a creditor whose debt will be met in preference to those of other creditors and who thus has the best chance of being paid in full on the bankruptcy of an individual or the winding up of a company.

## preferential hiring
A US term for an agreement under which an employer agrees to give first choice of jobs where vacancies occur, to members of a particular trade union.

## preferential shop
It is actually a firm where it has been agreed that members of a particular trade union shall get first choice of jobs, as in preferential hiring, as also promotional and other advantages over non-union members.

## premium
It refers to the following:
1. The consideration payable for a contract of insurance.
2. An amount in excess of the issue price of a share or other security.
3. An amount in excess of the nominal value of a share, bond, etc.
4. The difference between the spot price for a commodity or currency and the forward price.
5. The price paid by a buyer of an option contract to the seller for the right to exercise the option.

**Dictionary of Business**

## prepayment
It is the settlement of a debt before it is due, for instance, the early repayment of a mortgage.

## prestige advertising
Advertising aimed at promoting the public corporate image of a company, rather than particular products.

## pre-test
It refers to the following:
1. Test of a product, packaging, advertising presentation, etc. before its launch more widely.
2. Test given to a trainee before taking a training programme to test his/her suitability for the programme.

## preventive maintenance
It denotes the practice of checking and repairing a machine on a scheduled basis before it fails. The schedule is based on some historical information on the time between failures for the population of machines. The opposite of preventive maintenance is emergency maintenance, where the maintenance is done after the machine fails.

## price
It can be defined as the sum of money asked for a product or service at a particular time in a particular market. It is distinct from the cost to the producer of producing the product or service, and from the value of the product or service to the purchaser.

Price

## price discretion
It is a condition where a salesperson has the authority to vary the price of a product in order to make a sale.

## price discrimination
It refers to the sale of the same product at different prices to different buyers. It is normally practised by monopolists. It requires that a market be subdivided to exploit different sets of consumers and that these divisions can be sustained. Pure price discrimination rarely exists, since sellers usually differentiate the

product slightly. Examples are rail travel, air travel and different types of theatre seats.

### price/earnings ratio
It is the market price per ordinary share divided by earnings per ordinary share after tax. This ratio is expressed as the multiple of the latest reported earnings that the market is willing to pay for the ordinary shares. It expresses the market value placed on the expectation of future earnings, viz. the number of years required to earn the price paid for the shares out of profits at the current rate.

### price elasticity of demand
It is the way in which demand varies with changes in price of a product or service. Demand is elastic if a small change in price produces a large change in demand. It is inelastic if demand does not vary significantly with changes in price.

### price leadership
It is a system where competing companies operate similar pricing policies, charge similar prices and prices increase in line with each other as a result of one of the companies giving a lead to the others.

### price-lining
It is the policy of charging a standard price for a number of products though their production costs may be very different.

### price mechanism
It refers to the process in a free market economy by which prices are determined by the buyer's need and preparedness to pay and the supplier's ability and desire to supply. Price mechanism aims at maintaining levels of market prices for producers.

### price plateau
It is a price band which is accepted by customers as being reasonable for a particular product which is part of a range of products sold at different qualities and prices. This may lead a manufacturer to restrict price increases until evidence is obtained of the acceptability to customers of a higher price for the product.

### price sensitive
The term is used for product or service for which demand

is likely to fall off quickly if the price is increased.

## price stabilisation
It is a pricing policy aimed at avoiding widely fluctuating prices. The marketeer with this objective sets prices to match those of the competitors or to maintain existing price differentials.

## price theory
It is a theory that, at the microeconomic level, defines the role of prices in consumer demand and the supply of goods by firms. At a broader level, it explains the role of prices in markets as a whole.

## primage
In business, it refers to the following:
1. A small percentage added to a freight charged to cover the cost of loading or unloading a ship.
2. An extra charge for handling goods with special care when they are being loaded or unloaded.

## primary labour markets
It refers to markets offering firm-specific skills and therefore tending to be synonymous with internal labour markets. People with general skills are in secondary labour markets.

## prime rate
It is the rate of interest at which US banks lend money to first-class borrowers. It is similar in operation to the base rate in the UK. In India, there is prime lending rate (PLR), i.e. the rate at which the RBI lends to banks.

## prior charge
Loan or debt which has a first claim on the assets of a company in the event of liquidation or winding up.

## private bank
It denotes the following:
1. A commercial bank owned by one person or a partnership.
2. A bank that is not a member of a clearing house and therefore has to use a clearing bank as an agent.
3. A bank that is not owned by the state.

## private company
It is a limited liability company which has a relatively small number of shareholders and is not permitted to offer its shares to the public.

## private sector
It is the part of an economy that is not under government control. In a mixed economy, most commercial and industrial firms are in the private sector, while sectors of strategic importance like defence is in public sector.

## privatisation
It is the process of selling of a public sector undertaking (PSU) to the private sector. Privatisation may be pursued for political as well as economic reasons.

## proactive inhibition
It is a condition where a person's mindset, as a result of previous work, learning or experience, makes it difficult for him/her to learn and retain new skills or information.

## probate
It is a certificate issued by the court, on the application of executors appointed by a will, to the effect that the will is valid and that the executors are authorised to administer the deceased person's estate. When there is no doubt about the will's validity, probate is granted in common form on the executors filing an affidavit.

## procedural agreement
It is an agreement, either a separate or a part of a collective agreement, outlining the procedures to be followed by the relevant trade union or management in the event of their having a grievance or being in dispute.

## procedure
It is a generic term for the following:
1. A collection of steps that the organisation is responsible for implementing to ensure that policies and process requirements are met.
2. A series of activities carried out to accomplish a task or operation.
3. Also a specified way to carry out an activity or a process.

## process capability
It can be defined as the measured, built-in reproductibility of the product turned out by the process. Such a determination is made by using statistical methods. The statistically determined pattern or distribution is compared to specification limits to decide if a process

can consistently deliver the product within those parameters.

## process failure mode and effects analysis

It is an analytical technique used by a manufacturing team as a means to assure that, as far as possible, potential failure modes and their associated mechanisms have been considered and addressed.

## process manufacturing

It is a type of manufacturing where a product is produced or transformed through mixing, chemical reactions, etc. Examples include refining crude oil into gasoline, extracting aluminium from ore, combining materials to make some chemical or paint. Process manufacturing is opposed to discrete manufacturing.

## process mix

It refers to the proper mix or balance between manufactured components and bought out components in the production of goods.

## process production

The term is used for continuous and capital-intensive manufacture of a product, using plant designed to fit the technological requirements of the process, instead of needing to accommodate a large number of successive worker operations.

Process production was one of the three major systems of production identified and described by Peter Drucker, the other two being mass production and unique-product production.

## procurement

It refers to the procedures for obtaining goods or services, including all activities from the planning steps, preparation and processing of a requisition, to receipt and acceptance of delivery, etc.

## producer price index (PPI)

It is a measure of the rate of inflation among goods purchased and manufactured by UK industry. It measures the movements in prices of about 10,000 goods relative to the same base year.

## product comparison

It is a market research survey

in which respondents are asked to state to which

See the difference?

Product comparison

particular brand each of a number of different attributes is most applicable.

## product design quality

The term is used for the degree to which the product design contributes to the creation of a high quality product. Product design quality is the output of the knowledge workers who generally work in marketing, design, development, quality assurance and operations. The objective is how to integrate a quality philosophy into the knowledge work areas of marketing, design and development.

## product diversification

It refers to the development, manufacture and marketing of alternative or different products.

## product elimination

It refers to the process used to withdraw a product from a market, owing to some defect or problem, in an orderly manner so that it does not disrupt the sale of other products marketed by the same company.

## product features

These are features described to a customer when promoting the product. These are:

1. Functional features which are the quantitative or qualitative aspects of a product that either are non-existent in competing products or exist to a lesser extent.

2. Tangible features which are those which do not directly relate to the product's performance but in some way distinguish a product from equally performing competing products.

## production control

It refers to planning the manufacture of components and the assembly of finished products to meet sales requirements and ensure that the planned program of production is achieved through translating sales requirements into a production plan; preparing detailed manufacturing timetables; scheduling work; and regularly monitoring performance.

## production planning
It describes aspects of production control especially concerned with analysing sales demands and developing production programme to satisfy the demands.

## productivity
It is defined as the ratio of an output measure divided by an input measure. It shows how well a country, industry, business unit, person or machine is using its resources. It is a relative measure. A company's productivity can be compared to that of another company or of itself over a period of time. Total factor productivity is measured in monetary units. It describes the relationship between input and output of an industrial unit, etc. input being measured in workforce, machines, materials and money, while output in products and services.

## productivity bargaining
It is a system of establishing pay levels for a particular company or plant with productivity agreements that incorporate methods of increasing productivity and changes in work arrangements along with a wide range of terms and conditions in a package deal.

## productivity ratios
These are the ratios used in performance measurement. Relating physical input measures to output gives productivity ratios. They may include output per person and output per unit of material used.

## product layout
It is an approach to organise the physical configuration of a facility that is driven by the steps required to build a particular product. (See the figure on next page)

## product liability
It refers to the liability of manufacturers and other persons for defective products. The persons liable for a defective product are the producer, i.e. the manufacturer, including

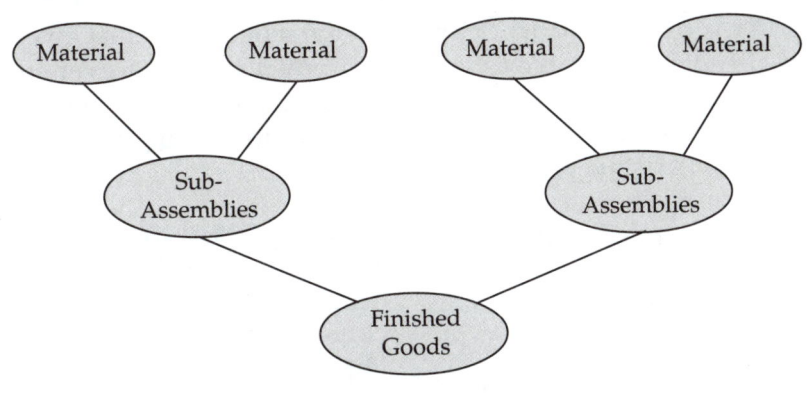

**Product layout**

producers of component parts and raw materials, any person who holds himself to be a producer by putting his name or trade mark on the product, or a person who imports the product.

## product liability or service liability

It is a generic term that describes the onus on a producer or others to make restitution for loss related to personal injury, property damage or other harm caused by a product or service.

## product life-cycle

It is the complete life of a product ranging from early planning and preparatory investment, design, production, sales build-up, maximum sales, declining sales to withdrawal of the product. The stages of a normal product life-cycle are sometimes summarised as (a) the research and development stage; (b) the introductory stage; (c) the market development stage; (d) the exploitation stage; (e) the maturation stage; (f) the saturation stage; and (g) the decline stage.

## product-market strategy

Also called Ansoff matrix, it is a marketing planning model wherein companies can either sell existing or new products. They can sell them either in existing markets or in new markets. The resulting two-by-two matrix gives the following four alternative strategies for increasing sales:
1. To concentrate on selling more existing products in existing market.

**Dictionary of Business**

2. An organisation can modify or improve its existing products and sell these to current customer.
3. To sell existing products to a new market.
4. Another strategy is to develop new products for new markets.

## product mix

It refers to a combination of products and product ranges produced by a company. One of the objectives of a company policy should be to produce the optimum product mix in terms of profitability, bearing in mind both the market potential and the company's own production and technical resources.

## product orientation

It is the attitude of a company that believes that the product comes first and is followed by persuading customers to buy it.

## product planning

It implies determining the products to be produced, the particular design features of the products, the quantities to be produced and the prices at which they are sold.

## product-plus

It is a term used in marketing for the selling point that gives a product the edge over its competitors and can be built upon by advertising and sales promotion.

## product position

The term is used for the way a product is seen by consumers in terms of its important attributes, viz. the place it occupies in consumer's minds, relative to competing products.

## product strategy

It is a company's new product development policy, about the revitalisation and development of new products for both existing and new markets, and the withdrawal of products that are not profitable

## profitability

It is the capacity or potential of a project or an organisation to make a profit. It is measured by return on capital employed and the ratio of net profit to sales.

## profiteer

It is used for a person who makes excessive profits by charging inflated prices for a commodity that is in short supply.

Dictionary of Business

## profit margin
It is the ratio of profit to sales, or profit as a percentage of sales.

## profit planning
It implies planning the direction and control of a company or organisation's future operations towards its profit goals.

## profit-pool concept
It is the identification of a number of minor purchases surrounding a major purchase, and the identification of the money value and profitability of each of these related sales.

## profit-sharing scheme
It denotes a method by which some of the profits of a business are distributed to some or all employees in the form of cash or shares. Such scheme provides for such distributing to be made annually to employees fulfilling certain basic conditions, viz. at least a particular length of service.

## profit variance
It denotes the variance between the standard operating profit, budgeted to be made on the items sold, and the actual profits made.

## pro forma invoice
It is a sales invoice sent in certain circumstances to a buyer, usually before some of the invoice details are known. In commodity trading, a pro forma invoice may be sent to the buyer at the time of shipment, based on a notional weight, although the contract specifies that the buyer will only pay for the weight ascertained when foods reach the port of destination.

## programme analysis and review
It is a management technique and approach used in government departments for analysing and assessing whether resources are in fact being used effectively in a project or programme.

## programmed text
The term is used for teaching material presented or programmed step by step in a manner that can be adapted to the needs of the individual trainee.

## progress chasing
It means ensuring that manufacturing work is

completed according to plan. It involves speeding up or rescheduling work; arranging timely delivery of raw materials, sub-assemblies or bought out parts; expediting the transfer of components and sub-assemblies between different parts of the factory and identifying the causes of delays in order to take the corrective action as required.

### progressive consumer
Opposite to retrogressive consumer, the term is used for a consumer who would be receptive to an offer of a better product or service at a slightly higher price.

### progressive part method
It refers to a method where an operation to be learned or a course to be taken is divided into parts which are learned separately but when each is completed it is integrated with what has already been learned, so that there is a coherence in training and skill.

### progressive tax system
It denotes income tax system which levies an increasing amount of tax as the income rises. The increase may be on either a slab scale or a slice scale. It is considered a fair and equitable system of tax.

### project cost
It implies the total cost to provide the business-driven and technology-based product or service. The main costs include the hardware, software, services, installation, maintenance, support, training, and internal staffing costs, etc. planned for the project. The apportioned salaries and benefits constitute internal staffing costs.

### project cost management
It is a subset of project management that includes the processes required to ensure that the project is completed within the approved budget. It can be called the compound of resource planning, cost estimating, cost budgeting and cost control.

### project description
It denotes an initial, high-level statement describing the purpose, plans, objectives, and benefits, general approach to development as well as the characteristics of a product or service required by an organisation.

Dictionary of Business

## project initiation
It is the conceptual development phase of a project, and can be described as a process that leads to approval of the project concept and authorisation to begin detailed planning.

## project integration management
It is a subset of project management that includes the processes required to ensure that the various elements of the project are being co-ordinated properly. It is composed of project plan development, project plan execution, and overall change control.

## projectised organisation
The term refers to an organisation having a number of project teams with a pool of specialists available to be called on by the project manager for particular projects.

## project management
It refers to the following:
1. The application of knowledge, skills, resources, tools, techniques, processes and systems to project activities in order to meet or even exceed stakeholder needs and the expectations from a project.
2. The planning, organising, scheduling, directing and controlling of a one-time activity to meet or exceed constraints on scope, schedule, cost, etc.

## project network diagram
It refers to any schematic display of the logical relationships of project activities. The diagram is always drawn from left to right to reflect project chronology.

## project oversight
The term is used for a process that employs a variety of quality control, inspection, test measurement and other observation processes to ensure that planned project objectives are achieved in accordance with an approved plan. It includes technical as well as management oversight, and is generally done by an independent entity trained or experienced in management and technical review methods.

## project period
It is the total amount of time during which the government official or department

authorises a guarantee to complete the approved work of the project described in the application. The periods of more than one year are divided into budget periods.

### project plan
It is a formal, approved document which guides both project execution and project control. The primary uses of the project plan are to prepare in the form of a document, planning assumption, decisions, and project baselines, facilitate communication among stakeholders and to describe how the project will be executed and controlled.

### project procurement management
It is a subset of project management that includes the processes required to acquire goods and services from outside the performing organisation. It is comprised of procurement planning, source selection, contract administration and contract close out, among other things.

### project purchasing
It is the policy of purchasing at one time all the materials and components required for a particular project or contract. It is opposite to stock purchasing of items to be drawn from stores as and when required.

### project quality management
It is a form of project management that includes the processes required to ensure that the project will satisfy the major needs for which it was undertaken. It focuses on quality planning, quality assurance and quality control.

### project scope
It is the sum of the products and services to be provided for a project and establishes the limits of a project. The project scope defines the five w's, viz. who, what, where, when and why, for a project.

### project time management
It is a subset of project management that includes the processes required to ensure timely completion of the project. It focuses on activity sequencing, activity duration estimating, schedule development and schedule control.

### project transition checklist
It is a document that ensures that the activities of the planning phase have been finished, reviewed and

approved so that the project may move from the planning phase into the execution phase.

## promoter
The term is used for a person involved in setting up and funding a new company, including preparing its Articles of Association and Memorandum of Association, registration, funding directors, and raising subscriptions. The promoter partakes of a position of trust with regard to the new company and is not supposed to make an undisclosed profit or benefit at its expense.

## promotional mix
It is a combination of techniques used by an organisation to project its image and promote its products or services.

## prompt day
It is the day on which payment is due for the purchase of goods. In some spot markets, it is the day payment is due and delivery of the goods is made.

## prompt note
It refers to a reminder to a purchaser of the money due from him/her and of the date on which it becomes due.

## proof of delivery
It is a signed receipt showing the date of delivery to the consignee. It generally has the signature of an agent. If the goods are part of a consolidation arrangement, delivery to the consolidator is sufficient.

## proprietary specification
It denotes a specification that restricts the acceptable products or services to that of one or more manufacturers or vendors. A common example is the use of a brand name specification that would exclude consideration of proposed equals. All sole source specifications are proprietary, but all proprietary specifications are not sole source. Proprietary items can be made available from several distributors through competitive bidding.

## prospectus
It is a statement of a company's or organisation's present strength as well as future plans, etc. published as part of a quest for support or investment. When a company goes public, it offers its shares for sale, and the prospectus is presented for assessment.

## protection
It is a term used for protecting

a home industry or industries from foreign competition in the home market by legislation, tariffs, or subsidies.

### protective output norm
It is a situation where a work group informally holds down production levels, e.g. under productivity restriction.

### protective practice
It denotes insistence by trade unionists on what they see as the interests of job security and security of tenure, on restricting the way in which production and other techniques are operated.

### protocol
It describes the rules governing the communications between different computers or computer peripherals. The protocol is a formal statement of how data is to be set out when messages are exchanged and are prioritised in order of importance.

### prototyping
Similar to evolutionary design process, it is a strategy in system development in which a scaled down system or portion of a system is constructed in a short time, tested and then improved in several iterations. A prototype is an initial version of a system that is quickly developed to assess the effectiveness of the overall design being used to solve a particular problem.

### provision
It is defined as the amount written off in the current year's profit and loss account for a known or estimated loss or liability.

### provision for bad debts
It is a provision calculated to cover the debts during an accounting period that are not expected to be paid. In banks, provision is mandatory according to prudential norms, as per the status of loan.

### Pty
It is a short term for proprietary company, the name given to a private limited company in Australia and the Republic of South Africa.

### public corporation
It is a state-owned organisation set up to provide a national service such as All India Radio or to run a nationalised industry.

## public relations (PR)
It can be defined as the planned and sustained effort to establish and maintain mutual understanding between an organisation and its public. PR is concerned with influencing points of view, while advertising is largely concerned with propagating its message through advertisements, which have been paid for.

## public utility
The term describes an organisation that provides the public with services like water, civic amenities, power, transport, telecommunication, etc.

## public warehouse
It is a business that provides short- or long-term storage to a different type of business, usually on a month-to-month basis. A public warehouse normally uses its own equipment and staff.

*Public warehouse*

However, agreements may be made where the client either buys or gets equipment at subsidised rates. Public warehouse fees are usually a combination of storage fees.

## puffery
It refers to the practice of exaggerating a product's good points in advertising or other promotional media. Tall claims of this kind are sometimes taken literally by consumers.

## purchase order
It is a document used to approve, arrange and process purchased items and is used to communicate a purchase to supplier. It is also used as an authorisation to purchase. Such order states quantities, costs and delivery dates.

## purchasing power
It can be defined as the ability to purchase goods and services. In times of inflation, a loss of purchasing power occurs when monetary assets are held because of the decline in the purchasing power of the currency.

## purchasing power parity (PPP)
It refers to the theory that, after adjusting for the

exchange rate, the cost of a good should be the same in all countries. The rate of exchange between two currencies should be such that each currency has exactly the same purchasing power in its own economy.

### pure risk
It is a term for the risk inherent in such factors as accident, fire, flood, health, hurricane, etc. as distinct from the speculative risk inherent in the element of business or an exchange risk due to currency rate fluctuations.

### push strategy
It is a strategy that makes use of a company's sales force and trade promotion activities to create consumer demand for a particular product. The producer promotes the product to wholesalers, who promote it to retailers, and retailers to consumers.

### push versus pull systems
These are two decision variables which all production systems deal with. Suppose that we have a factory supplying two warehouses in the region. With a push system, the people at the factory decide when and how much to ship to each of the two warehouses based on demand and inventory position information. With a pull system, we segregate the problem so that people at each warehouse decide when and how much to order from the factory based on their need.

### put and calls
These are options to sell (put) or buy (call) fixed quantities of specific securities including shares at specified prices at the stock exchange within a given period of time.

### pyramid selling
It is a system of selling in which purchasers buy the right to sell a product and, often, contract to handle a minimum quantity of it. The right to sell the product carries with it a title such as agent, salesman, sales supervisor or area manag

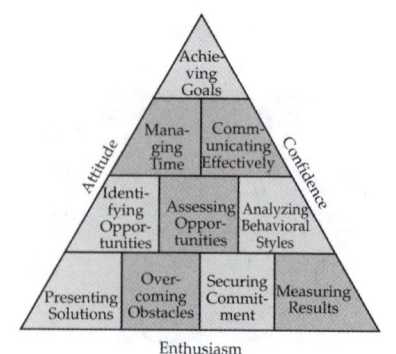

**Pyramid selling**

# Q

### qualified acceptance
It is an acceptance of a bill of exchange that changes the effect of the bill as drawn. If the holder refuses to take a qualified acceptance, the drawer and any endorsers thereon must be notified, otherwise will no longer be liable.

### qualifying distribution
A distribution from a company that results in advance payment of corporation tax. Such distributions include dividends and distributions from any company assets to shareholders.

### qualitative forecasting techniques
These are techniques used to forecast future trends like the demand for a product, when there is little meaningful data for use as the basis of statistical techniques. Such techniques include making use of sales-force estimates, and surveys of user expectations.

### quality
It is a generic term for the following:
1. The totality of features and characteristics of a product or service that has the ability to satisfy stated or implied needs.
2. Degree to which a set of inherent characteristics fulfils requirements.

### quality assurance
It denotes the following:
1. All the planned or systematic actions considered necessary to provide adequate confidence that a product or service will satisfy the given requirements for quality.
2. That part of quality management which is focused on providing confidence that quality requirements will be fulfilled.

### quality audit
It is a systematic and independent examination and evaluation to determine the following:
1. Whether quality activities

and results comply with planned arrangements.
2. Whether these arrangements are implemented effectively.
3. Whether they are suitable to achieve objectives.

## quality control and reliability

The term refers to techniques for ensuring that during design, production, and servicing, both work and materials are within limits that will produce the desired product performance and reliability.

## quality function deployment (QFD)

It is a method for ensuring that the customer has a say in the design specification of a product. It uses interfunctional teams from production, engineering and marketing. The process begins with market research, studying customer behaviour, consumers' preferences to define their need, and then breaking these needs down into customer requirements. Such requirements are then weighted on the basis of their importance to the customer.

## quality initiative

It is a formal effort by an organisation to improve the quality of its products and/or services. It generally involves top management development of a mission statement and long-term strategy.

## quality loop, quality spiral

It refers to the conceptual model of interacting the quality of a product and/or service in the various stages, from the identification of needs, to the assessment of whether these needs have been satisfied.

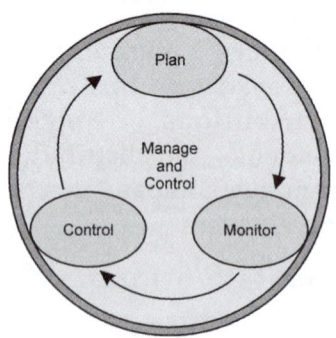

Quality loop

## quality management

It denotes the following:
1. The aspect of the overall business management function that determines and implements the quality policy.

2. A collection of quality plans, procedures, specifications, and requirements attained through quality assurance and quality control.

## quality market
It is a market in which quality of goods matters more than their price.

## quality planning
It implies the following:
1. Identifying quality standards which are relevant to the project and determining how to satisfy them.
2. A structured process for defining the methods, may be that used in the production of a specific product, or family of products.

## quality protection
The term is used for measures introduced as part of a quality control programme to guard against below-standard components or products.

## quality system audit
It is a documented activity performed to verify, by examination and evaluation of objective evidence, that applicable elements of the quality systems are acceptable and have been developed, documented and effectively implemented as per specified requirements.

## quality system review
It is a formal evaluation by management of the status and adequacy of the quality system in relation to quality policy and new objectives resulting from changing circumstances.

## quartering
Clocking-in-system under which an employee loses a full 15 minute's pay if he or she is even two-three minutes late.

## quasi-subsidiary
The term is used for a company, trust, partnership, etc. that does not fulfil the definition of a subsidiary undertaking but is directly or indirectly controlled by the reporting entity, and gives benefits for that entity that are in substance no different from those that would have been available in case it was a subsidiary.

## quid pro quo
It literally means something for something, i.e. something given as compensation for something received.

Contracts require a quid pro quo because without a consideration they would become unilateral agreements.

### quota restriction
It implies the following:
1. Where goods or services supplied to an organisation or person are restricted to a specified limit or quota for a given period of time.
2. Where, a work group working to loose piece work rate hold down output so as not to draw attention to the looseness of the rates. Workers who do not join their colleagues in quota restriction are called ratebusters, particularly in the USA.

### quota sampling
It is another term for random sampling, used particularly in market research when interviewers are given a quota of interviewees or informants broken down by required classification like social position, age, sex, etc.

### quotation
It refers to the following:
1. The representation of a security on a recognised stock exchange. A quotation allows the shares of a company to be traded on the stock of exchange.
2. A bid and offer price indicated by a dealer in financial obligations.
3. An indication of the price at which a seller might be willing to offer goods for sale.
4. An offer to carry out specified work, or to provide a specified service, for payment.

# R

### rack jobber or raker
In the UK, the term refers to a wholesaler who regularly maintains and merchandises racks and displays of goods in retail shops.

### rake-off
A slang for a share of the profit from a deal or enterprise, especially one paid illegally.

### rally
It implies a rise of share prices in a financial market, after a fall. It comes about by a change of market sentiment. However, if the change has occurred because there are more buyers than sellers, it is known as technical rally.

### random access storage
It is a flexible form of computer storage which affords instant access to any of its files or locations.

### random sampling
It means picking out of individual items on a basis that gives every individual item in the group an equal chance of being selected. The basic techniques of random sampling have a wide range of industrial and commercial applications—from production control to the selection of samples in market research.

### random variations
The term is used for variations from a planned level of performance. They may arise from external influences, or may be inherent in some elements of the process.

### random walk
It is a market research technique in which interviewers walk along prescribed routes calling on houses selected on random sampling principles for interviewing the householders on some products.

### ranking method
It is a simple method of job evaluation in which jobs are ranked according to an informal assessment of their overall importance to the organisation. Its method is

quick and inexpensive but becomes difficult to sustain when organisations become larger and more complex.

### rate buster
It is a US term for piece work worker who takes advantage of loose rates to earn high bonus payments rather than joining fellow workers in quota restriction or holding back production to the level of the bogey agreed unofficially by the work group.

### rate fixing
It is a shop floor practice common in the engineering industry by which piece work rates for the production of particular components are fixed by rate fixers on the basis of their experience of similar work.

### rate of exchange
It can be stated as the price of one currency in terms of another expressed in terms of how many units of the home country's currency are needed to buy one unit of the foreign currency. In the UK, however, it is expressed as the number of units of foreign currency that one unit of the home currency will buy. The latter method is called indirect rate.

### rating
It denotes the following:
1. An insurance term for measuring risk to determine premium rates.
2. In finance, it refers to determining creditworthiness of customers and potential customers using trade references and credit agencies.

### rating agency
It is an agency that monitors the credit backing of institutions and of bond issues and other forms of public borrowings. It may also give a rating of the risks involved in holding specific stocks. Moody's and CRISIL are rating agencies.

### ratio analysis
It refers to an analysis of accounting ratio to evaluate a company's operating performance and financial stability. Ratios like return on capital employed and gross profit percentage can be used to assess profitability.

### rationalisation
It is a reorganisation of a firm, enterprise or industry to

increase its efficiency and profitability. It may include closing some manufacturing units and expanding others, and merging different stages of the production process.

## real estate
The term refers to landed property including its natural resources and additions such as permanent buildings.

## real learning time
It refers to the time taken for a trainee to become capable of working at the speed and quality of an average experienced worker.

## realisable account
It is an account drawn up on the dissolution of a partnership. The account is debited with the assets of the partnership and any expenses on realisation. It is credited with the proceeds of any sales made. The difference between the total debits and credits is either a profit or loss on realisation, which must be shared between the partners in the profit-sharing ratio.

## rebalancing
It denotes the following:
1. The adjustment of a hedge in order to improve its effectiveness in the changed circumstances.
2. The adjustment of an investment portfolio over time to better reflect its underlying strategy.

## rebate
It is a discount offered on the price of a good or service, often one that is paid back to the person who pays, e.g. a tax or a duty drawback.

## recession
It can be defined as a slowdown or fall in economic growth rate. It marks a decline in gross domestic product in two successive quarters. A severe recession is called a depression.

## reciprocal costs
These are costs apportioned from a service cost centre to a production cost centre that carries out work for the original service cost centre. Cost appointment can be calculated either by the use of simultaneous equations or by a continuous appointment method.

## reciprocal trading
It is a trading in which a supplier of goods or services gives an undertaking to a

customer to buy for the latter certain goods and/or services in return.

## recorded delivery
A postal service offered by the UK Post Office that provides a record of posting and delivery of inland letters for an extra fee. The advice of delivery is also offered for a further fee.

## recourse
It refers to the right of redress of the aggrieved, should the terms of a contract not be fulfilled.

## redemption
The repayment of shares, stocks, debentures, or bonds. The amount payable on redemption is usually specified on issue. However, the redemption date, or dates, may or may not be specified on issue.

## reducing balance method
It is a method of spreading the cost of a fixed asset over its estimated useful life. The amount of depreciation charged each year decreases over the life of the asset. The percentage rate chosen is applied every year to the balance remaining from the previous year. It can be illustrated as below:

| | £ |
|---|---|
| Initial cost | |
| Depreciation 1st Year 20% | 1,00,000 |
| | 20,000 |
| Balance | 80,000 |
| Year 2 20% | 16,000 |
| Balance | 64,000 |
| Year 3 20% | 12,800 |
| Balance | 52,200 |

It is also called diminishing balance or declining method and is distinct from straight line method.

## re-exports
It implies goods that have been imported and are then exported without having undergone any material change while in the exporting country. Countries with major re-exports distinguish re-exports from domestic exports in their balance of payments accounts.

## reference groups
It is a term used in marketing for specially structured groups of people brought together for the purpose of examining consumer buying motives.

## reference rate
It refers to the following:
1. An interest rate relative to which a bank prices its

products, also called as its base rate.
2. An interest rate relative to which financial markets price their products, e.g. the London Inter Bank Offered Rate (LIBOR).

## reference tariff

In Eurozone, it is a tariff or scale of charges which is not restricted to the upper and lower limits of a forked tariff but any charges or rates outside the reference fork must be published as such. Such a reference tariff is used for inland waterways and bulk transport under the Common Transport Policy of the European Union.

## refer to drawer

These are words written on a memo of cheque that has been returned unpaid by a bank, usually because the account of the person who drew it has insufficient funds to cover it and the manager of the bank is unwilling to allow the account to be overdrawn or further overdrawn.

## reflation

It is the policy aimed at expanding the level of output of the economy by government's fiscal or monetary policy. This could involve increasing the money supply and government expenditure on public works, subsidies, etc. or reducing taxation and interest rates.

## register of charges

It denotes the following:
1. The register maintained by the Registrar of Companies on which certain charges must be registered by the companies. A charge is created when a company gives a creditor the right to recover a debt against some asset of the company. The types of charge that must be registered in this way, and the details that must be given, are mentioned in UK Companies Act. Failure to register the charge within 30 days of its creation renders it void, so that it cannot be enforced against a liquidator or creditor of the company.
2. A list of charges that a company must maintain at its registered address or principal place of business.

## registered company

It implies a company or corporation registered with the Registrar of Companies with whom it has deposited its Articles of Association, Memorandum of Association,

**Dictionary of Business**

annual accounts, etc. as required by the Companies Act.

## registered office
It is the official address of a company, to which all correspondence can be sent. Statutory registers are kept at the registered office, the address of which must be disclosed on stationery, including letterheads, e-mails, company websites, and the company's annual return.

## registrar of companies
It is used for an official charged with the duty of registering all the companies. The registrar is responsible for carrying out a number of administrative duties connected with registered companies, including maintaining the register of companies and the register of charges, issuing certificates of incorporation, etc.

## regression analysis
It is a statistical technique in marketing that attempts to measure the extent to which one variable is related to two or more other variables, often with the aim of predicting future values of the dependent variable.

## regression analysis
It is a technique, common in market research, which uses trends in one type of activity as a guide to the likely future level of another, related activity. Thus, a general rise in standards of living may be used as evidence for a forecast of increased sales of electronics and even luxuries like cars, ACs and microwave ovens.

## regressive tax
It refers to a tax in which the rate of tax decreases as income increases. Indirect taxes fall into this category. Regressive taxes are said to fall more heavily on the poor than on the rich.

## requisitioning
It refers to the taking possession of property by a government, usually during a national emergency, with or without the consent of the owner. When the emergency has ended, the property may be returned to its owner. In it, the ownership does not pass to the government as it does in a compulsory purchase.

## reinsurance
It may be termed as insurance of insurance, especially of

large-scale risks, with several insurers or brokers agreeing to share the risks involved.

## reintermediation
It denotes the creation of a new intermediary between customers and suppliers to provide such services as supplier search and product evaluation.

## relevance
The term is used for an accounting principle that the financial information provided by a company should be, (a) of such a nature that it is capable of influencing the decisions of users of that information, and (b) provided in time to influence those decisions.

## relocation
It is the change of an office, factory, or other place of work from one place to another, often as a result of a merger, takeover, etc.

## remedial frames
It refers to frames in an intrinsic branching program to which a trainee is referred in order to correct a wrong answer or to make up for a lack of understanding revealed by an answer or answers.

## rent
It can be defined as a payment for the use of land, usually under a lease. The most usual kinds are ground rent and rack rent. Rack rent is paid when no payment has been made for the lease and such rent represents the full value of the land and buildings.

## reorganisation
In the US, it is the process of restructuring a company that is experiencing financial difficulties. Protection against creditors can be sought under Bankruptcy Reform Act, 1978. If the creditors cannot agree on a plan, the company's assets are liquidated and the proceeds distributed by the court.

## replacement analysis
It is a technique used to establish the optimum time to replace plant and machinery, allowing for depreciation, after assessing effectiveness of existing equipment and potential of available new equipment.

## replacement demand
It is a term used in marketing for demand associated with consumers or users scrapping and replacing consumer

durables or industrial capital goods. Other types of demands are repeat demand, consumer goods demand, and expansion demand.

### repositioning
It implies changing a product's formulation, design, packaging, presentation, price, brand image, or even brand name to reposition it in the minds of the customers and in relation to its competitors.

### repudiation
It is an act of refusal of one party to pay a debt or honour a contract.

### repurchase
It refers to an agreement under which one party sells a financial asset to another on terms that provide for the seller to buy it back later at an agreed price. The seller is paid in full and makes the agreement to raise ready money without losing the holding.

### reputed owner
It refers to a person who acts as the owner of certain goods, with the consent of the true owner. If that person becomes bankrupt, the goods are divided among the creditors and the true owner is estopped from claiming them, i.e. the law of estoppel applies.

### reserve
It denotes to the following:
1. It can be defined as part of the capital of a company, other than the share capital, arising from retained profit or from the issue of share capital at more than its nominal value. Reserves are distinct from provision in that for the latter there is a known diminution in value of an asset or a known liability, whereas reserves are in the nature of surpluses.
2. The term is also used for a provision in the project plan to mitigate costs and schedule risk. It is often with a modifier so as to provide further detail on what types of risk are meant to be mitigated. The specific meaning of the modified term varies according to application.

### reserve assets
The term denotes the following:
1. Money held by a bank that is not committed to outstanding loans, and is

therefore available to cover shortfalls.

2. Gold and foreign currency held by a central bank, e.g. RBI, in case of India, for invention in foreign exchange markets.

## reserve price

It is the price below which the vendor is not prepared to sell at an auction or sale. It is also called floor price or upset price.

## resident

The term is used for a person living or based in the UK to whom one of the following applies for a given tax year:
1. The person is present in the UK for 180 days or more during that year.
2. The person pays substantial visits to the UK, averaging 90 days or more for four or more consecutive years.
3. A UK resident or resident company is subject to tax on income earned anywhere in the world.

## residual income method

It is a method of measuring and controlling divisional performance which tries to align divisional goals with those of the company as a whole. It measures return on investment (ROI), allowing for capital charges at various rates, intra-company trading at open market prices and values of assets at net book value.

## resolution

It is a binding decision made by the members of a company. If a motion is put before the members of a company at a general meeting and the required majority vote is in favour of it, the motion is passed and becomes a resolution.

## resource levelling

It denotes any form of network analysis in which scheduling decisions are driven by resource management concerns such as limited resource availability or difficult-to-manage changes in resource levels.

## resource scheduling

It is a technique used for allocating resources to the different sections of an organisation or project at the right time. It is an integral part of critical path analysis.

## restrictive covenant

It is a clause in a contract that

**Dictionary of Business**

restricts the freedom of one of the parties in some way. Employment contracts, for example, usually include a clause in which an employee agrees not to compete with the employer or be employed with a competition for a specified period after leaving his/her employment.

### restrictive trade practices (RTP)

It refers to the following:
1. A trading practice or agreement that is not in the public interest, particularly, in the UK, as defined in the Restrictive Trade Practices Act, 1956, the Resale Prices Act, 1964 and the Fair Trading Act, 1973.
2. Agreements between traders that are not considered to be in the public interest. In UK, under the Competition Act, 1998, any agreement between two or more suppliers of goods or services restricting prices, conditions of sale, quantities offered, processes, areas and persons to be supplied, etc. must be registered with the Office of Fair Trading.

### retail banking

The term is used for involving with private customers by banks and other financial institutions.

### retail gravitation

In marketing, it is the situation in which the people use particular kinds of retail outlet, or can be attracted to them.

### retail price support

It is the subsidy paid to a retailer by a producer or wholesaler to maintain a foothold in a market.

### retained earnings

It refers to profits not distributed by way of dividend payments, but retained within the organisation as part of a company's capital reserves.

### retrogressive consumer

He is a consumer who is keen to economise on an existing product or service. It is in contrast the progressive consumer, who would be receptive to an offer of a better product or service even at a slightly higher price.

### return on assets managed

It is a method of assessment of company and management performance. It is expressed as sales minus the cost of goods sold as a percentage of assets managed minus liabilities. In this computation, assets managed are treated as the sum of all fixed assets at current replacement cost plus all inventories, stocks, debtors and prepayments, cash in hand, bank balance, bills receivable, selling rights, goodwill, patent if any, and unquoted investments, etc.

## return on capital (ROC)

It implies a method by which an average expected profit is estimated on several years of a proposed project or enterprise, and then expressed as a percentage of the capital employed.

## return on capital employed (ROCE)

It is an accounting ratio expressing the profit of an organisation for an accounting period. It is expressed as a percentage of the capital employed and is one of the most frequently used ratios in financial analysis.

## return on investment (ROI)

It refers to the following:

1. A figure of merit used to help make capital investment decisions is calculated by considering the annual benefit divided by the investment amount.
2. An estimate of the financial benefit in money invested on a particular investment.

## revaluation

It refers to the following:
1. Writing up the value of an asset to its current market value.
2. A change made by a country in the official rate at which its currency is exchanged for other currencies. The term is usually used for upward changes in a currency's exchange rate.

## revaluation account

It is an account in a partnership to which a new partner is admitted or if an existing partner dies or retires, to revalue the assets and liabilities to their current market value. The differences between historical values and the revaluations are debited or credited to the revaluation account.

**Dictionary of Business**

## revaluation of assets
It is the revaluation of the assets of a company, because of the reason that they have increased in value since they were acquired or due to the fact that inflation has made the balance sheet values unrealistic. The Indian Companies Act makes it obligatory for the directors of a company to state in the directors' report if they believe the value of land differ materially from the value in the balance sheet.

## reverse engineering
It is defined as taking a finished product and analysing it to find out how it is made or how it works. In the case of a mechanical device, this usually involves disassembling it.

## reverse takeover
It implies the following:
1. The buying of a larger company by a smaller company.
2. The purchasing of a public company by a private company. It may be the cheapest way that a private company can obtain a listing on a stock exchange, as it avoids the expenses of flotation, etc.

## reverse takeover bid
Takeover bid where the company making the bid has the objective of having the management of taken over company run the resulting combined company.

## re-work
It means repeated or revised work, generally because it was done inadequately the first time.

## Ricardian approach
The term is used for David Ricardo's theories governing the distribution of wealth between the owners of land, capital, and labour. While recognising the influence of capital costs on prices, Ricardo stated that the effect of rises in wages on prices depended on the proportion of capital and labour used in the production process.

## rigging a market
It refers to an attempt to make a profit on a market, usually a security or commodity market, by overriding the normal market forces. It involves taking a long position or a short position in the market that is sufficiently substantial to influence price levels.

Dictionary of Business

## right of recourse
It is the right to reclaim or recover a bad debt such as a dishonoured bill of exchange.

## right of resale
The right that the seller in a contract of sale can resell the goods in case the buyer does not pay the agreed price. If the seller tells the buyer that the goods will be resold and the buyer still does not pay within a reasonable time, the seller may resell them and recover from the first buyer, the damages for any loss, etc.

## rights issue
It is a new issue of shares in a company offered to shareholders in proportion to their existing holdings and on advantageous terms. An individual shareholder may accept the offer or may renounce all or part of their rights in favour of others.

## risk
It is defined as any component that affects the project being completed on time and within budget. It denotes the possibility of suffering a loss. In a development project, the term describes the impact to the project, which could be in the form of diminished quality of the end product, increased costs, or delayed completion.

## risk analysis
It is a technique to identify and assess factors that may jeopardise the success of a project or achieving a goal. It also helps define preventive measures to reduce the probability of these factors from occurring and to identify measures to successfully deal with these constraints when they develop.

## risk assessment
It is a systematic assessment by an employer of the risks to health and safety of employees while at work.

## risk capital
It refers to venture capital long-term loans in situations or businesses with a high degree of risk.

## risk premium
Also called market-risk premium, it is the difference between the expected rate of return on an investment and the risk-free rate of return over the same period. If there is any risk element at all, the rate of return is higher than if no risk were involved.

## rival unionism
It is a situation where two or more trade unions are competing for members and recognition in the same industry or company.

## rolling contract
A contract for a specified period of time but in which the demand is constantly renewed from the present.

## rolling plan
It is a long-term plan that is revised regularly, and at each revision it is projected forward again for the same period as the original plan. A two-year rolling plan might be revised each year, so that at the end of a year one, plan is revised and fresh future projections are made.

## roll-over credit
It implies a medium-or long-term bank loan in which the rate of interest varies with short-term money market rates such as LIBOR or SIBOR (Singapore inter-bank offered rate) because the bank has raised the loan by short-term money market or interbank market borrowing.

## royalty
It is a payment made for the right to use the property of another person for gain. This is usually an intellectual property such as a copyright, e.g. in a book or a patent as in an invention.

## rough-cut capacity
The term is used to determine estimated load on main pieces of equipment or resources. It may use production plan or master production schedule. Such capacity is used as a check to verify that manufacturing resources are adequate to execute the production plan.

## routing
The term is used along with the bill of material (BOM) in manufacturing operations. While the BOM contains the material requirements, the routing contains the specific steps required to produce the finished items. Each step in the routing is called an operation.

## running costs
These are costs directly or indirectly related to keeping equipment or an enterprise in operation. These costs include wages, rents, interests, payments, taxes, day-to-day services, consumable equipments, replacement of goods sold, etc.

# S

### safe custody
It denotes service offered by most commercial banks, in which the bank holds valuable items belonging to its customers in its strong room. These items may be documents such as deeds and bearer bonds, but they may also include items of value like gold, diamonds, jewellery, etc. The bank is bailee for these items and its liability will depend on whether or not it has charged the customer for the service and terms of the customer's own insurance.

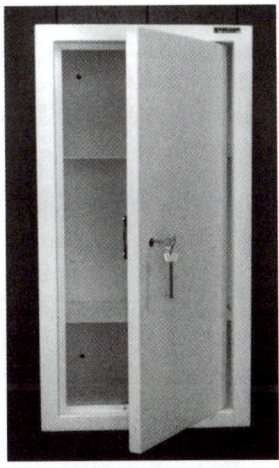

Safe custody

### safe working conditions
It is the statutory duty of the employer to use reasonable care to ensure that his/her employees have safe working conditions, where they have no hazard, risk, threat or disturbances.

### safety stock
It is the average inventory on hand when an order is received. In an independent demand inventory system, the safety stock should be a function of the standard decision of the demand during the replenishment lead time.

### salaried partner
A partner in a partnership who, by agreement, draws a regular salary.

### salary classes
These are salary brackets used in calculating entitlements and contributions under certain pension schemes.

### salary progression
It is the rate at which the salary of an individual whose

job is placed in a salary grade, can progress through the grade. Such progression may take place in fixed increments or may be at different rates, depending on performance appraisals.

## salary review

It refers to the re-examination of employees' salaries with regard to performance or inflation. It is generally used in an annual basis, company policy and/or individual contracts of employment.

## sales and operations planning

It is a horizontal communication process in which key managers from sales and operations meet to develop realistic plans. Such planning is the set of vital communications and decision-making processes for developing the company's plan that balances market demand with resource capability. Such planning process provides a way to draw out functionally conflicting objectives and resolve them so as to develop a true manufacturing, marketing contract, integrate all the functions of the business by developing a 'single set of numbers' from which all other plans and schedules can be developed. The plans take into account projections made by the sales, and marketing departments, the resources available from manufacturing, engineering, purchasing, and finance.

## sales chain

It can be defined as the process or chain along which a product passes from the producer to the end user. The classic sales chain is the one from manufacturer to wholesaler to retailer to consumer. However, there are now several variations on this pattern, either shortening or extending the sales chain.

## sales coverage

It is the ratio between the number of potential customers in an area and the number which can be effectively serviced by a salesperson.

## sales force management

It encompasses planning, organisation, recruitment, training and motivation of the sales force within a marketing strategy. It includes setting sales objectives and evaluating the results obtained by the sales force.

## sales mix
It refers to the combination of quantities of a variety of products that comprise total sales.

## sales order processing
It denotes administrative work involved in checking customer's orders, including the creditworthiness of the customer, and raising the necessary documents for despatch or production.

## sales orientation
It refers to a strategy that concentrates on selling products, whether they meet consumer needs or not.

## sales promotion
It refers to activities and techniques not involved in direct selling but used with the intention of bringing a company's potential customers into contact with its products and services. These activities include advertising, public relations, merchandising, exhibitions, demonstrations, deals, offers, and sampling.

## sales representative
He is the person who sells the goods and services of a company or group, either as an employee or as part of a contractual sales force. Additional responsibilities might include generating new sales leads, publicising changes in products or prices, gathering information about competitors, products, etc.

## sales response function
It is the relationship between the likely sales of a particular product during a specified period and the level of support it receives from the market.

## sales revenue
It refers to the amount receivable for goods or services supplied during a particular period of time.

## sales target
It is the envisaged volume or value of sales that should be obtained for a product, a market or a sales force.

## sample survey
It can be defined as market research or survey based on an examination or a representative part of the total population in an area or region.

## sampling
The term is used for technique

**Dictionary of Business**

which involves collection of attitudes, facts, etc. from a number of people or items in the total population which is appropriate to the survey.

## sampling orders
These are trial orders for a product by a prospective buyer who may place large orders if the samples meet his/her requirements.

## satisfice
It means to obtain an outcome that is good enough. Satisficing action is at variance with maximising action, which seeks the biggest or optimising action, which seeks the best. However, doubts have arisen in recent times about the view that in all rational decision-making, the agent seeks the best result. Instead, it is argued, it is often rational to seek to satisfice.

## scab
Also called black leg, it refers to the worker who continues working during a strike or who takes a striker's place.

## scalability
It is the ability to scale hardware and software to support larger or smaller volumes of data. It can be defined as the ability to increase or decrease size or capability in cost-effective increments with minimal impact on the unit cost of business and the procurement of additional services.

## scalar principle
It is a concept in management that subordinates should communicate with their senior colleagues only through the intermediate superiors and follow the chain of command.

## scatter diagram
It is a diagram that depicts the relationship between two or more variables. It shows how data vary in a frequency distribution.

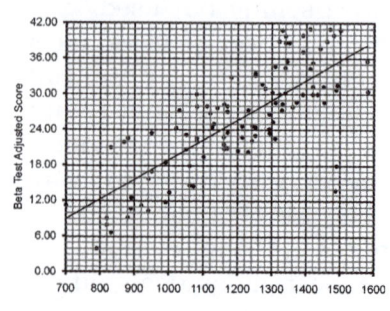

Scatter diagram

## scenario
In business, it refers to the long range position of the organisation in relation to

estimates of the various technological, market, economic, and social forces that will impact its future development.

### science park
It refers to the area especially developed as a site which is attractive to companies in the high technology industries like computer software, hardware, communication, electronics or pharmaceutical research.

### scope creep
It denotes any increase in the project scope that happens incrementally and is subtle in recognition.

### scope definition
It implies decomposing the major deliverables into smaller, more manageable components to provide better control.

### scope planning
It means developing a written scope statement that includes the project justification, the major deliverables and the project objectives.

### scrambled merchandising
It is the offer for sale by a retail outlet of goods other than its normal wares.

### scrap
It refers to the following:
1. The number units of products or raw materials that are defective and cannot be sold or reworked to saleable product.
2. Material outside of specifications and possessing characteristics that make rework impractical.

### search engine
It is a modern term for a service provided on the Internet that enables the user to search for terms which are important for trade and business. Some such as the widely used Google, Bing, and Yahoo are free and attempt to capture information from the whole range of material available on the net. Others are subscription-based but provide added-value services.

### seasonal unemployment
It can be defined as unemployment that occurs as a result of the seasonal nature of some jobs. The building trade, for example, employs very few people during the rainy season. Agricultural

work is also seasonal. There is unemployment in the off-season.

### secondary banking sector
The term is used for financial institutions and fringe banks that carry out a wide range of banking activities but do not have the proven resources of a clearing bank, member bank or commercial bank.

### secondary boycott
In the UK and USA, it refers to the situation where pressure is applied to the employer by persons other than those actually in dispute with him or her. The sympathy strike is one of the most common forms of secondary boycott.

### secondary labour markets
These are labour markets in which people have limited skills or general skills rather than the firm-specific or technical skills.

### secondary picketing
It is picketing favour of a trade dispute by individuals or groups not directly party to the main dispute.

### second penetration products
These are high technology products, e.g. car spare parts which evolve and develop within a few years of the original product.

### secret reserves
These are funds accumulated by a company but not disclosed on the balance sheet. They can arise when an asset has been deliberately undervalued by providing more depreciation, or some other method has been used to account for a transaction with the intention of not showing the effect on the balance sheet.

### secured liability
It implies debt incurred against the pledging of a specific asset by the borrower so that the lender can be sure of recovering through the value of the asset if the debt itself is not repaid.

### security
It can be defined as the guarantee given by the borrower as a safeguard for a loan. The term is also used more loosely to mean debentures, shares or any other negotiable documents with a cash value.

## self-assessment
It is a system that enables taxpayers to assess their own income tax. Post assessment the tax return must be filed within the stipulated time.

## self-liquidating
It denotes the following:
1. An asset that earns back its original cost out of income over a fixed period.
2. A loan in which the money is used to finance a project that will provide sufficient yield to repay the loan and its interest and even yield a profit.
3. Also a sales-promotion offer that pays for itself, e.g. a coffee mug with a jar of coffee.

## self-selection store
It is a type of self-service store in which the customer selects from the goods on display, but normally with the added facility that staff is there to pack the goods, provide guidance as well as collect payment.

## self-service store
It is a store where the customers select from the goods on display, paying for those they have collected at a check point before leaving the store.

Self-service store

## selling overheads
These are expenses incurred by an organisation in carrying out its selling activities. They may include salaries of sales personnel, advertising costs, sales commissions, discounts, etc.

## semantic differential
In marketing, it is a term for the use of pre-coded questions to discover where informants' attitudes to a product, etc. are on a given scale.

## semi-skilled worker
He is a reasonably skilled worker, not as highly skilled as a craftsman who has served as an apprentice.

## semi-structured decisions
These are decisions in which some aspects of the problem are structured and others are unstructured. Structured

means clearly defined and well-understood, while unstructured are a bit vague.

### sensitive market

It implies a market in commodities, securities, etc. that is sensitive to outside influences owing to its instability. For example, a poor rice crop may make it sensitive, with buyers anxious to meet their requirements but are unwilling to show their hand and the risk forcing prices up.

### sensitivity analysis

It is a method of analysing the sensitivity of a decision to a change in any of the assumptions used in making it. For example, a company might analyse how its future performance might be affected by lowering the price of a product, or offering a discount.

### sequestration

It is the confiscation of the property of a person or a company who/which has not complied with a court order. This, however, is resorted to in serious cases only.

### service guarantee

It is a set of two promises offered to customers before they buy a service. The first promise is the level of service provided. The second promise is what the provider will do if the first promise is not kept. Advantages of such a guarantee include helping to retain customers who are about to defect, helping the organisation to learn from its mistakes and improving its service offerings, providing some opportunity to advertise service quality.

### service mark

It describes the design, device or trade mark used to establish the identity of a service offered to the public.

### set off

It is an agreement between the parties involved to set off one debt against another or one loss against a gain. A bank is empowered to set off a credit balance on one account against debit balance in another if the accounts are in the same name and in the same currency. But a notice of bank's intentions to set off is necessary.

### settlement

It denotes the following:
1. The payment of an

outstanding amount, invoice or charge.

2. A disposition of land, or other property, made by deed or will under which a trust is set up by a settlor.

3. The voluntary conclusion of civil litigation or an industrial dispute, following an agreement between the parties to this effect.

## set-up cost

It refers to the marginal cost of a set-up. It usually includes the labour and the materials cost associated with the scrap generated by the set-up. Allocated overhead should not be included as a part of the set-up cost. The cost of a set-up at bottleneck resource should include the opportunity cost of entire system. The cost of a set-up at a clear resource should be only the marginal cost of the labour and materials.

## shadow director

The term is used for a person upon whose instructions directors of a company are accustomed to act, although that person has not been appointed as a director. Such a director influences the running of the company. Some provisions of the Indian Companies Act, including wrongful trading and the regulation of loans to directors, are also applicable to shadow directors.

## shake-out

It is the process of making employees redundant.

## Shamrock organisation

It is an organisation with flexible manning. The concept was developed by Professor Charles Handy of London Business School, based on an organisation with a small core group of permanent employees supported by a changing population of peripheral workers.

## share of production plan

It is a type of payment-by-results scheme in which payment is dependent on company or organisation performance, not individual worker performance.

## share option

It is a benefit offered to employees, especially new employees, in which they are given an option to buy shares in the company for which they work at a favourable fixed price or at a stated discount to the market price.

## shares

The term is widely used for a part of the equity capital or ownership of a company. Particular types of shares include preference shares, ordinary shares and deferred shares. Some methods of selling shares to the public are issue by tender, offer for sale, placings, public issue by prospectus, and rights issues. A public company may also issue bonus shares to its existing shareholders.

## share splitting

It defines the division of the share capital of a company into smaller units. The effect of a share split is the same as a public issue, although the technicalities differ. Share splits are usually carried out when the existing shares reach a high price that trading in them becomes difficult or is limited.

## sharpbender

It implies a firm that has been underperforming its rivals in an industry, but suddenly improves and maintains its performance to go above the average. Such improvement may be caused by a new management team, significant new product success, or other major changes in its business strategy.

## shell company

It refers to the following:
1. Company which exists on paper but does not apparently trade or operate, and is possibly being used as a cover for illegal or unethical activities.
2. Company registered for the purpose of its name and registration to be sold subsequently to someone needing a readymade company.

## shift premium

It refers to extra payment made to shift workers, over and above day rate, to compensate for the social inconvenience of shift working.

## shift working

It is an arrangement by which a group of workers at the end of a working day of normal lengths is succeeded by another group which carries on with the same work. This arrangement may be a continuous process plant or in certain public services that have to be provided at all times.

**Dictionary of Business**

## shipping and forwarding agent

The term is used for an agent who provides services including arranging efficient through-transport from the exporter's factory to the overseas buyer's premises; arranging import of materials, including customs clearance, etc. advising on modes of transport; expediting export documentation; and warehousing, container services, etc. if required.

## shipping documents

These are documents that an exporter of goods delivers to a bank in the exporting country in order to obtain payment for the goods. The bank sends them to its branch or agents in the importing country, which/who releases them to the importer against payment. Once the importer has these documents, he can claim the goods at the port of destination. The documents usually consist of a bill drawn on the buyer/importer of goods, commercial invoice, bill of lading, insurance policy or certificate, and certificate of origin, consular invoice, etc.

## short covering

It is the purchasing of goods that have been sold short so that the open position is closed. The dealer in commodities, securities, or foreign exchanges, hopes to cover the short position at below the price at which he/she had sold in order to make a profit.

## short interval scheduling

It denotes assigning tasks and a planned quantity of work to certain employees to be completed within a specified period of time. The basic concept is that performance can be improved and controlled if work is assigned and monitored over short periods of time.

## short selling

It refers to selling commodities, precious metals, shares, currencies, etc. that one does not have. A short seller expects prices to fall so that the short sale can be covered at a profit before the goods have to be delivered.

## short-time working

It is the condition where shortage of work leads an employer to reduce hours of work to a part-time basis. Yet another reason for introducing short-time working is breakdown in supplies of components.

### shrinkage
It refers to losses as a result of stock deterioration, scrap or waste.

### shut down
It is temporary closing of a factory or plant.

### sickness and accident policy
Insurance policy providing income temporarily, in many cases up to a maximum of one year, in the event of sickness or accident of an employer.

### side deal
It is a private deal between two people, for the personal benefit of one of them, as a subsidiary to a transaction between the officials of a company, government, etc.

### single line store
It refers to a retail shop carrying only a selection of related merchandise, e.g. all kitchen-ware or garden accessories, etc.

### single point of contract
It is a service quality that suggests that a customer should have to talk to only one person for the delivery of a service. In a multipoint contact system, a customer waits a long time in a queue only to be told by the unfriendly service worker that they have to go and see someone else and never builds any relationship with any service worker and no service worker ever takes any 'ownership' of the customer's needs. Thus, the single point of contact principle has many advantages, like the firm builds a closer relationship with the customer, the customer does not have to wait in multiple queues, much less information is lost in the hand-offs between multiple service workers, the job environment is more satisfying for the service workers because they get to own the entire set of the customer's needs.

### single-task role
It is the role that is concerned primarily with one task only. A role concerned with a variety of tasks is known as a multiple-task role.

### sit-down strike
It is a strike in which workers

come to their place of work, but refuse to either work or to go home. They also refuse to leave the workplace until an agreement has been reached. It is opposite to work-in strike where the workers refuse to leave the place of work and continue working.

## sit-in

It is a form of industrial action in which workers pursue the right of work and occupy their factory on a 24-hours-a-day basis to rule out the possibility of a lockout.

## situation profile

It refers to a profile used in establishing the payment system for a firm, a department, a section or an individual. Lupton and Gowler have identified the following profile dimensions use:
1. Number of job modifications per job.
2. Length of the job cycle.
3. Degree of automation.
4. Recorded job stoppages.
5. Rate of product change.
6. Percentage of job elements specified by management for operator.
7. Average length of job stoppages.
8. Time required to fill the vacancy, including training time.
9. Number of unions negotiating separately in the firm.
10. Number of stoppages due to pay disputes.
11. Average age of workforce.
12. Percentage of labour costs to total cost.

## SI units

It refers to an international metric system of units used for commercial purposes. It is based on the seven basic units: metre, kilogram, second, ampere, kelvin, candela, and mole. Derived units with special names are: hertz (frequency), joule (energy), volt (potential), and watt (power). These units are used with a standard set of multiples and submultiples, including hect- (×100), kilo (×1000), centi- (1/100), and milli- (1/1000).

## six sigma

The term has the following three different meanings depending upon the context:
1. It is the structured application of the tools and techniques of total quality management on a project basis to achieve strategic business results.

2. In management philosophy, six sigma is a customer-base approach realising that defects are expensive. Fewer defects mean lower costs and improved customer loyalty. The lowest cost, high value producer is the most competitive provider of goods and services.

3. It is a way to achieve strategic business results.

It processes products having less than 3.4 defects or mistakes per million opportunities. Many successful six sigma projects do not achieve a 3.4 ppm (parts per million) or less defect rate (or 99.99966 per cent good). To implement the six sigma management philosophy and achieve the six sigma level of 3.4 defects per million opportunities or less there is process that is used. Such process includes five steps: (a) define, (b) measure, (c) analyse, (d) improve, and (e) control.

## skewness

It implies a sample that is biased in some way or a distribution curve that is asymmetrical rather than representing a normal distribution.

## skilled man worker

He is a craftsman in a particular occupation or trade who is able to apply the required skills and know-how to basically non-repetitive work with a minimum of direction and supervision.

## skimming

It is a pricing policy designed to maximise profit margins by putting a product on sale at a high price and then reducing the price in stages to saturate the market. Penetration pricing is an opposite approach to seize as large a share of the market as possible and as early as possible by putting the product on sale at a low price.

## slack time

It is the difference between the amount of time an activity takes and the amount of time allocated to it in network modelling. Activists that constitute the critical path in a project are those for which there is no slack time.

## sliding-parity

Also called crawling-peg, it is

## slip chart

a concept that offers a compromise between fixed parity and floating exchange rates by spreading any currency devaluation or revaluation over several months.

## slip chart

A chart that records scheduled times for stages in a project on a vertical axis and real or actual times on a horizontal axis, using the same scale on each axis so that a line at 45 degrees will represent the ideal path of events.

## slowdown

It is a situation in industrial action in which workers reduce their pace of work but do not actually withdraw their labour. It has similar effect as go-slow or work-to-rule.

## slump

A condition in which economic and industrial activity is at its lowest. Slump is marked by deflation and mass unemployment.

## small print

It is an illegal practice of setting out conditions of sale and liabilities of buyer and seller in small type size or with use of complex jargon.

## smart card

It is a plastic card that contains a microprocessor that stores and updates

Smart card

information, used in performing financial transactions. Unlike an ordinary credit card, debit card or cash card, a smart card memorises all transactions in which the card is used.

## smokestack industries

The term is used for the manufacturing industries which are now in decline in the major economies and are giving way to the growth of hi-tech and service-based industries.

## snap time
It is time a meal or meal break is taken. The term is common in traditional industries and manual work.

## social audit
It refers to the study of the social impact of company or national policies, including how far they are being affected by social expectations. Such study ranges across the employment of disabled worker, pollution control, utilisation of resources, safety, time lost through industrial action, equality of opportunity, and the social effects of investment policies.

## social investment
It refers to investment in parts of an economy's infrastructure that are concerned with social needs such as transportation, health care, civic amenities, education and housing.

## social security
It is a government system for paying allowances to the sick and the unemployed, as well as maternity benefits and retirement pensions. Other low-income members of society are also eligible, like the disabled and single-parent families.

## socio-technical system
It is a system of organisational development in which the main objective is to jointly optimise the conditions for task performance and for the satisfaction of human needs.

## soft currency
It refers to a currency which is unstable because of balance of payments deficits or international speculative dealing and therefore, having the risk of devaluation.

## soft landing
The term is used for a situation in which an economy slows down but does not go into a recession.

## soft sales promotion
It is sales promotion that is not concerned with actually making the product itself more attractive, as in the reduced price offers and increased quantities but with drawing attention to the product in peripheral ways like competitions or personality promotions that do not intrinsically have anything to do with the quality or quantity of the product or service.

## soldiering
The term is used for time wasting or restrictive labour practices.

## sole proprietor
It is a generic term for an individual who runs an unincorporated business on his/her own. Usually, a sole proprietor of a business is known as a sole trader, and a sole proprietor of a professional practice, like an accountant or solicitor, is called a sole practitioner.

## solus offer
It refers to offer of sale of a single product or service. It is in contrast with multiple offer where several products are included in a single offer for sale. An add-on sale is one made to a customer satisfied on earlier occasions.

## solus position ad
It is the advertisement position in a newspaper or journal that is among editorial material and separate from other classified ads. Solus advertisements are costlier than normal position ads.

## special agent
It implies an agent appointed to act for his/her principal in a particular matter. It may be a restrictive appointment, authorising the agent to act only within the terms specified or it may be the conferring of special powers which would not apply to a general agent.

## special resolution
It is a resolution of the members of a company that must be approved by at least three-fourths of the members to be valid. Members must have been given at least 21 days notice of the meeting at which the resolution is proposed to be presented along with details of the special resolution.

## specific risk
It is the risk associated with each of the individual assets in a portfolio, as opposed to the systematic risk associated with the market as a whole. It can be eliminated by diversification. Since specific risks can be eliminated in this way, there is no requirement for a risk premium for taking specific risks.

## specific unemployment
It denotes unemployment in particular industries. It may be caused by a slump in a particular industry.

## speculative risk
It is the inherent risk in the element of business speculation in a project or enterprise. It may be distinguished from pure risk of factors such as accident, poor health, or a natural disasters.

## spend management
It is a systematic attempt to optimise a company's spending by achieving best value for money in all the areas of its expenditure. This is to be distinguished from simple cost cutting, which achieves only short-term benefits. Spend management begins with an analysis of current spending behaviour and develops a strategic approach, integrating areas like procurement, contract management, supply-chain logistics, among other images.

## spin-off
The term is used for a commercially valuable product or process that emerges as an unexpected benefit from a research project in another field.

## spot market
A market where goods or securities are dealt in at prices for immediate delivery. It is opposite to a forward market which deals in futures, or promises to buy or sell at a future date.

## spread
It denotes the following:
1. The difference between the buying and selling price made by a market on the stock exchange.
2. The diversity of the investments in a portfolio.
3. The simultaneous purchase and sale of a commodity futures in the hope that movement in their relative prices will yield some profit.

## squeeze
The term is associated with controls imposed by a government to restrict inflation. An income squeeze limits increases in wage and salaries, while a credit squeeze limits the amounts that banks and other moneylenders can lend.

## staff status
It consists of terms and conditions of employment and fringe benefits. It is associated with executive and often, white collar status. A characteristic of staff status is sometimes the receipt of a

Dictionary of Business

monthly salary, rather than a weekly wage or hourly rates, etc.

### stagflation
It is a condition which exists at the same time as limited economic growth or economic stagnation.

### staggered working day
It is a system where working hours are arranged to be different from the hours traditionally worked by other firms in the area, usually with the aim of allowing employees to avoid rush hour travel, etc. The staggered working day system usually calls for all the workforce or work group to work the same hours.

### stale cheque
It is a cheque that has not been presented for payment within six months of being written. The bank will not honour it, returning it marked 'out of date'. However, such cheque can be revalidated by the drawer.

### stamina building
It is the process of building up the performance of trainee operators to acquire the speed and sustained effort needed in the production situation.

### stamp duty
It is a tax collected by stamping the legal documents to give effect to certain transactions. The rate of duty is, some percentage of the consideration given, the charge being rounded up to the nearest £100.

### stamp trading
Trading prevalent in some European countries, in which a retailer gives a small discount, not in cash but in the form of trading stamps or coupons which the customer redeems for goods supplied by the trading stamp company when sufficient stamps have been collected.

### standard
It is a generic term for mandatory requirements employed and enforced to prescribe a disciplined uniform approach to software developments, viz. mandatory conventions and practices that are in fact standards.

### standard costing
It refers to a system of cost ascertainment and control in which pre-determined standard costs and income for products and operations are

**Dictionary of Business**

set and compared every quarter with actual costs incurred as well as with income generated in order to establish any variances. As companies tend to become less labour-intensive there has been a decline in the use of such systems.

It is a management tool used mainly in mass production. Costs for standard parts of processes are established by work study or past experience, actual costs are then constantly against the standard costs.

### standard deviation

It is a measure of the variability of a random variable. The sample standard deviation is the square root of the sample variance and is defined by,

$$x_1, x_2 - xn$$

The standard deviation of the return from some investment is used as a measure of risks inherent in that investment.

### standard marginal costing

It is a system of cost ascertainment and control in which specified standards for marginal costs and income generated for products and operations are set and then periodically compared with actual marginal costs incurred and income generated in order to see if there are any variances.

### standard performance

It is a work study term for the rate of output which qualified workers are supposed to achieve without excessive exertion, as an average over the working day and adhering to the specified method as workers are to apply themselves to their work.

### standard time

It refers to the total time in which a job should be completed at standard performance, allowing for relaxation or compensating rest, contingency and where applicable, unoccupied time and interference, etc.

### standard transportation problem

It is the problem of finding the cheapest feasible pattern of shipment from origins to destinations. These problems can be solved by using operational research techniques like transportation tableau or Vogel's approximation method.

## standby credit
It refers to the following:
1. A letter of credit that guarantees a loan or other form of credit facility. The bank that issues it, promises to refund the amount borrowed if the borrower defaults on repayment.
2. In a note issuance facility, standby credit is a third-party guarantee to honour an issue to an investor who may have a low credit rating.

## standby pay
It refers to payment made to workers for making themselves available or on call for work, irrespective of whether, it is necessary to perform the work or not.

## standing order instruction
It is an instruction by a customer to a bank to pay a specified amount of money on a specified date or dates to a specified payee. Standing orders are widely used for such regular payments as loan instalment and recurring deposit every month.

## standstill agreement
It implies the following:
1. An agreement between two countries in which a debt owed by one to the other is kept in abeyance until a specified date in the future.
2. An agreement between an unwelcome bidder for a company and the company, in which the bidder agrees not to buy more of the company's shares for a specified period.

## start-up costs
These are costs involved in launching a project or enterprise, over and above the normal running costs once the enterprise is operational. Accomplishing break-even point means recovering both start-up costs and cumulative running costs.

## statement of desires
It is a statement that something is hoped for, but does not imply any action to be taken to ensure the desired outcome.

## statistical control
It refers to the condition describing a process from which all special causes have been removed, based on a control chart by the absence of points beyond the control limits and by the absence of

**Dictionary of Business**

non-random pattern or trends within the control limits.

### status symbol
It implies the following:
1. Prestigious products or services obtained more for the image they create than for their usefulness.
2. Also to executives and perks, any items like size of office, type of accommodation, car, etc. which indicate the seniority or level of an employee.

### statutory books
These are books of account that the Indian Companies Act requires a company to keep. They must show and explain the company's transactions, disclose the company's financial position at a given time, and enable the directors to ensure that the accounts are prepared according the provisions of the act.

### stewardship accounting
Simple but orderly recording and monitoring of incomes and expenditures, but to a less detailed extent than financial accounting or management accounting.

### stilling tests
These are confusion tests used in selection of workers for specific jobs, in which the person being tested tries to identify letters, numbers or forms printed in colours that become confused with the background in case their vision has a colour defect.

### stinkers
The term is used for difficult piece work jobs or those with tight rates. They are different from loose rates on which bonus is earned comparatively easily are known as gravy jobs or fat work.

### stock cover
It is the length of time to which present stocks will last if sales continue at the same rate as in the immediate past.

### stocking agent
The term is used for the middleman who provides warehousing facilities and handles stocks for which he is often paid a fixed sum. He does not purchase the goods he is selling but receives commission on sales.

### stock-in-trade
It implies the goods and/or services that an organisation normally offers for sale.

### stockist
It implies the trader discount and buying terms, and credit

terms from a manufacturer in return for an undertaking to hold specific levels of stocks of a range of products.

## stock losses

These refer to the decreases in the value of stocks compared with the price or cost at which they were originally produced or purchased.

## stock out

The term is used for cost to a company of not having an item in stock. The costs may be tangible, viz. lack of raw materials causing production delay, or intangible, e.g. inability to satisfy customers' order causing lost sales.

## stockpile

It denotes the following:
1. An unusually large stock of a raw material held by an enterprise in anticipation of a shortage, or planned production increase, etc.

Stockpile

2. A large stock of strategic materials, food, etc. built up by a government in anticipation of a war, or anticipated decrease in supply.

## stock policy

It is an insurance policy covering the goods stocked and sold by a commercial company for specified risks like fire or theft or for all risks. Policies are paid for the stock, not the price at which it might be sold.

## stock profits

These are profits accruing from increases in the value of goods or stocks components, materials, etc. compared with the prices for which they were originally obtained. It is opposite to stock loss.

## stock turnover

It denotes the following:
1. Ratio of sales to stock-in-trade.
2. Ratio of cost of sales to stock-in-trade.

## straight line depreciation

It is a simple linear method of spreading the cost of a fixed asset over its estimated useful life. It comprises dividing the cost, less estimated scrap value, of an asset by its estimated economic life.

## stranding

It refers to a running aground of a ship as a consequence of an unusual event. For the purposes of marine insurance, it does not include running aground and being refloated.

## strategic alliance

It denotes agreement between two or more firms to engage in an activity on a shared basis. The outside activities of each partner are not affected by the alliance, which is designed to build on the expertise of each member and the manner in which they complement each other.

## strategic behaviour

It can be defined as the behaviour of firms or individuals that is aimed at influencing the structure of a market. In traditional economics, situations like monopoly or oligopoly were resorted to because of technological conditions and the state of demand. Nowadays, a particular firm or individual can influence its competitors in the market in various ways, for example, by starting a price war if other firms attempt to enter the market.

## strategic business unit (SBU)

The term is used to identify distinctive businesses during corporate planning.

## strategic drift

It may be termed as limitations placed on strategic choice by assumptions made in the past and the application of previously tried remedies.

## strategic gap analysis

It is a method of examining a business strategy and establishing whether or not it will meet a desired objective. If there is a performance gap between the hoped-for and expected states, it can be closed by means of a modified strategy, which will have to be formulated.

## strategic group

It is a group of firms within a market or industry that is examined to determine the position each holds in terms of range, coverage, supply and distribution. Analysis of a strategic group shows which companies are the closest competitors.

## strategic management accounting

It is a management accounting system organised

in such a way that it is capable of providing the information required for long-term strategic decision-making as opposed to the more traditional approach of providing short-term costs. Such accounting, for example, provides information that will assist in the pricing strategy for new products and decisions relating to the expansion of capacity.

## strategic misrepresentation
It is a tendency for those presenting projects for approval to deliberately understate costs and overstate benefits. It is a matter of policy and thus distinct from optimism bias, planning fallacy, or simple miscalculation. Those who favour such a policy argue that many worthwhile projects would never get approval if the true costs were revealed at the start.

## stratified sampling
It is a sampling procedure in marketing wherein a population is divided into two mutually exclusive and collectively exhaustive strata and then, a probability sample is drawn from each stratum.

## strike
It can be defined as organised temporary withdrawal of labour or refusal to work by employees seeking to get a grievance addressed or a demand met. It may be an official strike with trade union backing, or an unofficial strike without formal trade union backing. The effect of a strike is measured in striker-days or working days lost.

**Strike**

## strike-breaker
It is a blackleg or scab, i.e. someone who supplies blackleg labour during a strike.

## structural unemployment
It refers to unemployment arising from long-term changes in demand for products and/or skills.

## sub-culture
The term is used for the

values and way of life of a particular group of people. It gives an idea about their views and attitudes in respect of the general culture of the country or society in which they live in. The existence of such a sub-culture is particularly marked in industries like mining where the workers and their families usually live together in isolated communities.

## subjective goodwill

It refers to the goodwill of a company calculated by deducting its net tangible assets from the net present value of its estimated future cash flows.

## sub-optimisation

It can be described as a situation that arises when the individual components of a system fail to work together for achieving maximum synergy. It can result from poor communication of objectives at a strategic level, or across component boundaries, either through ineffective use of the available tools, or it may be due to the development of sub-cultures that do not take cognisance of overall objectives of the organisation.

## subpoena

It implies an order made by a court instructing a person to appear in court on a specified date to give evidence of specified documents. The party calling for the witness has to bear all reasonable expenses.

## subrogation

It refers to the right of an insurer who has paid a claim for loss or damage to goods of taking over the rights of the insured for taking legal action against the parties causing the loss or damage.

## subsidiary company

It is a company controlled by another which holds more than 50 per cent of its voting capital.

## subsidy

It can be described as a type of grant paid to a supplier of goods or services, often by government, so that the goods or services are made available at less than the market price. It can be given on various types of goods such as petrol, fertilisers, etc.

## substantiality

It is the extent to which a market segment is sufficiently

large or profitable to provide an attempt to service it.

### substantive agreement
It is an agreement made after collective bargaining between management and trade union representatives on issues such as a wage payment system, a disciplinary code, etc.

### substitute awareness effect
An effect that depends on the relation between a customer's price sensitivity and his/her awareness of the existence of substitutes.

### sucker effect
It is a theory that some individuals will reduce their individual effort when working on a group task because they apprehend that they may contribute more to the group than others but get the same reward.

### sue and labour clause
It is a clause in marine insurance policies extending the insurance to cover costs incurred by the policyholder in preventing a loss from occurring or minimising some loss that could not be avoided.

### sugging
It is the unethical practice of deliberate deception by telemarketers posing as market researchers.

### sunk costs
In business accounting, it is the expenditure that has already been incurred and that cannot be recovered. Such costs are not relevant to any subsequent spending decisions.

### supermarket
In UK and USA, the term is used for retail outlet of more than 2,000 sq. ft. operated on a self-service basis with at least three check-out points.

Supermarket

### supplier credit
It is credit allowed by a bank or finance institution to enable an individual or company to invest in the manufacture and/or factoring of goods and

services until they are sold. It is opposite to buyer credit.

## supplier qualification and certification

A supplier qualification by a customer happens when it has been established that the supplier is capable of providing a part. A supplier becomes certified when it has delivered parts with perfect quality over a pre-specified time period. At that point, inspection is no longer required. In some cases, the two firms share the savings.

## supply chain management

It can be defined as management that applies total system approach to managing the flow of information, materials and services, from raw material suppliers through factories and warehouses, to the ultimate users. It should result in lower total system cost and higher service levels. However, the benefits of such changes need to be shared between the players in the supply chain.

## support activities

These are activities of indirect labour and services that serve, but are not central to, the manufacturer of a product, etc.

## support buying

It is buying of currencies or commodities by a government agency, or central bank, in order to support or maintain their market position.

## suspense account

It is an account in which credits and debits or charges are entered temporarily until they can be put to their proper permanent account.

## swap

It denotes the means by which a borrower can exchange the type of funds most easily raised for the type of funds required usually through the intermediary of a bank. There may be a currency swap that will enable them to exchange the currency they hold for the needed currency, and interest-rate swap, in which borrowers exchange fixed interest rates for floating-interest rates. The essence of a swap is that the parties exchange the net cash flows of different types of borrowing instruments on an over-the-counter market.

## switching cost
It is the customer's cost of switching from one supplier to another. It is often in the supplier's best interest to increase the customer's switching costs so that the customer does not go to other suppliers.

## symbolic models
It implies simulation of business or other situations in symbolic or mathematical form.

## syndicate
It denotes the following:
1. Association of businesses for a specific purpose such as a joint project.
2. Small group of course students or delegates segregated from the rest of the course for undertaking specific project or investigation.

## synergy
It is a system of combining two or more courses of action which is more effective than pursuing them individually.

## synthesis
The term can be defined as the translation of input requirements, including performance, function and interface into possible solutions including through satisfying those inputs.

## systematic risk
It refers to the element of risk in a portfolio of investments that cannot be reduced by diversification, as it is common to all securities of the same general class. The compensation that an investor requires for undertaking such risks forms the basis for the risk premium calculation, and arbitrage pricing theory.

## systems analysis
It is an analysis of methods required by an organisation or system and, use of computer in creating and designing solutions.

## systems engineering
It is the design and organisation of a complex of resources and devices to perform specified strategies and functions in the most beneficial manner.

## systems selling
It is a sales system where a group of products that perform related functions is sold as a package instead of as separate products.

# T

### 360° feedback
It implies a system that provides employees with all-round performance feedback from colleagues, managers, and customers. It also compares the individual's self-perception with performance ratings.

### 3i, investors industry
It is a industry that provides long-term loan capital and share capital to small- and medium-sized firms which are not otherwise obtainable through traditional banking facilities or to bring a new issue.

### 3pl (third-party logistics)
The term describes a business that provides one or many of a variety of logistics-related services. Such services generally include public warehousing, contract warehousing, transportation management, distribution management, freight consolidation, etc. A 3pl provider may take over all receiving, storage, value added, shipping and transportation responsibilities for a client and conduct them in the warehouse, using the 3pl's equipment and employees.

### tacit knowledge
It denotes highly personalised knowledge that is hard to formalise and communicate. Tacit knowledge consists of know-how, skills, models, beliefs and perspectives which are by and large, based on experience.

### tactics
These are detailed plans and approaches to the implementation of decisions and the best way of achieving results.

### tainted goods
Also called blacked goods, these are products or supplies that have been boycotted by a trade union.

### take-home pay
It is pay actually received by an employee after adding on bonus earnings, etc. and making tax, insurance and other deductions.

## takeoffs
It refers to the effects, good and bad, of using sales agents in export markets.

## takeoff stage
It refers to the stage of national economic growth following the traditional society and pre-takeoff stages. This stage is marked by the trends towards industrialised society, accelerating to a rapid rate of change.

## tallyman
The term refers to the tradesperson who collects regular payments from customers without invoicing them or giving receipts on each occasion.

## tangible assets
These are assets that are real but are not intended for resale, e.g. land and buildings; plant and machinery; furniture, fixtures and fittings; cars or other vehicles, etc.

Tangible assets

## tapered increase
A situation where a collective agreement gives greater increases in pay to the lower paid than to the higher paid.

## tardiness
It refers to an order that has past the due date (or due time). Tardiness is zero if the order is on time or is early. Average tardiness is a common measure, but should be used with caution, because it only considers orders that are tardy. For example, a firm has hundreds of orders that are tardy with an average of three days. The firm may improve its on time performance for nearly all orders.

## target marketing
It refers to marketing where the seller identifies many market segments, one or more of these segments, and develops products and marketing mixes.

## tariff
A duty imposed on a commodity when it is imported into a country or customs union.

## task-based appraisal
In performance appraisal procedures, etc., it is a type of report in which a senior manager comments on a more junior executive's performance in the particular areas of work allocated to the latter.

## tax
It refers to the following:
1. Money that individuals and corporations have to pay to the government so that it can spend on maintaining public services. People/companies pay tax according to their income/profits.
2. To put tax on somebody/something.

## tax burden
It is defined as the total loss of real income suffered by an individual or organisation as the result of a tax. This may not be the same as the tax obligation imposed by law, because there may be a shifting of the incidence of taxation to others.

## tax credit
It is the tax allowance associated with the dividend paid by a company. The shareholder is given allowance for the tax paid at source by the tax credit at the same rate. If it is 10/90, a dividend of £9000 received by the shareholder has an associated tax credit of £1000.

## tax evasion
It refers to attempts, successful or unsuccessful, at reducing income tax payable by illegal means like concealing income or inventing deductable expenses.

## tax haven
The term is used for a country which offers low tax rates and other special advantages to foreign companies.

## tax holiday
It is tax relief or exemption granted to a firm, etc. for a specific period of time. It is used, for example, to encourage exports and general industrial development.

## tax relief
It is a deduction from a taxable amount, usually given by statute. Some times, income tax reliefs are given in respect of income from tax-exempt sources such as investment in some mutual funds and post office schemers, insurance policies, etc.

**Dictionary of Business**

## team building
It is the process aimed at improving the ways in which work groups function, by means of improving group processes or organisational systems and structures.

## technical performance measurement
It is the continuing prediction and demonstration of the degree of anticipated or actual achievement of some particular technical objectives. Achievement to date is the value of a technical parameter estimated or measured in a particular test and/or analysis.

## technical position
It describes the amount of stock of a particular share in relation to the demand for it.

## technician
He/she is the person employed to use his/her skills within a laid down framework.

## technology agreement
It is an agreement between employer and trade union or other employee representatives on the employment and training procedures to be followed relating to the introduction of new technology, with the objective of averting a showdown and maintaining amicable industrial relations.

## technology transfer
It is a term for the transfer of technological knowledge to a third party, which occurs when a patent holder grants a licence to another firm to use a technology, process, or product. In many cases, this transfer takes place between countries, when an entrepreneur establishes an overseas subsidiary or grants a licence to a local producer. Thus, it can be described as a means by which countries gain new technology or update their existing technological base.

## telecommunication
It implies transmission and reception of signals by broadcast or transmission lines.

## teleconferencing
It is a telecommunication facility enabling users in two or more locations to participate in a live exchange of information or views. It may involve the transmission of voice only (called audio

**Dictionary of Business**

conferencing), voice, and pictures (called videoconferencing). The main business advantage is that teleconferencing saves the time and money spent in travelling to meetings.

## telemarketing
It refers to the teleselling but is supplemented by the addition of market research and sales follow-up activities.

## telephone banking
It is a facility enabling customers to use banking services by means of a telephone link.

## teletext
It is an information service in which pages of text are transmitted to office for display. The information is given under various headings, with a menu call-up system, and includes latest stock exchange prices.

## temporary employee
It refers to an employee who is employed for a specified period or for a specific task. As per law, such employee is entitled to be treated no less favourably than a permanent employee if he is doing the same or similar work. It is open to the employer to justify less favourable treatment if there is some valid reason.

## tender
It denotes the following:
1. A written offer to purchase something at a stated price.

**SHORT TENDER NOTICE**

PPIB invites well-reputed authorized firms stationed in Islamabad / Rawalpindi for the supply of Heavy Duty Digital Photocopying Machine.
The tender documents containing detailed information, terms and conditions can be obtained during working hours from the office or can be downloaded form PPIB website: www.ppib.gov.pk
Tender should reach this office by February 3, 2007 by 1500 hours which will be opened on the same day at 1530 hours.
The competent authority reserves the right to reject or accept any tender without assigning any reason.

Sami Rafi Siddiqui
Director IT/Administration
**Private Power & Infrastructure Board (PPIB)**
50, Nazimuddin Road, F-7/4, Islamabad
Tele: 9201848, 9206357

Tender

2. Also a means of auctioning an item of value to the highest bidder. Tenders are used for allocating valuable construction contracts, or for the sale of government's securities.

## terminal bonus
It is an additional amount of money added to payments made on the maturity of an insurance policy or on the death of the insured person. This is given out of the profit produced by the investment of the insurer.

## terminal market
It is a commodity market in a

trading centre such as New York, London or Paris, instead of a market in a producing centre such as Kolkata or Singapore.

## term loan
It refers to a bank loan to be repaid by means of monthly, quarterly, or half yearly instalments. It may be short-term, medium-term or long-term.

## term shares
These are shares which cannot be sold for a specified period of time. Such shares enable organisations such as building societies and land banks/mortgage banks to operate more confidently and without fear of a sudden outflow of capital.

## terms of trade
The term is used for the trading prospects of a country expressed as an index of export prices divided by an index of import prices. When a country's terms of trade improve, it can purchase more imports for a particular volume of exports.

## terotechnology
It is the technology of installation, commissioning, maintenance, etc. of plant, machinery and equipment, using information received as feedback. The aim is to reduce long-term costs and maintenance.

## territorial rights
In business, these encompass interests and standpoints of the different kinds of function such as personnel, finance, marketing, factory line management, etc.

## test battery
It is a range of complementary psychological tests for a wide range of abilities for the purposes of personnel selection, vocational guidance, etc. Well-known test batteries include the engineering apprentice test battery (UK) and the general aptitude test battery (US).

## test in depth
It is an accounting term for a detailed check on an aspect of the accounts of a company or organisation. This test may take the form of a detailed examination of a particular transaction.

## test requirement
It is the stimulus, measurement, power, loads and any special test

**Dictionary of Business**

equipment or procedure considered essential to validate proper operation of a device or some pre-determined design control or product specification definition.

### testable
It implies a set of requirements considered testable if an objective and feasible test can be designed to determine whether each requirement has been met.

### thin capitalisation
It is a term for an arrangement in which a company is incorporated with a small share capital and financed with a large loan from its parent company, to benefit from tax relief on the interest payment on the loan.

### thin market
The term describes market for a security, commodity, currency, etc. where there are currently few transactions. In this market, the spread between bid and offer prices will be wide and any sizeable transactions will have a direct effect on prices.

### threat matrix
It is a graphical method of classifying threats to an enterprise according to their seriousness or probability of occurrence. Assessments are entered in the appropriate box of a matrix. It is used in corporate planning or SWOT analysis.

### threshold agreement
It is an agreement between employer and employees whereby increases in pay are awarded automatically whenever the cost of living index rises by a specified amount.

### threshold worker
It refers to a worker or an employer beginning his/her first employment.

### throughput accounting
Throughput is the rate at which an organisation generates money through sales. Eliyahu M. Goldratt defines throughput as the difference between sales revenue and unit-level variable costs such as materials and power. Cost is most important driver for regarding business operations decisions. Since the goal of the firm is to make money, operations can help this through three items of throughout accounting, viz.

inventory (I), operating expenses (OE) and throughput (T). Inventory equals materials costs and other truly variable costs with no overhead. Operating expenses equal overhead and labour cost. Throughput rate is equal to revenue materials cost plus out of pocket selling costs. When a company applies throughput accounting to the bottleneck, it must look at key performance measurements like output, downtime, and yield rate.

### tied indicator
The term is used in marketing for a product whose sales performance may be related to the likely future performance of other products.

### tiger markets
It is a colloquial term for four economies in the Pacific Basin that experienced rapid growth from the 1960s to the 1980s due to heavy exports. They are South Korea, Singapore, Thailand, and Taiwan.

### tight rate
It is a situation in which the piece work rate for completing a job, as established by a rate fixer, is of a type that makes it difficult for a worker to earn bonus earnings. There is a danger in it that the workers will not even try to earn bonus and will fall back on daywork level of earnings, which will adversely impact production output.

### timecard
It is a card on which an employee's arrival times are recorded, computation of wages.

### time preference
It denotes relative value to an individual or company of present consumption as against future consumption. It necessitates balancing the attractions of the rate of interest to be expected if income is invested against the rate of time preference.

### time-scaled network diagram
It refers to any project network diagram drawn in such a way that the positioning and length of the activity represents its duration. The diagram is a bar chart that includes network logic.

### time-series analysis
It is a marketing research

**Dictionary of Business**

technique for forecasting sales, in which past sales are broken down into trends, cycles, seasons, etc.

## tipping point
It is the point at which a new idea, behaviour, or product suddenly breaks out from being a minority or of limited interest and becomes a mass trend. The idea was popularised by Malcolm Gladwell's book, *The Tipping Point*, which analysed why some trends achieve exponential growth while others fail to do so.

## tort
It refers to a civil wrong other than the one relating to a contract. The law of tort is concerned with providing damages for personal injury and damage to property resulting from negligence.

## total cost approach to distribution
Abbreviated as TCD, it is a popular management technique in the USA, for identifying and aggregating the more obscure distribution-related costs as well as the more obvious and commonly recognised distribution costs. It helps in cost-cutting, particularly in large and complex organisations.

## total cost of ownership
It is a calculation of the fully burdened cost of owning a component. The calculation helps consumers and enterprise managers assess both direct and indirect costs and benefits related to the purchase of IT components. For the business, purchase of a computer, the fully burdened costs may also include service and support, networking, user training and software licensing.

## total income
It can be simply put as an individual's income after expenditure has been deducted from the gross income from all sources.

## track sheet
It refers to production control documentation giving instructions on the use and flow of materials in a production line. The term is popular in the US.

## trade advertising
It is an advertising that is aimed at members of the distribution channel of a product or service rather than at the consumer. It is

sometimes beneficial to draw the attention of the trade to a product either in addition to consumer advertising or instead of it.

## trade association
It is an association of companies in the same trade, formed to represent them in negotiations with trade unions, or other trade associations, and to keep members informed about new developments affecting the trade.

## trade bloc
It is a group of nations united by trade agreements between themselves, e.g. the European Union.

## trade discount
It is a reduction on the recommended retail price of a product or service offered to distributors because they buy regularly in bulk. The difference between the retail price and the discounted price provides the retailer with his overheads and profit margin.

## trade drive
It is a system for arranging trade fairs and other activities aimed at promoting goods and services, particularly in an overseas market.

## trademark
It is the motif and/or wording registered by a manufacturer and used to make his/her products immediately recognisable. A trademark has to be registered separately in each country where it is used.

## trade name
It is the name under which a company trades, or a product is sold. It may be part of a trademark.

## trade-off
It implies weighing up the use of alternative approaches to achieve an objective such as to select the optimum alternative, conceding some points in exchange for other advantages.

## trade promotion
It refers to sales promotion aimed at retailers and other distributors by offering them incentives like bulk discounts and dealer competitions.

## trade secret
It refers to knowledge of some process or product, belonging to a business, disclosure of which would harm the business's interests. Indian courts generally grant

injunctions to prohibit any threatened disclosure of trade secrets by employees.

### trade union
It is an organisation that exists to represent workpeople and employees collectively in matters of pay and terms and conditions of employment.

### trade union federations
These are formal groupings of trade unions for the purpose of negotiation with employers.

### trade union recognition
It is the extent to which a union is recognised by management, extending to the representational rights of joint consultation or even beyond, i.e. to the negotiating rights of collective bargaining.

### trading down
It can be defined as the policy to achieve high turnover and attract high volume of customers by concentrating on lower quality products. The term may also imply provision of minimum of customer services, viz. no credit or delivery facilities.

### trading halt
It denotes the following:

1. The cessation of trading on a financial market when price movements reach the permitted limit.
2. The halting of trading in a particular security, normally as a result of a major news development or some destabilising rumour.

### trainability test
It is a term designed to assess a person's potential for learning new skills. It may also be designed to test a more general trainability.

### training credits
The term has been defined as an entitlement to train to approved standards for young people who have left full-time education to join the labour market. Such credits aim to motivate young people to train by giving them purchasing power in the training marketplace.

### training design
It is a design prepared by a training officer in an attempt at getting the optimum mix of variables he/she can control or regulate, effectiveness, etc.

### training plan
It is a program of training

needed to equip the employees of a firm or unit with further skills for sustaining the present and envisaged operations of the firm. Such plan may be arrived by following the manpower analysis and the drawing up of a job cover plan. It should incorporate information on the availability of both trainees and instructors at the required times according to the plan. It should cover, among other things, costings including trainees' employment costs, subsistence and travel allowances to trainees, course fees, costs of materials, facilities and space used for training, etc.

## transfer pricing

It implies allocation of costs to division, departments or cost and profit centres with the aim of charging out the internal transfer of goods and services in an attempt to control more accurately, the movements within an organisation and decentralise decision-making.

## transhipment

It is the shipment of goods or container to an intermediate destination, and from there, to another destination, sometimes by changing the means of transport. For example, goods received at Mumbai port are transhipped to Kolkata by means of another ship or steamer.

## transportation tableau

The term is used for a matrix used to assist in solving the standard transportation problem. There is one row for each origin (factory) and one row for each destination and thus one cell for each combination of origin and destination. The capacities and requirements are noted on the border of the tableau. Such tableau is used to determine the feasible solution, which is the one which satisfies delivery requirements at the lowest total cost.

## treasury bills

These are promissory notes used by the UK and the US governments to raise short-term loans, either at a fixed price to government departments or by tenders invited from discount houses and money brokers, who use these bills as security for dealing in the money market.

**Dictionary of Business**

## trend
In business, it is the prevailing tendency like a sustained upward movement in price levels.

## trend bucker
It is a US term for a corporation whose earnings remain high at times of economic recession, the time when many other businesses are performing badly. There were some trend buckers in India during the global recession of 2008-09.

## triadic product test
The term is used in market research for a product test in which each informants are presented with three unmarked products, two of which are identical, and asked to pick out the one which is different. In such test, it is difficult for candidates to make guesswork.

## trial balance
It is a bookkeeping term for checking whether all the debit and credit items in a double-entry ledger are in balance. The items are picked from trial balance to prepare balance sheet and profit and loss account.

## trigger price mechanism
It refers to minimum price specified by the government for certain imported goods. If the price falls below the level set, then the authorities investigate to ascertain whether dumping is involved.

## trim costs
It refers to the firing of employees and the reduction of plant and equipment with a minimum reduction in production.

## truncation
It means transfer of money between bank branches electronically, without physical movement of cheques, drafts, etc.

## trustbuster
It is a term in US and UK for government officer concerned with probing and dissolving illegal business organisations or associations.

## trustee
He is a person who holds the legal title to property but who is not its beneficial owner. In trust to land, there must be at least two trustees. The trustee may not profit from the position but must act for the

**Dictionary of Business**

benefit of the beneficiary, who may be regarded as the real owner of the property.

## turnkey contracts
These are contracts for the provision, control and management of a wide range of integrated services supplied as a package by one organisation.

## turnkey system
It implies the planning and execution of a major capital project, in which one company is responsible for its overall management, so that the client only has to literally turn the key in order to start the operation.

# U

### unabsorbed cost method
It is an accounting method where overhead expenses are allocated to an anticipated or budgeted total volume of production per unit of output. Since the expected volume is not achieved, some overhead costs may remain unallocated.

### unamortised cost
The term to the following:
1. The historical cost of a fixed asset less the depreciation accumulated against that asset up to a specified date.
2. Also used for value given to a fixed asset in the accounts of an organisation after revaluation of assets, less the total depreciation shown against that asset.

### uncalled capital
It implies that part of the capital of an enterprise which is authorised but shareholders have not yet been asked to subscribe it.

### uncleared effects
The term denotes financial documents including bills lodged with a bank for collection, still held by the bank pending the completion of the collection.

### unconstitutional strike
The term is used for strike called, in breach of an agreed procedure. An agreed procedure, or disputes procedure, lays down a system such as the engineering procedure in the UK, through which a grievance should be processed before a strike can be called constitutionally.

### uncontrollable costs
These are costs which cannot be reduced and affect a manager or management's budget and area of activity. These include group services, rents, etc. Changes in government policies may also introduce uncontrollable costs for management such as tax, tariff, duty, etc.

### undermanning
The term is used when a plant is manned by too few

employees for it to operate at a high level of efficiency.

## underwriter
He is a person or firm that guarantees the purchase of the full issue of stocks, shares, etc. irrespective of the result of the offer for sale.

## undischarged bankrupt
It implies a person whose bankruptcy has not been discharged. Such person may not be eligible for obtaining credit without first informing the creditor that he/she is an undischarged bankrupt.

## unearned increment
Increase in value of asset or stock which does not result from any effort or action by the owner, e.g. appreciation of the price of a plot of land. This may happen, for example, where land formerly used for farming is needed by the community as building land.

## unemployment benefit
It refers to the payment made to a person who is available for employment as a compensation for the fact that he/she is unable to obtain work and a regular income.

## union label
It refers to the following:

1. Mark attached to a product to identify it as having been produced by the members of a particular trade union.
2. A form of boycott by trade unions. A common boycott in the USA is one in which preference is given to goods made by trade union labour, ignoring those which do not have a union label.

## union reference
It is a situation where a trade union or its representatives seek to use a dispute procedure or a grievance procedure. If an employer takes such a step, it is called an employer reference.

## unique selling point
It is a sales feature peculiar to a particular product or service and therefore stressed in advertising and sales presentations.

## unique-product production
It is one of the three major systems of production identified and described by Peter Drucker, the others being mass production and process production. He defined the basic principle of unique production as "organisation into homogeneous stages", which are

## unit cost

Cost per individual item or unit of production. It can be expressed as cost per quantity of output, per machine hour, or per hourly labour rate.

## unit load

It is a term for material handling that describes any configuration of materials that allows materials to be moved by the handling equipment as a single unit. While smaller manually handled configurations could be considered unit loads, larger configurations would be moved by a lift truck such as palletised loads, crates, etc.

## unit trust

It denotes the following:
1. An investment fund shared by a large number of different investors. It is an open-ended fund, which means that the fund gets bigger as more people invest and smaller, as people withdraw their money.
2. It is a trust or organisation run by professional managers. It invests, over a wide portfolio of investments, funds subscribed by the public. The investors, in return, receive units which represent equal shares in the investment portfolio. The trust undertakes to buy back units from investors when requested. A unit trust subscriber receives his income from his share of the return on the portfolio investment.
3. A trust scheme in the US in which investors purchase redeemable trust certificates. The money collected is used by the trustees to buy such securities as bonds, which are usually held until maturity.

## unlimited accounts

These are businesses that are eligible for any amount of credit. This category includes large stores and companies which enjoy a good reputation worldwide.

## unlimited liability

It can be defined as a liability to pay all the debts incurred by a business. For a sole proprietor or a partner in a firm, liability is not limited to the amount he or she has agreed to invest. All his debts of the business must be paid

Dictionary of Business

out of the assets of the business but also, if necessary, out of his/her personal assets.

## unlisted securities
These are securities in companies that are not on an official stock exchange list. As such, they are not required to satisfy the standards set for listing. Unlisted securities are usually issued in relatively small companies and their shares usually carry a high degree of risk.

## unloading
It is a slang for selling goods usually in large number and often in export markets, at a relatively low price. It is also called dumping.

## unsocial hours
These are collateral hours of work that do not coincide with the hours worked by most other people and must to some extent interfere with social and family life of people who work during these hours. For example, shift working involves working some unsocial hours.

## upset price
Also called reserve price or floor price, it is the pre-determined price below which an item is withdrawn from sale at an auction or public sale.

## upward delegation
It implies passing work on to a more senior person in order to achieve a more efficient distribution of work.

## usance
It is the time allowed for the payment of short-term foreign bills of exchange. It varies from country to country but is normally 90 days.

## usury
It refers to an excessively high rate of interest. In Muslim countries, all forms of lending on interest are condemned.

**Dictionary of Business**

# V

## validation
It refers to the following:
1. The evaluation of a product at the end of the development life-cycle of an enterprise to ensure that it complies with the requirements and the criteria set forth by the customer and performs exactly as expected.
2. Confirmation by examination and provision of objective evidence that the particular requirements for a specific product, etc. intended use can be consistently fulfilled.

## value
It can be described as the sum of money or equivalent a purchaser or user is prepared to pay for a product or service. It is distinct from the price of a product or service and from the cost to the producer, of producing the product or service.

## value added tax (VAT)
Tax levied at each point where goods or services are exchanged in the course of production and distribution until they reach the ultimate consumer. At each stage, the tax is levied on the difference between the cost of the inputs, i.e. the goods or services bought in at the beginning of the stage, and the sale of the outputs sold at the exchange point at the end stage.

## value analysis
It is a technique for analysing design, production and marketing of existing products to ensure that operation at each stage is as economic as possible. It aims at enhancing the product's value and/or reducing its cost.

## value proposition
1. The term describes how you have positioned your product in the market. For example, a firm offering a very low priced product that has few features, is trying to give value proposition to the customers based on price and not on features.
2. It is also denoted as a

statement of differentiated and timely value of a product or service, which meets a need or solves a problem for an individual customer. It consists of a package of benefits from which the customers are persuaded that they derive greater value than from a competitor's offering.

### value received

These are words that appear on a bill of exchange to indicate that the bill is a means of paying for goods or services to the value of the bill. These words are mandatory in a bank draft.

### value satisfactions

A term in marketing for the reasons that lead a consumer to buy a particular product or service. These reasons include logical benefits such as product performance; psychological benefits like prestige, aesthetic appeal; and apparent benefits like value for price and the satisfaction of dealing with a particular company.

### variable cost

It implies cost that varies directly with the level of business activity and may be constant per unit of production. A cost that varies only indirectly with changes in the level of activity is called a semi-variable cost. The opposite of a variable cost is a fixed cost which remains constant whatever the level of business activity.

### variable expenses

These are expenses that vary with output. These are opposite to fixed expenses which remain constant regardless of the level of business activity.

### variables

The term is used for those characteristics or part thereof that can be measured. Examples are length in millimetres, resistance in ohms, weight in kilograms and the torque in foot pounds.

### variance

It denotes the following:
1. Dispersion of a frequency distribution. It is calculated as the summation of the squares of the differences between each item and the arithmetic average of the distribution divided by the number of items.
2. In accounting, it is the difference between budget or standard costs and actual costs.

**Dictionary of Business**

3. Difference between the standard or budgeted levels of cost or income for an activity and the actual costs incurred or income achieved. If the actual performance is better than standards, then there is a favourable variance while if actual performance is not as good as standard there is an adverse variance.

4. In statistics, variance is a measure of the dispersion of a distribution of outcomes.

### variance analysis
It is an analysis of the effect, influence and importance of different parameters in a complex business situation.

### variation
It is the inevitable difference among individual outputs of a process. The sources of variation can be grouped into two major classes, viz. common causes and special causes.

### variety reduction
It implies the standardisation and rationalisation of product range, raw materials and stocks of parts. Such reduction is undertaken periodically by a special project team which studies the problem, reports its findings and helps to implement the proposals.

### Veblon effect
The term is used for high level of consumption or affluence which leads to increased demand for higher priced products or services.

### Venn diagram
It is a diagram in which relationships are identified by circle, triangles, squares, etc.

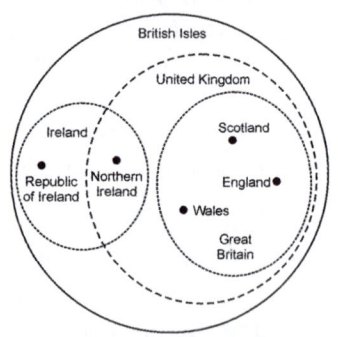

**Venn diagram**

### venture capital trust
Abbreviated as VCT, it is an investment trust that provides risk capital for businesses of the same kind that qualify under the Enterprise Investment Scheme in UK. The trust managers accept sums of money from investors who wish to share in the profits of the trust. This form of investment has certain tax

advantages in the UK, as any profits are free of capital gains tax.

### vertical integration
It has been defined as the "acquisition, amalgamation, or reorganisation of a number of formerly separate companies which extend activities back towards the supply of raw materials and components and/or forward to various elements in the production, marketing and distribution chain".

### vested interest
It denotes the following:
1. In law, it is an interest in property that is certain to come about rather than one dependent upon some event that may not happen.
2. Also an involvement in the outcome of some business, scheme, transaction, etc. normally in anticipation of a personal game.

### vested rights
It is the provision in a firm's pension scheme that if employees leave the firm, they may retain their pension rights in the form of a frozen or paid-up pension.

### vestibule training
It is a form of training in which new employees learn the job in similar to actual working environment. An example is the training of airline pilots in a simulated cockpit. Such type of training is generally used when the use of actual equipment by untrained employees would be too risky.

### vicarious liability
It is the liability of the employer for wrongful acts of his/her employee which are committed within the scope of his/her employment.

### virtual auction
It is an auction conducted completely online, with no physical location.

### virtual office
It is comprised of home-based workers linked by a computing, communications and other high technology network to work as a conventional office.

### virtual organisation
It is an organisation that uses information and communications technology to enable it to operate without clearly defined physical boundaries.

### visible exports
It refers to exports of physically visible goods appearing as receipts in the

### visible imports
These are imports of physically visible goods appearing as payments in the current account of a country's balance of payments account.

### visible management
It is the policy ensuring that senior managers are known by sight throughout the organisation.

### vocational guidance
It is the assessment of an individual's abilities and aptitudes followed by advice on how these are matched effectively with appropriate training and suitable occupations.

### vocational training
It refers to training in a trade. In the UK, there is a national system of vocational training.

### Vogel's approximation method
It implies a technique for solving transportation problems of devising the cheapest possible way of shipments. The method considers the consequences of not choosing the best cell in each row and column of the matrix. It, therefore, selects the cell which is so important as cannot be missed.

### volume checking
It means examining all the accounts of a company or organisation in detail. In modern auditing it is more like examining the accounting systems and controls, making a detailed check of only part of the accounts as less in auditing by rotation.

### voluntary arbitration
It is arbitration where reference can be made to the relevant tribunal only if both parties to an industrial dispute agree to it.

### voluntary assumption of risk
It refers to the assumption that if an employee took a risk at work completely voluntarily, it must be shown that he/she expressly admitted that the employer should not be liable in case of accident. It is also called the doctrine of 'volenti non fit injuria'.

### voluntary redundancy
It implies negotiated redundancy between employer and employee or trade union, with individual employee opting to take redundancy to meet new manning levels sought by the employer.

# W

## wafer seal
It is a form of seal, usually a red paper disk, used on official or legal documents such as property deeds, in place of original sealing wax.

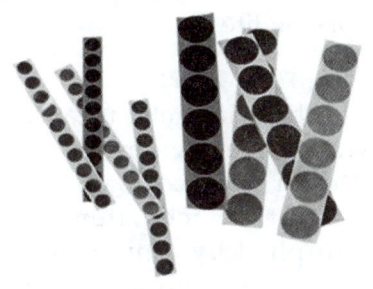

Wafer seal

## wage differential
It is the difference in earnings between workers with similar skills in different industries or between workers with different skills in the same industry. There may also be differentials between urban and non-urban wages, or between wages in different regions.

## wage drift
It is the tendency for actual pay to rise above nationally agreed levels.

## wage freezed
It may be termed as stopping increases in wages. In some countries, it is introduced by the government to control high inflation, as part of an incomes policy or prices and incomes policy.

## walking delegate
It refers to a trade union officer appointed to deal with local unions or to represent the union in dealing with employers.

## want
The term is used for what would be a demand for a product or service together with the fact that the possessor of the want lacks the purchasing power to translate it into a real demand.

## warehouse
It refers to any building in which goods are stored. The warehouse at or near a port in which goods are stored after being unloaded from a ship or before being loaded on the deck of ship is called public warehouse.

## warehouse management system

It is a software application that manages the operations of a warehouse or distribution centre. Application functionality includes inventory management, task interleaving, order picking, replenishment, packing, shipping, etc. Some systems use barcodes and radio frequency technology to provide accurate information in real time.

## warehousing

It denotes the following:
1. Storage of goods in a warehouse, etc.
2. Where nominee holdings in a company's shares are built up anonymously in preparation for takeover bid.

## warrant

It denotes the following:
1. A security that offers the owner the right to subscribe for the ordinary shares of a company at a fixed price. Warrants are bought and sold on stock exchanges and are equivalent to stock options.
2. A document that serves as proof that goods have been deposited in a public warehouse. It identifies specific goods and the ownership thereof can be transferred by endorsement. Warrants are also used as security against a bank loan.

## wear and tear

It can be defined as a diminution in the value to an organisation, of a fixed asset, due to the use and damage that it sustains throughout its working life.

## weighted average

It is the arithmetic mean in which the relative importance of each item is taken into account. Each item is multiplied by a number to give due weight to its importance.

## weighted-points plan

It refers to the method of evaluating suppliers by rating service, price, quality, etc. and weighting this according to their relative importance to the buyer.

## weighted sample

A term in market research for a sample with a specific bias, rather than random sampling.

## wheeler-dealing

It implies the practice of driving bargains according to commercial opportunity and without regard for ethical or moral considerations.

## whistle blowing
It refers to making public complaints or criticisms, usually of organisational wrongdoing or practices deemed to be unethical.

## white goods
These are major consumer products such as refrigerators, freezers, washing machines, etc.

White goods

## whole-job ranking
It is a job grading technique which consists of making a series of paired comparisons, where each job is compared with each of the other jobs to be graded until a rank order is built up right across the range of jobs.

## whole method
It is a method in an operation or a course, which is not divided into parts for training purposes but is learned as a whole.

## wholesale banking
It is interbank lending as well as lending to or by other large financial institutions, pensions funds, and government institutions. It also refers to the provision of banking services to large corporate businesses at special rates.

## wholesaler
The term is used for middleman who provides for buying, stocking and re-selling goods without having a special relationship with any particular suppliers. He/she also arranges the facilities of a forward warehouse and information to retailers, breaks bulk quantities, and offers a delivery service.

## wildcat strike
It refers to unconstitutional strike or unofficial strike called at short or no notice without going through the procedure agreed upon for setting right the grievances.

## window dressing
It refers to the practice that

tries to make a situation look better than it really is. It is used by accountants to improve the look of the company's balance sheet. For example, banks call in their short-term loans and delay making payments at the end of the financial year, in order to show exceptionally high cash balances.

## withdrawal

It denotes the following:
1. A term for withdrawing purchasing power from the circular flow of income in an economy, in the form of savings, taxation or imports.
2. The act of withdrawal money from one's saving or current account in a bank.

## withholding tax

It is part of an employee's wages or salary withheld by his/her employer as part or whole payment of income tax.

## without recourse

These are words that appear on a bill of exchange to indicate that the holder has no recourse to the person from whom it was bought, if it is not paid. The wording is also given in an opinion given by a bank about any of its clients, to some other company or institution which seeks it.

## work breakdown structure (WBS)

It is a product-oriented listing, in family tree order, of the hardware, software, services, etc. which completely defines a product or program. The listing results from project engineering during the development and production of material item. A WBS relates the elements of work to be accomplished to each other and to the end product.

## work experience

It refers to period spent in working environment by students with the purpose of gaining experience of employment for embarking career.

## work group

It refers to employees engaged in similar or related work. It tends to be linked by social as well as working ties. The term is used especially if the employees are on the same payment-by-results scheme.

## working capital

It can be defined as that part of a company's capital which is circulating or is in use rather than tied up in fixed assets, etc. A general criterion for identifying working capital is to subtract current liabilities from current assets.

## work-in-process
1. The term describes inventory that is currently being processed in an operation, or inventory that has been processed through one operation and is awaiting another operation.
2. Work-in-progress is actually an inventory account that represents the value of materials, labour and overhead that has been issued to manufacturing but has not yet produced a stockable item.
Depending on how fellow's accounting and inventory systems are set up, it may also include components picked for production usage.

## work package
It refers to a deliverable at the lowest level of the work breakdown structure, when that deliverable may be assigned to another project manager to plan and execute. It may be accomplished through the use of a sub-project where the work package may be further decomposed into activities.

## workplace bargaining
It denotes collective bargaining over local rates by pay and conditions of work in part of a plant or factory, conducted between shop stewards and local management.

## workshadowing
It refers to time spent on witnessing and noting the work performed by a manager or other employee.

## worksharing
The term is used for methods of sharing the available work between a greater number of workers through policies like reduced working hours and adoption of more labour-intensive working practices.

## work structuring
It is a concept developed in Holland for organising work and working conditions in a way that encourages workers' participation within working groups. Work structuring stimulates job enrichment by suiting job content to the capacities and ambitions of the individual employee.

Dictionary of Business

## work study
It implies techniques like method study and work measurement to examine all aspects of a particular area of work to make it more efficient.

## worst case scenario
It is the projection of possible future outcome that assumes worst possible situation.

## written-down value
The value of an asset after taking account of its reduction in value below the initial cost, because of its use in the trade.

## wrongful trading
It refers to the trading during a period in which a company had no reasonable prospect of avoiding insolvent liquidation. In such a situation, liquidator of a company may file a petition in the court for an order instructing a director of a company that has gone into solvent liquidation, to make a contribution to the company's assets. The court may order any contribution to be made that it deems fit in case the director knew, or ought to have known, the company's situation.

# X

## x-bar chart
It is a quality control chart that monitors the mean of the process. A sample of n parts is collected from the process every so many parts or time periods. The mean of the sample is plotted on the control chart and a determination is made if the process is under control or not.

## xd
It is abbreviation for ex-dividend.

## xerography
It is an electrostatic process for making photocopies and printing computer output with a laser printer.

# Y

### yield
It denotes the following:
1. Return or profit earned on an investment, in particular stocks or shares. It is usually expressed as a percentage of the money invested or the current market value of the stocks or shares, yield, earnings, price earnings ratio, etc.

2. The per cent of product produced that is not defective. This can be used as performance measure for a planning factor used to inflate the required production start quantity.
3. Agricultural produce per acres of land.

### yield gap
It is the difference between the average annual dividend yield on equities and the average annual yield on long-dated fixed-income bonds.

### yield management
Also called revenue management or perishable asset resource management, it is an approach to maximising revenue given that the capacity-related costs are relatively fixed. Yield management systems change prices and capacity allocations over time as the date of the event approaches. For example, it is said that airlines change their prices several times in a month. The goal is not to maximise utilisation, but to maximise revenue per unit or resource.

### yield variance
It is the calculation of the actual amounts produced, compared with norms or standards and expressing this variance as a percentage. The term is used in standard costing.

### yuppie
It is a slang in USA for a successful and ambitious young person, especially one from the world of business or finance.

### zero-based budgeting
It implies budgeting which requires managers, when preparing their budgets, to justify all their expenditures from a zero base rather than simply asking for increments to previously budgeted figures.

### z-chart
It is a graph, showing three aspects of production or sales volume, showing the total for the period (monthly or quarterly), cumulative totals and moving annual total.

### zone pricing
In marketing, it is a pricing strategy in which a company delineates two or more zones. All the customers within a zone pay the same price for a product. In it, more distant the zone from the company's headquarters or warehouse, the higher the price.

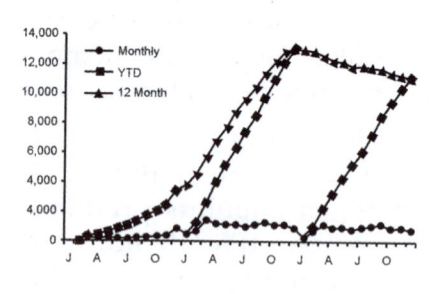

Z-chart

# Business Letters & e-mails
# WRITING GUIDE

*including Business English vocabulary and useful letter writing phrases*

## Business Letters

All business letters have one thing in common: the way they are formatted. In general, try to adhere to the following guidelines:

- Keep it simple and use the so-called *Block Style*, where all the elements of the letter are left-aligned (and not justified).
- Use a 1-inch margin all around.
- Use single-line spacing.
- Do not indent your paragraphs – leave a line-space between all paragraphs and elements of the letter, except for the last element (your name), before which you should leave three line spaces.
- Never use abbreviations unless quoting an official name.
- Omit your address if using headed paper on which this is clearly stated in the header or footer.

# Conventions

### The Date Line
Month Day, Year          i.e. May 27, 2015 (but NOT May 27th, 2015)

### Titles and Qualifications in Addresses
Company Position:   Title / First-Name / Surname, / Company Position
i.e. Mr John Martins, Managing Director

Post-nominal or Honorary Titles:   First-Name / Surname, / Lowest Qualification, Next-highest Qualification, Highest Qualification
i.e. John Martins, BA, MA, Ph.D

*when using a post-nominal or honorary title, do not include Mr/Mrs/Ms/Miss

### Abbreviations in Addresses
The only time abbreviations should be used is when they are part of an officially registered name, i.e. Manning and Sons Inc.
However, where the company's registered name includes the full word rather than the abbreviation, do not shorten it - copy the official name exactly,
i.e. Manning and Sons Incorporated.

### Care of
Never use the abbreviated form c/o. Always write the complete phrase
i.e. Mr John Martins,
Care of Maxwell Incorporated

Do not use 'Care of' if the addressee is an employee of the company or guest of the hotel whose address is being used. 'Care of' should only be used if the addressee is temporarily receiving mail at the offices of a given organisation.

### Addressing Women
Miss: used for an unmarried women.
Mrs: used for a married woman.
Ms: used if you do not know the addressee's marital status,
if they are divorced and have reverted to their maiden name, or,
if the addressee prefers this title.

### Punctuating the Address
Write the address as follows:

Name of Addressee         Mrs Aisling Foote
Name of Organisation      Bermuda High School
Street Address            25 Ramsey Street
City, State ZIP Code      Nell, Paget 1108

## Salutations

- Begin 'Dear'
- Follow the salutation by a colon {:}

**Where the Person's Name is known**
Use: Dear Mr/Mrs/Ms/Miss Surname:        i.e. Dear Mr Thompson:

**Where the Person's Name is NOT known**
Use: (a) Dear Sir or Madam   *or*   (b) Dear [Job Title]: (i.e. Dear Recruiter:)

Alternatively, if you are not sure <u>by whom</u> your letter will be read, as is the case with a Personal Reference for example, you may also use:

TO WHOM IT MAY CONCERN:

\* in this case, the entire phrase should be capitalised.

## Closing the Letter

- Always follow the closing remark with a comma, then three spaces and your name.

>   i.e.        Yours sincerely,
>   --- *LINE SPACE* ---
>   --- *LINE SPACE* ---
>   --- *LINE SPACE* ---
>   Miriam Chapman

**Where a Person's Name was used in the Salutation**
Any of the following are appropriate:
(a) Yours sincerely,     (b) Sincerely,     (c) Yours truly,
(d) Very truly yours,    (e) Sincerely yours,

The following is only appropriate when writing to someone of considerable authority or for extreme formality:     Respectfully yours,

The following are only appropriate when writing to someone with whom you have an established personal as well as business relationship:
(a) Kind Regards,  (b) Best wishes,  (c) Kindest Regards,  (d) Cordially yours,

**Where a Person's Name was NOT used in the Salutation**
Use:     Yours faithfully,

# The Main Types of Business Letters

## Cover Letters

When submitting a CV or job application, this will almost certainly have to be accompanied by a cover letter. Your cover letter should typically introduce you, explain why you are writing, highlight your key skills and experience, and include a request for an in-person meeting with the person to whom the letter is being sent (or someone from within their organisation).

First impressions are extremely important, and your cover letter is perhaps your best chance to make a good one on prospective employers, so take great care when writing same. The person receiving the cover letter, as well as getting a good indication of your skill set and experience, will also be able to gauge how effectively you communicate in written English based on the quality of your correspondence.

The tone of your letter will be determined by the nature of the job for which you are applying, but irrespective of the degree of formality expected, you should at all times appear professional, so do not let your letter stray beyond formal-to-neutral English into an informal style.

Here are some <u>General Tips</u> for writing cover letters:

- Where possible, address the person you are writing to by name, i.e. 'Dear Mr. Thompson' rather than 'Dear Sir or Madam'.
- Be clear and concise – limit your letter to one A4-page.
- Tailor your letter to the specific job for (or, if a speculative submission, company to) which you are applying.
- If possible, show that you have done some research and demonstrate your background knowledge of the company to which you are applying.
- Avoid waffle, jargon and long, complicated sentences.
- Use action verbs and the active voice to give the reader a sense of your confidence and enthusiasm.
- Avoid sounding over-confident or arrogant; do not do a hard-sell, but nonetheless put yourself forward as self-assured and very competent.
- Structure your letter in a logically-flowing manner and allocate one full paragraph to each main point discussed.
- Above all, proofread meticulously; your letter must be error-free and sound, both in terms of grammar and punctuation.

# Letters of Recommendation

There are two main types of Recommendation Letters:
- Employer Reference Letters
- Character Reference Letters

**Employer Reference Letters** are written by a current or former employer. They are typically requested by a prospective employer. Nowadays, for legal reasons, such letters tend to be very matter-of-fact, stating the dates from and to which the person was employed, their official job title, details of their role, and, in some cases, a general statement about their performance, i.e. 'Mary's time-keeping was excellent, she got on well with the other members of her team and performed her role to a very satisfactory standard.'

For legal reasons, employers will seldom provide very positive or negative appraisals, or discuss the person's performance at length. An Employer Reference is expected to be true, fair and accurate by law.

**Character Reference Letters** are written by work colleagues or friends of the subject as an endorsement of said's general character. You should begin a Character Reference by stating who you are (in what capacity you are writing), your relationship to the subject and how long you have known them. Identify the subject by full name. Use the main body of the paragraph to outline what you perceive to be the subject's character strengths and key personality traits, using examples to justify your observations.
A Character Reference is by definition a positive appraisal of the subject, but it should also be balanced. Therefore, it is in the subject's interests that your letter should not simply be full of praise, and highlighting one or two areas for improvement (in a positive way i.e. 'In the past, Jane has tended to allow strong personalities within the group to dominate her, and she has struggled to make herself heard. That said, she has now become more conscious of the need to assert herself, and, as time goes on, she is increasingly demonstrating that she has the confidence to share her opinions and get her point across effectively.') lends credibility to what is said.

- As it is seldom known who will read the correspondence, reference letters often begin with the salutation:   TO WHOM IT MAY CONCERN:
- Often, the letter writer will invite the reader to contact them if they require more information in the final paragraph. i.e. 'I am happy to provide more information if required and can be contacted on 01- 2748539 during office hours to this end.'

# Letters of Inquiry

There are several different types of Letters of Inquiry, such as:

- Prospecting Letters
- Letters of Interest (not job related)
- Requests for Information on a Product or Service i.e. pricing, availability etc.
- Proposition Letters

## Prospecting Letters

A Prospecting Letter is much like a Cover Letter, the difference is you are sending an unsolicited CV or declaration of interest in working for the organisation. The main aim here is to leave a good impression and ascertain whether or not the company is hiring, and, if so, whether they would consider you a suitable candidate for a vacancy. A Prospecting Letter will differ slightly from a Cover Letter in the sense that you will focus on what you know about the company in greater detail and emphasise how your skill set can benefit it.

## Letters of Interest

Here, you are expressing your interest in cooperating with the addressee's company in some way, for example, as a distributor of their products, so it is necessary to give a clear, succinct and detailed profile of your company and what it is you do, and to outline how your and the addressee's companies can work together in a mutually beneficial way. It is, essentially, an invitation to cooperate.

## Requests for Information

When writing such a letter, your objective is typically to get an answer to a very specific question i.e. the cost of a service, the availability of a service, the price of a service etc. This is a very simple form of transactional letter, and, as the function is not to convince the addressee of something, your language does not need to be persuasive in the same sense as it does with Letters of Interest and Prospecting Letters. Nor do you need to give detailed information about your person/company. Keep it short and to the point, but outline any information that might be relevant to the response, i.e. if requesting prices, give an indication of the number of units you would be ordering etc.

## Proposition / Proposal Letters

This type of letter is in a sense a Prospecting Letter but written by a company rather than a person. You are writing to highlight what it is your company does and outline why it would be in the addressee's interests to do business with you. Essentially, you are inquiring as to whether or not the addressee's company would be interested in your services, and inviting them to get in touch with you to explore the possibility of working together. You will need to go into considerable detail about your company's services and your proposal, and how it (the proposal) would benefit the addressee or their company.

- For all of the above types of letters except Requests for Information, you will need to use persuasive language and sell yourself or your product or service. However, do not put across an aggressive hard sell and maintain a formal register.

## Letters of Response

Although it is not compulsory to use a reference line(s), it is often quite practical to do so in a Letter of Response, as then the reader will immediately know what the letter is about. The reference line comes after the date, and may be in bold print, i.e.

> **Our Ref: Case 158**
> **Your Ref: Order 129**

Alternatively, or in addition, you can add a subject line. A subject line is basically a one-line summary of what the letter is about, and, following British convention, comes after the 'Dear [Name]' element. It may be in bold print and underlined, i.e.

**Findings of the investigation into your complaint dated 27 May, 2015.**

There are several **types** of **Letters of Response**:

## Acknowledgment Letters

Acknowledgement Letters, also known as Courtesy Letters, simply confirm or acknowledge that you have received correspondence from the addressee. Such letters should be kept short, and usually end with one of the following phrases:

(a) 'We will follow up in due course.'
(b) 'We will revert to you with a more complete response by [date].'
(c) 'We will take your proposal under consideration and revert to you should we have any additional questions or wish to pursue this matter further.'
(d) (in response to a job prospector) 'We will keep your CV on file and inform you should any suitable positions become available.'

### Follow-up Letters
Though a Follow-up Letter is not always a response (you may be following up on your own unanswered inquiry), it is typically sent after there has already been some bilateral communication. A Follow-up Letter can be something as simple as a short Thank-you Note, a Status Update, or a Status Request. You must remember to refer to the correspondence which you are following up in the first paragraph and, preferably, the Reference or Subject Line.

## Sales and Marketing Letters

The following are the main types of correspondence in this category:
(a) Marketing Letters
(b) Order Letters
(c) Confirmation Letters

### Marketing Letters
The purpose of a marketing letter is twofold. Firstly, it seeks to capture the target reader's attention. Secondly, it seeks to persuade them to consider a product or service. In this sense, such letters can be less formal, and may intentionally break letter-writing conventions so as to stand out. That said, it is vital to ensure that, irrespective of the choice of writing style, the reader is left with the impression that the company promoting itself is a professional outfit. Start by catching the reader's attention with an interesting or unusual statement, but do not lose focus on the main purpose of writing, which is to inform the reader in as full and simple a manner as possible about the product or service you are promoting. To this end, avoid technical jargon, and use simple, descriptive language when talking about functionality and key attributes.

### Order Letters
When placing an order, the primary function is to convey the information as simply as possible. Insert a table with the details of the order into your letter to promote understanding so as to minimise the chances of an error occurring in the order fulfilment process. Quote quantities, model/part/reference numbers, product names and prices both accurately and clearly, indicate the desired delivery timeframe and, where appropriate, prompt a discussion on costs.

### Confirmation Letters
It is essential to keep the customer informed throughout all stages of the order process. In your initial follow-up letter, you should enclose the invoice, and clearly state prices, delivery and payment terms. The customer should be sent a further follow-up message once the order has been dispatched, and feedback should be invited from the customer on the fulfilment process and their satisfaction with the product or service at a later date.

## Customer Relations Letters

There are several main types of Customer Relations Letters, including:
**(a)** Complaint Letters
**(b)** Adjustment Letters

### Complaint Letters
A Complaint Letter is a difficult thing to get right. You must strike a balance between outlining your position and stressing the problem you have had, and not coming across as unreasonable. If you succeed in doing the latter, you will be far more likely to get a favourable response. Adopt a formal and professional tone, begin by describing your dealings with the addressee or their company to date, clearly and succinctly state how you were inconvenienced, and state just as clearly what you would like to be done. Avoid threatening language that will escalate tensions unreasonably at such an early stage in the complaint process. Allow the addressee the right of reply, and, if you are still unsatisfied, then you may wish to consider an escalation of the issue at that point.

### Adjustment Letters
An Adjustment Letter is a response to a complaint. If you feel the original complaint was justified, start your letter by acknowledging your company's error, offer an explanation of how the error occurred, explain the procedures put in place to ensure there is no recurrence, and clearly state what you propose to do for the customer to resolve the matter or by way of compensation. If you feel the complaint was not justified, clearly state the case as to why this is your position in a professional manner, highlighting, if necessary, the fact that procedure was followed by your staff, or that events outside your company's control for which it could not be held accountable led to the incident. Remain at all times professional and use conciliatory rather than aggressive, defensive or dismissive language.
\* In any instance where a complaint has been upheld, it is essential to send follow-up messages to ensure the matter has been resolved to the customer's satisfaction.

## Letters of Resignation
A Letter of Resignation should contain language of the utmost formality, the tone should be polite and the message should be stated simply and clearly. First state the reason for writing and the date at which your resignation will come into effect. Say why you are resigning and, if appropriate, where you are moving to. Avoid being confrontational, or adopting an immodest, disrespectful or satisfied tone. You may need a reference from your current employer at some future point, so ensure where at all possible that you exit on good terms.

# Opening Phrases

## Examples

### When replying
- I write with reference to your letter of [date]...
- Thank you for your inquiry dated [date]...
- With reference to your letter dated [date], I wish to / would like to...
- Thank you for your correspondence dated [date]...
- In reply to your letter of [date], I wish to / would like to...
- I received with thanks your letter dated [date], and I would like to...
- I refer to your letter of [date].

### General opening phrases
- I am contacting you regarding...
- I am writing in relation to...
- I am writing to inform you that...
- I wish to enquire about...
- I am contacting you for the following reason...
- I wish to request / confirm / draw your attention to / highlight...
- I was forwarded your contact details by ... and would like to...
- I am pleased to inform you / confirm that...
- I would be interested in obtaining / receiving information about...

### For a Job
- Having seen/read your advertisement in [name of magazine / newspaper], I wish to...
- I wish to apply for the position of [name of position] as advertised in / on [name of magazine/newspaper / web source]...
- I wish to put myself forward for consideration for the vacant post of [name of position] as advertised in / on [name of magazine/newspaper / web source]...

### Complaint
- I wish to express my dissatisfaction with...
- I wish to make a formal complaint about...
- I am writing to convey my disapproval of the manner in which...

## Function: AGREEING

**Examples**
- I wholeheartedly agree that...
- I am in complete agreement with you regarding...
- I fully agree that / endorse your comments regarding...
- I concur that...
- We ('we' as in the addressee and you) are in agreement that...

## Function: DISAGREEING POLITELY

**Examples**
- Whilst I take your point that ... , my position is...
- I have given your remarks careful consideration; however,...
- Having taken your comments into consideration, I regret that...
- I have given due regard to your concerns/comments; however, from my perspective,...
- Regrettably, I cannot agree to your request for ... because...

## Function: CONFIRMING

**Examples**
- It gives me great pleasure to confirm that...
- I am delighted to confirm that...
- I am happy to be in a position to confirm that...
- I am pleased to be able to confirm that...

## Function: REQUESTING

**Examples**
- I would be grateful if you could...
- I would appreciate your immediate attention in this matter. Please...
- Could you please forward / inform me / confirm / send me ... ?
- Would it be possible for you to forward / send / confirm / investigate ... ?
- I would very much appreciate it if you could forward me / confirm / investigate / clarify...

## Function: REFERRING TO AN ENCLOSURE

### Examples
- Enclosed, please find...
- I have enclosed the following:...
- Please find enclosed...
- Enclosed, you will find...
- For your convenience/reference, I have enclosed the following documents:

## Function: APOLOGISING

### Examples

**General Apology**
- I am deeply sorry that...
- Please accept my humblest apologies for...

**Specific Apology**
- I wish to apologise for any inconvenience this matter has caused you.
- We deeply regret this incident and the manner in which it has inconvenienced you.
- Please accept my apologies for not replying sooner.
- I wish to apologise for the delay/inconvenience...
- I wish to extend you my sincere apologies for the manner in which you have been inconvenienced/treated.
- I apologise unreservedly for the manner in which you have been treated.

## Function: COMPLAINING

### Examples
**General Complaint**
- I wish to highlight the following issue I have had with your company...
- I wish to complain about...
- I wish to express my unhappiness/dissatisfaction with...

**Strong Complaint**
- I wish to convey my utter dissatisfaction with the manner in which I have been treated.
- I am thoroughly dissatisfied with the manner in which this matter has been handled.
- I am dismayed by the manner in which this case/matter has been handled.
- I wish to put on record my deep dissatisfaction with...
- I am extremely dissatisfied with...
- I am very unhappy with...

## Function: CLOSING REMARKS

### Examples
**Inviting a Reply**
- Please do not hesitate to contact me should you require more information.
- Please do not hesitate to contact me should you have any questions whatsoever or wish to discuss this matter further.
- Please reply at your earliest convenience.
- I look forward to receiving your reply in due course.
- I would welcome your thoughts on this matter and look forward to hearing from you in the near future.

**General Closing**
- Thank you for your time and consideration.

# Other Phrases

## To do with Pricing
- Please find our full price list enclosed.
- Please send us your full price list (at your earliest convenience).
- We are delighted to provide you with the quotation you requested, which you will find enclosed herewith.
- We can make you a firm offer of [amount]...
- Please note that our prices and terms are subject to change (without notice).

## To do with Orders
- We wish to place an order for the following items:...
- We wish to cancel our order of [date].
- We wish to amend our order as follows:...
- Please confirm receipt of our order of [date].
- I hereby confirm receipt of your order dated [date].
- Your order will be processed and dispatched by [date].
- Regrettably, the following items are not presently in stock:...

## To do with Payment
- Our terms of payment are as follows:...
- Enclosed, please find our most recent catalogue and price list.
- Our records show that payment is still outstanding as of [date] (for order number [number])

## Giving Bad News
- We regret to inform you that...
- Regrettably,...
- Unfortunately, we are not in a position to...
- After careful consideration, I regret to inform you that...

## Giving Good News
- We are pleased to announce/confirm that...
- I am delighted to be in a position to inform you that...

# British English
## vs
# American English

**130**

common words and phrases
used in business context

# British versus American

| British | American |
|---|---|
| analyse | analyze |
| Annual General Meeting (AGM) | Annual Stockholders Meeting |
| Articles of Association | Bylaws |
| authorised share capital | authorized capital stock |
| baggage | luggage |
| bank holiday | national holiday / federal holiday |
| barometer stock | bellwether stock |
| barrister, solicitor | lawyer, attorney |
| base rate | prime rate |
| bill (in restaurants) | check (in restaurants) |
| bonus or capitalisation issue | stock dividend or stock split |
| bridging loan | bridge loan |
| building society | savings and loan association |
| catalogue | catalog |
| chemist | pharmacist |
| cheque | check |
| company | corporation |
| creditors | accounts payable |
| current account | checking account |
| curriculum vitae (CV) | résumé |
| debtors | accounts receivable |
| defence | defense |
| dinner jacket | tux, tuxedo |
| directory enquiries | directory assistance |
| engaged *(telephone line)* | busy *(telephone line)* |
| enquiry | inquiry |
| enrolment | enrollment |
| estate car | station wagon |
| expiry date | expiration date |
| favourite | favorite |
| first floor | second floor |
| fill in *(an application form)* | fill out *(an application form)* |
| fortnight | two weeks |

| British | American |
| --- | --- |
| gilt-edged stock (gilts) | Treasury bonds |
| goods train | freight train |
| grey colour | gray color |
| ground floor | ground floor, first floor |
| ironmongers | hardware store |
| kiosk | newsstand |
| labour | labor |
| licence *noun* (verb: license) | license *noun + verb* |
| Memorandum of Association | Certificate of Incorporation |
| merchant bank | investment bank |
| motorway | freeway |
| ordinary share | common stock |
| organise | organize |
| overheads | overhead |
| petrol | gasoline / gas |
| profit and loss account | income statement |
| programme | program |
| property | real estate |
| quid: pounds | bucks: dollars |
| quoted company | listed company |
| rates | taxes |
| retail price index (RPI) | consumer price index (CPI) |
| ring off *(telephone)* | hang up *(telephone)* |
| sacked | fired |
| share | stock |
| share premium | paid-in surplus |
| shareholder | stockholder |
| shareholders' equity | stockholders' equity |
| stock | inventory |
| storey *(a 3-storey building)* | story *(a 3-story building)* |
| trade union | labor union |
| underground | subway |
| unit trusts | mutual funds |
| visible trade | merchandize trade |